Manchurian
LEGACY

Memoirs of a Japanese Colonist

Kazuko Kuramoto

Afterword by Dr. Kathleen Uno

Michigan State University Press
East Lansing

⊗ The paper used in this publication meets the minimum requirments
of ANSI/NISO Z39.48-1992 (R 1997) (Permanence of Paper).

Michigan State University Press
East Lansing, Michigan 48823-5245

10 09 08 07 06   3 4 5 6 7 8 9

LIBRARY OF CONGRESS CATALOGING-IN-PUBLICATION DATA
Kuramoto, Kazuko, 1927–
Manchurian legacy : memoirs of a Japanese colonist / Kazuko Kuramoto.
      p. cm.
ISBN 0-87013-510-4 (alk. paper)
ISBN 0-87013-725-5 (alk. paper)
1. Kuramoto, Kazuko, 1927– 2. Japanese—China—Manchuria—Biography.
3. Women—China—Manchuria—Biography. 4. Agricultural colonies—
China—Manchuria. 5. Manchuria (China)—Biography. 6. Manchuria
(China)—History—1931–1945. 7. Japan—History—1945– 8. World War,
1939–1945—Personal narratives, Japanese. I. Title.
DS731.J3K87 1999
951'.8042'092—dc21
[B] 99-6503

Cover design by Michael Smith of View Two Plus
book design by Michael J. Brooks

Visit Michigan State University Press on the World Wide Web at
www.msu.edu/unit/msupress

In loving memory of my parents
And for my family near and far

Manchurian
LEGACY

We are each of us angels with only one wing
And we can only fly embracing each other
—*Lucians de Creschenko*

Contents

Author's Note

This memoir includes my childhood memories of a then colonial city, Dairen, at the south end of Manchuria (the northeastern province of the People's Republic of China); how I saw World War II as a teenager, how we survived the hellfire of Manchuria at the time of Japanese surrender; how we were finally rescued and shipped back to Japan; how as a repatriate I survived in the ruins of postwar Japan; and how I came to the United States as a young adult.

When Japan awoke from its two hundred years of self-imposed national isolation in 1868, it saw the world of "dog eat dog" imperialism, especially in the Far East, and plunged into the world of imperialism itself. Following the Meiji Restoration era of rapid modernization, industrialization, and militarization, Japan emerged as a world power. It defeated China in the Sino-Japanese War of 1894–95, gaining Formosa (Taiwan) from China. Ten years later, in the Russo-Japanese War of 1904–5, Japan defeated Czarist Russia and won the lease of Liaotung Peninsula at the south end of Manchuria along with the railroad rights for all of Manchuria, according to the terms of the Treaty of Portsmouth. The treaty also granted Japan the southern half of Sakhlin Island, formerly Russian territory, and placed Korea under Japanese control. Korea became a Japanese territory five years later, in 1910. It was a time of Japanese expansion in Asia, and Dairen, the port at the south end of the newly acquired Liaotung Peninsula, was Japan's entrance to Manchuria.

In late 1905, shortly after Japan's victory over Russia, my maternal grandfather was sent to Dairen with the Japanese police forces. Under the protection of the Kwantung Army (the Japanese field army in Manchuria) and with liberal financial support from Tokyo, Dairen was a rapidly expanding, tax-free commercial port city, the largest of its kind in the East, representing the international power of Imperial Japan. I was a product of this almighty Japanese imperialism.

I was born in Dairen in 1927, at the peak of Japanese expansion in Asia. As a member of the third generation of my family in Dairen, I was born into a society of Japanese supremacy and grew up believing in Japan's "divine" mission to save Asia from the "evil" hands of Western imperialism, which at that time included the British in India and Hong Kong, the French in Indochina, the Dutch in the East Indies, and the United States in the Philippines. The poorly armed Asian countries had been colonized by Western imperialists as early as the seventeenth century, bit by bit. This colonization process was seen as a serious threat to the small island country of Japan. "You are Japan's only future, a glorious future," adults around us used to say. We believed it with passion. "Japan is the God-chosen sacred country," they also told us, and we believed that too. "We are the leaders of Asian countries." Yes, yes, of course we are. "We must liberate Asia from the evil hands of the Western imperialists." I joined the Red Cross Nurse Corps to help my country win the war, the World War II in the Pacific theater— "Asia for the Asians!" But, alas, the following year the war ended. Japan surrendered unconditionally under the threat of the world's first atomic bomb.

The fall of Imperial Japan struck us like a thunderbolt from the suddenly darkened sky. Many Japanese have since claimed that they had expected it for some time, or even from the very beginning, but most of us were caught completely by surprise. I now wonder if it were more so with us in Manchuria because we were away from mainland Japan and did not directly experience the daily bombing runs of the B-29s. Suddenly, the more than a million and a half Japanese in Manchuria found themselves in the middle of no-man's-land, stripped of any means of protection or direction, surrounded by enemies: Russians crossing the Siberian-Manchurian border in the northeast; Chiang Kai-shek's nationalist army coming in from the southwest; and numerous local Chinese guerrillas, who had been suppressed by the Kwangtung Army for more than forty years, surfacing within.

The exact death toll among the Japanese in Manchuria at that time will probably never be known. The Japanese government, which started the repatriation of its army survivors and of overseas Japanese from its lost colonies and territories immediately after its surrender, did not extend a helping hand to those of us in Manchuria. We were left to somehow survive on our own for more than a year. Some say that the government was misinformed about our condition because the communication between Tokyo and Manchuria had been cut off, while others say that there was an international conflict over the new ownership of Manchuria. I do not know. All I know is what I saw and experienced as a teenager, a very limited personal experience in a circumscribed area, mainly in the city of Dairen. That my family was one of the very lucky ones to be rescued unharmed is still a small wonderment to me to this day.

Like most Japanese, then and now, I had buried the memories of war deep within and had no desire to recall them. Yet, as I became well settled in the small town of Ontario, Oregon, watching my young daughter grow into her teenage years as well as observing the American teenage students in my Japanese class at Ontario High School, I began to remember my teenage days in Manchuria. I also became aware of how little people knew about what had happened on the other side of the Pacific during and immediately after the war, especially in Manchuria. Most Americans did not even know where Manchuria was. And then when I read stories of Japanese-American—Issei and Nisei—experiences in the United States before and during the war, the suffering that they had gone through, I thought of my parents and grandparents, who had also left Japan at the turn of the century but had gone in the opposite direction, to Manchuria. While those who came to America suffered prejudice and injustice, those who went to Manchuria practiced that prejudice and injustice against the native Chinese in Manchuria. The price for this injustice was high, and many paid for it later with their lives. The irony of all of this struck me. I had a story to tell to the American public, I thought, if only I could write in English.

English is my third language, after Japanese and Chinese. I knew my English would be quite inadequate to express myself. After failing to find the necessary help locally, I wrote to well-known author Bill Hosokawa, whom I had never met but had admired for his well-researched books on Japanese-American history, asking for help. He was quite hesitant at first, because of his busy schedule, but showed some interest in the topic of Manchuria. I started sending him my draft, chapter by chapter, written with my stiff, textbook English. Perhaps out of his long years of habit as an editor, he corrected my English, page by page, and mailed them back to me. The pages were mailed usually from Denver, where he lived, but sometimes they were sent from other towns where he was on business, corrections having been made while flying. When the manuscript came to the point where I left Dairen, which was where I intended to end my story, Mr. Hosokawa tried to persuade me to continue on to write what I had seen and done in postwar Japan. I flatly refused to do so. I had no desire to reveal my most miserable experiences in postwar Japan. I was not ready to face them. Thus the project remained unfinished, or "incomplete," as Mr. Hosokawa put it then.

It was after I retired from teaching Japanese at Ontario High School that I became more serious about the possibility of writing this story on my own. I took classes first at the local city college, then progressed on to Eastern Oregon State University, where I earned my B.A. I went on to Boise State University to continue my study as an English major in graduate school. This was where I met Dr. Ballenger, a professor of writing, who knew how to draw stories out of students, even a student like me who had once refused to remember a certain period of her life. I began to see myself in a different light and somehow managed to write short stories (nonfiction) and essays based on my postwar Japan experiences, as well as on my childhood memories of Manchuria. Then, when I read one of my short stories to the class one day, I saw many of my fellow students, as well as Dr. Ballenger himself, in tears. The story I had read was about my father, or rather about Japan as it was some fifty years ago, as seen through my memory. I was elated. I could, perhaps, reach American readers with my writing! Thus encouraged, I started to rewrite my memoirs from the very beginning, in a totally different form and from a different perspective. I tried to write with more insight and reflection, as suggested by Dr. Ballenger, and remembering what Bill Hosokawa had said ten years before, I went on, with complete honesty, to cover my days in postwar Japan.

Because of my inadequate writing skill in English, I feel that there are many words still unspoken. Still I was impelled to write this, not only to share my story with the American public, but also as a way of dealing with my undying longing for Dairen; as a way of reaching out to my forgotten self and overcoming my self-doubt, rebuilding my self-esteem, and confirming my identity as a Manchurian-born Japanese American. But most of all, I have written this as a tribute to the memory of my loving parents.

Kazuko Kuramoto

Part One

Dairen, Manchuria

East Asia before World War II

CHAPTER 1

The Young Patriot

MY FATHER HAD a mole on his face, just below his forehead, in the center where his eyebrows met. It protruded as if half a red bean had been glued there, only it was soft and bouncy to the touch of my fingertip. As a toddler, I used to press this "button" to make him "beep, beep" for me. Every night, after dinner, he'd take a hot Japanese bath, change into kimono bathrobe, and sit cross-legged on a large sitting pillow in the family room, ready to enjoy the day's newspaper. I would then run to him, before he could start to read the paper. He would act surprised to see me, but then help me to get into the front of his bathrobe, and let me securely sit in the warmth of the kimono front. Astride his stomach, my arms spread over to his sides like a frog sample in a biology class, and my face nuzzling against his chest, I would peacefully breathe in the lingering smell of hot bath. Sometimes I'd fall off to sleep, listening to the crackling of the newspaper over my head. Sometimes I'd ask him for "the finger dance" on my face. It was the dance performed by his two fingers—middle and index—like the long legs of a comic dancer, starting from my chin with a simple tune and phrases of no origin, most likely Father's own creation. He'd start it with his rather shy and off-tune song, "jumping over the ditch," making his finger-legs jump over my expectant, smiling mouth. With the next line, "going to view the flower," the dancing legs would hop onto my giggling round nose. (In Japanese, the words for flower and nose are phonetically the same.) The next line, "walking around the ponds," took the dancer to a quick gliding around my eyes, like a figure eight on ice. The

1

dancer now would happily skip up across my forehead to the tune of "passing over the field," which would quickly turn to "deep into the wood," as his hand ruffled my hair, as I wiggled and laughed in his arms. Then he'd yell, "Look, I found a mushroom!" gently pulling my ear, then quickly over to the other side of my head to proclaim, "Oh, my, there's another one!" Or, sometimes I'd stand up on his lap, pushing away the newspaper, holding onto his neck. I'd stretch my arm to reach my favorite "button" on his face, and press it with all my might. He would then "beep, beep" for me with a smile, and I would giggle with delight. I remember those scenes well because I have watched him do the same with my two younger sisters, as they took my place in Father's kimono front. I smiled with each of my sisters when they giggled, knowing exactly how it felt inside his kimono front, warm and secure, and remembering the lingering smell of hot bath.

Father's newspaper reading was a daily ritual, as far as I can remember. He never laid the newspaper on the table or on his desk. He always held the paper up high in front of himself like a Shinto priest reading a ceremonial message to his gods. Once in a while, we, my sisters and I, would hear a heavy breathing sound of "phew, phew" from behind the paper he was holding. We soon figured it out that this was Father's way of holding back his tears. It was a time of war (World War II) and the paper was filled with the stories of heroic soldiers such as the young kamikaze pilots, the suicide attackers. Two of our brothers were serving in the Japanese Imperial Army, and those articles were too close to Father's heart. We understood this, and respectfully fell quiet and left the room whenever his "phew, phew" started.

Another thing he did when his emotions got the better of him was to rub his nose—his large "lion's nose," as we called it—with the back of his hand. I remember him rubbing his lion's nose when my oldest brother received *aka-gami* (the red paper), the official draft notice from the Japanese government. And again when my second oldest brother received the same. Both times, he put the red paper on the altar set up in front of the enlarged picture of Emperor Showa, put his hands together, and prayed while my sisters and I watched his back with uncertainty. He prayed for a long time, then rubbed his lion's nose as he quietly walked away, leaving us in an uneasy silence. We had been told over and over that it was the utmost honor and privilege to be drafted into the Japanese Imperial Army. An occasion of joy and pride. But Father rubbed his nose. Was he about to cry? Why the long prayer? And why did Mother fall quiet suddenly? We suspected that even Mother was crying in secret. Yet everyone acted joyful, and we had send-off parties for them.

I especially remember the send-off party for my second oldest brother, Kay. It was held in the big room upstairs. Mother cooked the *seki-han* (red rice), the sweet rice cooked with red beans, which was the special dish for all happy occasions. She cooked many other dishes as well, as she did for New Year's Day. As Kay and his friends sang their school song, one of his friends got up to do a cheerleading routine, bellowing the name of their school.

"*Kanpai!* (Bottoms up!)" Everyone toasted to their school.

"*Banzai!*" someone shouted.

"*Tenno-heika, Banzai!* (Long live the emperor!)" Someone else made it more formal.

"Hey, don't forget to holler it with your last breath!" another added. Japanese soldiers were expected to salute the emperor with their last breath on the battlefield.

"Hell!" Kay stood up suddenly. "To hell with it. I salute my mother!" Kay held up his sake cup and shouted, "*Okaa-san, Banzai!* (Long live Mother!)"

A sudden hush filled the room. Then everyone followed Kay's lead, hurriedly and cheerfully.

"Yeah, right. *Okaa-san, Banzai! Okaa-san, Banzai!*" they toasted Mother.

Mother, covering her mouth, ran out of the room and disappeared down the stairway. Father's nose rubbing expanded to face rubbing.

Father rubbed his nose again when I decided to join the Red Cross Nurse Corps in order to follow my brothers' footsteps to the battlefield. It was March of 1944. I was about to graduate from the *Futaba Gakuin*, a private junior college for girls, and was working toward my degree to be a kindergarten teacher. I was a romantic, dreaming of spending my life playing with innocent young children while writing the poetry and novels that I had always loved. How little I knew about myself! One day, a piece of paper nailed to a telephone pole changed the course of my life completely. It was a poster with a large picture of a Red Cross nurse in navy blue dress uniform, asking for high school graduate girls to join the force.

"This is it!" I stopped short in front of the poster, squeezing my schoolbag against my pounding heart. It was a sudden revelation to me, a sudden awakening. I felt that I had finally found what I had been looking for.

3

I gazed at the picture with reverence. The young woman's face was tilted slightly upward as if she were looking into Japan's glorious future, her mouth pursed with determination, her straight shoulders pulled back with pride; a perfect picture of a young patriot. I was glued there, and read everything that was on the poster: qualifying age, application procedure, the patriotic history of the Red Cross, and its deep commitment to the ongoing battlefield action.

I hurried home and proudly announced my decision to join the Red Cross, expecting cheers and praise from the whole family. But to my surprise, my parents were dumbfounded, while my sisters stared at me with disbelief. I did not understand it. Didn't we make a big show of pride every time someone was drafted or enlisted? Was patriotism a privilege granted only to men and boys?

I was born after three brothers. My mother used to tease me that had I been another boy she might have given me to one of our family friends who was childless, and to tell me how glad she had been when I was born: a little girl, at last! This had always made me feel "special," as if I had done her a great favor just to be born a girl, which had led me to believe that girls were somehow better than boys, and that I meant more to my mother than my brothers did. So I grew up feeling "special," even after my sister was born four years later, followed by another three years after that. Thinking back on my childhood, I now wonder if each one of my five siblings grew up feeling "special."

Now, out of the blue, I had declared that I would join the Red Cross Nurse Corps to dedicate myself to the great cause—to save Asia from the evil hands of Western imperialists. How vividly I still remember my mother's panic and my father's heavy silence. The whole house turned silent. My mother wept silently and my sisters accused me silently. But I was obstinate.

After three or four days of heated argument as I tried to win my father's consent, my parents finally called my grandfather and two of my favorite aunts, Aunt Masu and Aunt Kiku, to help them talk me out of "my sudden impulse," as they called it. Aunt Masu and Aunt Kiku were the youngest of my mother's siblings, born in Dairen years after my grandparents had settled in the newly acquired Japanese colony following the victory in the Russo-Japanese War of 1904–5. *Masu* means Manchuria in classic Japanese, *Kiku* is the chrysanthemum, the imperial crest of Japan, signifying the loyal spirit of the samurai pioneer who had come to Manchuria to realize the national dream of the expansion of Imperial Japan.

"Remember, your brothers are already serving the country. Giving two men from one family is more than called for," Grandfather said coaxingly.

"Every subject of the emperor must do his duty. I wish to do mine," I replied without giving in. I had fallen in love with patriotism: self-sacrifice, total dedication, honor, and the possibility of the ultimate heroic death. It touched the root of my romantic nature.

"Look what Japan is facing," I argued with passion, "Japan must save Asia from the Western invasion. The British are in India and Hong Kong, the French are in Indochina, the Dutch are in the East Indies, and the Americans are in the Philippines. They are helping themselves to bits and pieces of underarmed Asian countries. This must be stopped at any cost."

It was not hard for me to recite what I had been taught all my life. My generation had grown up with Japan's military propaganda. World War II in the Pacific theater was then called *Dai To-a Senso*, the Great East Asia War. It was a sacred war, of course, and Japan was the self-appointed savior and leader of *Dai To-a Kyo-E-i Ken*, the Great East Asia Co-Prosperity Sphere. The sacred war had started with a bang, as any sacred war should, with the divine blessings of our ancestors. But, alas, it did not last long. The day of my sudden awakening to patriotism was in early March 1944. The war against the United States and her Allies in the Pacific was moving into its third year, much too long a time for Japan's limited military resources. The first year's succession of victories at Guam, Wake Island, Hong Kong, British Malaya, Singapore, Sumatra, Borneo, and Burma had almost exhausted Japan's military resources, and the Allies had started to win back all of the key positions in the Pacific, closing in on mainland Japan. After winning back the New Guinea air base, the Allies started dramatic air raids on Tokyo and other major cities in Japan. The casualties mounted day after day. The shortage of nurses and doctors was a well-known fact. No one could openly deny a young girl's patriotic desire to join the Red Cross Nurse Corps. My parents were trapped. I remember my father standing in front of the pot-belly stove, noisily stirring up the already burning coals, eternally rubbing his lion's nose.

". . . and I thought the girls were safe from the war," Mother wept.

"Now, now, let's be practical," Aunt Masu, the most practical of the clan, cut in. "It's not as if Kazuko is taking off to war right away. She'll have to go through three years of schooling and training. The war will be over by then, I am sure."

They looked at one another. Why, of course! Why hadn't they thought of that! This settled the family feud, and I won my father's consent. Yet my mother was still softly sobbing. I broke my mother's heart with my fantasy of heroism, and this guilt was held against me by my sisters for a long time.

It was unprecedented for the Japanese Red Cross to enlist local girls of Japanese ancestry in Manchuria to form an entire unit of freshman cadets. The media treated us like war heroes even before we entered the training school. The local newspaper placed our story on the front page. We were interviewed and photographed, and our declarations of naive patriotism were given equal treatment with the main news of war, making us feel like Joans of Arc, if not Florence Nightingales. I enjoyed the attention, even though it did not quite match the celebrations that my older brothers had received when they were drafted—the send-off parties with red rice and all of us going to the Dairen port to ship them off to Japan with the three loud cheers of *Tenno-heika, Banzai!* echoing high into the sky. I did not receive the *aka-gami*, the red paper. I was not drafted. But I got the attention of a war hero in my own way. And my mother cooked the red rice for me.

The training school for the nurse cadets was on the third floor of the Red Cross Hospital in west Dairen. Our dormitory was in a smaller building in the compound behind the main hospital across the Japanese-style rock garden with pine trees, a pond, and a bridge. The nurses' training was originally a four-year program, as with other college curricula, but as the war dragged on and casualties mounted, senior students were called to active duty, soon followed by juniors. Consequently, the sophomores and the freshmen were put to work around the hospital. We spent mornings mopping the floors, cleaning up the blood-stained mess after surgery, and running errands for the doctors and nurses. Afternoons were spent in intense classroom study or outdoor training, practicing first aid and carrying mock patients on stretchers. I soon realized that we were being trained to be of immediate use on the battlefield, if and when it became necessary to ship the untrained students to the front line. They were pushing us to grow fast, much too fast.

One particular lesson still stands out in my memory of the Red Cross training. Early in our training, we were required to witness an autopsy, something for which we were not quite ready. We were led into an all-white lecture hall and were seated on the bleachers. A gurney holding something covered by a white sheet was wheeled in. When a young assistant pulled off the white cover, we gasped. There on the narrow bed lay a corpse. I felt the blood drain from my face.

"This coolie died of an accident," the assistant's voice echoed far away in my head like a line from the yellowed pages of some ancient horror story. Unreal. The body on the bed glistened from its shaven head to its stiff toes. The coolie, a Chinese laborer who had lived at the bottom of society, probably had never been as clean as this while he lived. The "polished" body was two-tone. The upper part of the body was deeply tanned while its lower part, from the waist down, was ghastly pale. It told this dead man's life story, that he had labored half naked all his life under the dry, harsh Manchurian sun. And now he lay stiff on the table for an autopsy.

"If any of you don't feel well, you may leave the room," the chief nurse said, and I saw a few girls leave their seats in a hurry, covering their mouths. I was nailed to my seat. I watched the doctor measure each of the wounds on the corpse's head while the assistant took down notes, and then he proceeded to open its stomach skillfully, explaining the function of each organ. I was in a daze, my mouth dry, my heartbeat drumming in my head.

None of us talked about this experience during the rest of the day, going through the motion of daily tasks as if nothing had happened. But that night at the dorm, after the lights-out, muffled whimpers filled the darkness. I was sobbing too, and sobbed myself to sleep. After all, we were only teenage girls.

Yet that was a part of my training. I was determined to take anything that was required. In fact, I welcomed the military-like discipline. The lifestyle of the Red Cross training school in those days closely resembled that of the Japanese Imperial Army. Every action we took was done by an order and according to strict regulations. From the early morning roll call, reciting the oath of loyalty to the Emperor, to the lights-out, every minute was tightly scheduled. The way we stood, the way we sat, the way we walked, the way we marched and saluted, everything was uniform and regimented. Still, I rather enjoyed the change. It was refreshing.

I did suffer the complete loss of privacy, however. The chief nurse had the full right to go through our private belongings and to censor our letters coming in and going out. It seemed that I was getting more letters than anyone else, with many parts blackened out. I wondered if my friends were getting my letters all blackened out. The chief nurse also didn't like the books I had brought in. One of them was a beautifully bound copy of *Correspondence between Goethe and Schiller*, a compilation of personal letters exchanged between the two great intellectuals of the eighteenth-century Germany. It had been given to me just before I joined the Red Cross by a boy I had grown up with. This, *The Sorrows of Young Werther*, and several other books that I loved were confiscated by the chief nurse.

"Some literature is detrimental to young minds," the chief nurse had said.

"I had such high hopes for you," she sighed when she returned the confiscated books to me to be sent back home, as if I had let her down. Then she pulled out a letter and placed it in front of me. I recognized the letter and blushed with embarrassment. It was a letter that I had written a friend some time ago, before I was aware that she censored all of our personal letters.

"So you think the Red Cross is a 'glorified prison,'" the chief nurse continued, her icy stare fixed upon me. I remembered writing it. I had written it lightheartedly. A joke, supposedly. But I did not try to excuse myself. I was no longer embarrassed. I was angry. Furious. I stared back at her: then why act like a warden?

I also did not get along with the upper-class cadets. The very first time I ran into an upper-class cadet in the hallway I greeted her with my usual cheerful "Good Morning!" She stopped short, blocking my way, and saluted me with the stiff, fifteen-degree bow of Red Cross salute, saying, "Good Morning, Freshman Yamasaki," her steady eyes fixed on my dumbfounded, flushed face. I learned to keep my smile in check after that experience.

From the first day of my training, I was aware that those of us who had been born and raised in Dairen were somewhat different from the sophomores who had come from small towns and villages in Japan. For one thing, most of us had bobbed hair, not long enough to pull back into a librarian's knot as the Red Cross required. And in the dorm after school, we dressed in casual blouses and skirts while the sophomore girls dressed in cotton kimonos like our parents and grandparents did. The only time we wore kimono was during the new year holidays, and then they were colorful silk kimonos. Our high school uniform was a sailor-collared middy blouse, navy blue in winter and white in summer, with navy blue pleated skirt.

Our behavioral patterns also were quite different. We were more casual and out-spoken, not easily intimidated, while still keeping our respectful distance, and while the sophomore girls spoke *Kyushu* (southern Japan) dialect with a strong *Kyushu* accent, we spoke Japanese without an accent simply because no local dialect existed in colonial Dairen, and with better vocabulary, possibly because our parents were better educated. We had come from different cultural backgrounds—Japanese as we all were. This was a case of city girls versus country girls, or the new breed versus the traditionalists, and I must have represented the new breed to the sophomores, for I became the target of their "nit-picking." Often I was called into the room where the sophomores congregated. There I was made to sit by myself under a bright light, facing a group of serious-looking sophomores who took turns accusing me of being a snob or disrespectful, or whining about such trivial things as my dress being too short or bright-colored, or my salute not being quite fifteen degrees. However, they did not really succeed in making my days as miserable as they hoped. I took it all in stride and went about my business. It did, however, leave with me a lasting conviction that we, the colonial-bred, were different from the people of mainland Japan.

It was around this time that Kunio, the boy who had given me the copy of *Correspondence between Goethe and Schiller*, came to see me. Having a visitor in the middle of the week was a rare occasion, a special treat. I hurried to the visiting room, flung the door open, and found Kunio standing awkwardly in the middle of the barren room, neatly dressed in his college uniform.

"Kuni-chan!" I cried out in delight as I ran into his open arms. (*chan* is an endearment used among families or childhood friends.) He gave me a quick hug and stepped back to hold me at arm's length to take a second look as if to make certain that this antiseptic-smelling girl in a white nurse's uniform was indeed me, the girl with whom he had had the private joy of sharing books and thoughts.

He was a sober-minded boy, tall, slim, and rather pale, with contrastingly willful bushy eyebrows. He had been my next door neighbor until his family had moved to Port Arthur, thirty miles west of Dairen.

"I asked for an emergency visit with you because I am leaving for Tokyo in a few days. I told them I was your cousin," he grinned.

"You mean, you've been accepted at Tokyo Imperial University?" I cried out. Tokyo Imperial University was the most prestigious in Japan, and it had long been Kunio's dream to be accepted there.

"Oh, I am so happy for you, Kuni-chan, you deserve it! You're so smart, smarter than anybody I've ever known!"

Kunio had always been an avid reader and loved to talk to me for hours about the books he had read and was inspired by, and had urged me to read the same.

9

"You are not majoring in literature, are you?" I asked, suddenly concerned. Literature majors were not allowed deferment from military duty, while some science majors were allowed to continue their studies.

. "But I am. German literature."

"Oh, no! Then there's no way you can finish college."

"Didn't you know? There's no longer any deferment for any major. And the draft age has been lowered to twenty, too."

"Twenty? Then you don't even have a year left!"

"I know. But that's exactly why I am taking German lit. I want to study what I love as long as I can, even if it may be only a month, a week. . . ." His voice faded into a bitter whisper. I moved closer, picked up his hand and pressed his fingertips against my lips. I didn't know what to say.

"So how have you been? Are you happy here?" He changed the subject abruptly, pulling his band back.

"Me? Happy here? Sure, why not?" I said, looking away. But Kunio turned me to face him, looking into my eyes as he had always done when he demanded an honest answer. I blushed and added, "Well, I had to make a few adjustments, of course, but I am getting along. I'm okay."

The beautiful book you gave me, I can't keep it here with me, I wanted to tell him. That, and all the other books I loved. Books meant a lot to me.

"Are you sure you're all right?" Kunio insisted.

"Yes, yes, I'm all right," I smiled. What could Kunio do, or anyone else for that matter, about my little private skirmishes with the upper-class girls and the chief nurse? This was a part of the Red Cross life that I had chosen for myself.

"I wrote you a letter." Kunio pulled a thick envelope from inside his jacket.

"Oh!" I was taken aback. So he had traveled all the way from Port Arthur just to hand-deliver his own letter. I had known he resented the censorship of personal letters, but had not expected him to deliver his own letter. It must be much more than an ordinary letter, I thought. My heart throbbed.

"It turned out to be a rather long one. Do you mind?"

"Oh, no. Of course not. You know I like your letters."

"You may not like this one."

"That's all right."

The envelope, which simply said "To Kaz-chan" on the front, was bulging out of shape.

"Do you have a pocket?" he asked.

I fumbled around my skirt but the side pockets were too shallow to hold the envelope. Without a second thought, I unbuttoned my blouse top enough to make an opening for the letter. Kunio came closer to drop the letter in as we used to when I wanted to borrow a book that might not meet Mother's approval. The letter caught the edge of my bra. Kunio jumped back, staring at me, almost accusing me, of becoming a woman when he wasn't looking. I turned back, quickly pushing the letter down, and buttoned my blouse all the way up to my neck. I was embarrassed to tears. Kunio waited, and then gently turned me around to face him.

"Sorry," he said as he looked into my eyes, "but you're beautiful."

"Thanks." I buried my face in his jacket, hiding my embarrassment.

"Now, you take good care of yourself, Kaz-chan, okay?" he whispered. "The letter I just gave you may well be my last words."

"Oh, Kuni-chan! Don't say that!" I cried out, shaking my head furiously. Yet I understood the impact of his letter. I understood it painfully well. There was no way of knowing what lay ahead of us. The distance between Dairen and Tokyo had become more than physical mileage. The youngest of my three older brothers was in Tokyo, attending a college, but we had not heard from him for months. His delicate health had kept him out of the army so far, but we knew Tokyo and many other cities in Japan had been severely bombed. And even in the narrow strait between Korea and southern Japan, which was the only way to get to Japan from Manchuria, Japanese passenger ships had been bombed and destroyed. Kunio knew that he might not even get to Japan safely, let alone survive in Tokyo. So he wanted to leave his last thoughts with someone, and he chose to do so with me. It would be a legacy; Kunio's legacy to me.

"Don't cry." He held me tightly, crushing the letter between us. Then he touched my forehead lightly with his lips.

"We will keep in touch. I promise," he said. I nodded like an obedient little child, and watched him walk away.

After the lights-out that night, I read his letter with the help of a small flashlight. It was, as expected, the letter of an angry young man shaking his fists at his fate, at his country, at his government. At the same time, it was the letter of a brokenhearted youth crying out for a chance to live. And finally, it was a letter of farewell to a girl he had grown up with but might never see again. Above all, however, it was a frightening statement. Kunio called Manchukuo, the country that had been set up in Manchuria by the Japanese government in 1931, Japan's puppet country. He went on to say that the brotherly bond between Japan and Manchukuo that the

11

Japanese government claimed existed was nothing but hypocritical pro-paganda. What really existed, he said, was a relationship between the oppressor and the oppressed, with a deep-rooted hatred on the part of the oppressed. Finally, Kunio claimed, the war Japan had waged in the Pacific for the last three years was nothing but a manifestation of a hunger for more military power, the Japanese themselves being the vic-tims of a government controlled by the military. "It is a crime," Kunio continued, "to blindly prolong a war that has long lost its cause, at the cost of our lives. What are they trying to prove," the letter screamed in fury, "at the cost of our entire generation?"

Had Kunio lost his mind? For a fleeting moment I honestly doubted his sanity. It was called *shi so han*, a thought crime, to think anything crit-ical of the government, and there was no crime more serious than tak-ing a stand against the government. We had been taught to respect and obey the government without question. Where did he get these deeply disturbing ideas and information? I wondered. Yet I knew that Kunio would not have expressed these thoughts had he not truly believed in them. To make things more horrifying, it dawned on me that Kunio might not be alone in these beliefs. I wondered how many of the young men going off to fight for their country really believed in its cause. I remembered the send-off party for my second oldest brother Kay and his *kanpai* toast to Mother instead of the emperor. It had been passed off as a joke, but hadn't Kay been expressing the same sentiment as Kunio was, that he would rather die for his mother than for the emperor? And hadn't he been just as angry as Kunio was for having to give up his own life for a cause that he did not really understand or believe in, but was imposed on him nevertheless?

I was frightened for Kunio. This was no joke. This was a highly articu-late written statement. More than enough had been written to cause him to be thrown into jail as *shi so han*, a thought criminal. No one must see this letter, I decided, and held it tightly all night. Next morning, I wrapped the letter in my nightgown and pushed it deep into the folded futon, guarding against the chief nurse's unannounced inspection.

Waiting for the lights-out the next night, I read through the letter again, line by line, and finally decided to dispose of it. I waited until everyone in the room was asleep, then tore each page to shreds and stole away to the bathroom with the shredded letter stuffed inside my paja-mas. In the quiet of the night, the sound of the toilet flushing seemed to echo through the whole dormitory.

I flushed the letter down the toilet, but Kunio's words have haunted me ever since. Even while I was going through the motions of everyday life I was constantly arguing with Kunio's letter—Japan was fighting to protect all Asian countries against Western invasion. There had been British colonies, French colonies, and Dutch colonies all over Southeast Asia. And from the north, the Russians would have taken Manchuria and Korea a long time ago if it had not been for Japan. If Japan had not stood up for herself in 1904, we would have been a slave country to Czarist Russia, along with Manchuria and Korea. Yes, somebody had to stand up and fight to stave off the European invasion of Asia. How could Kunio dare call this a hunger for more power? As for our relationship with Manchukuo, hadn't Japan been protecting Manchukuo from the Russians? And who had developed and cultivated the otherwise untamed vast field of the Manchurian sub-continent? Not only had Japan developed some six-thousand miles of railway network throughout Manchuria, it had developed coal mines, steel industries, farmland, and countless other industries and businesses. How could this be called military exploitation?

I became aloof and withdrawn to the point that it drew the attention of the forever watchful chief nurse. Twice more I was called in to her office for extensive questioning and pep talks, but this only made me withdraw further into myself.

I was in this confused state of mind when I was called home for my grandfather's funeral. Grandfather had died in his sleep, a *Dai-oh-jo* (great rebirth), a perfect way to end his peaceful existence. He had come to Dairen as a Japanese police inspector and *kendo* (fencing) instructor in 1905 with his young wife and their oldest daughter, Sumi, my mother, at a time when the city was growing rapidly under Japanese military protection, and he had had a son and three more daughters while in Dairen. He enjoyed the life of the privileged and died without suffering. I remember seeing a picture of him in his police uniform, much like that of the military, but by the time I was born he was already retired and my memory of him is closely connected with the affluence and luxury of colonial society. A tall and handsome man with white mustache carefully pinched upward at the ends, he was always dressed in kimono and *haori* (top coat of kimono), *hakama* (loose trousers over kimono), and white *tabi* (socks), proudly displaying the fact that he was a son of *Nambu Hanshi*, the upper class *samurai* of northern Japan. As if to make up for his missing sword, he always carried a slim walking stick with him, which he would hold up in *kendo*'s challenging position with a sharp shout of

"Hutt!" whenever he encountered one of us grandchildren playing out-side the house, invariably winning our laughter and hugs.

Since his only son, my uncle Hideo, had been promoted to an execu-tive position in the Manchurian Railroad Company and transferred to the main office in Mukden, located in south central Manchuria, my grandparents had been living with their third daughter, my aunt Masu, and her family. Aunt Masu sent her car to the Red Cross to pick me up. Several of my classmates came to the front door of the hospital to see me off, or rather to see the chauffeur-driven black car. Privately owned cars were rare in 1944 in Dairen. Aunt Masu was rich and made no secret of it. She was practical and unpretentious in her own way, which was often mistaken for arrogance.

Grandfather's body was still laid in his down-filled silk futon, as if his sleep had never been disturbed. His white mustache was freshly pinched upward, as he had always done himself. Once, his barber had trimmed his prized mustache too short and blunt, and those tips had kept droop-ing, ruining his proud resemblance to General Araki, the war minister and a hero to many Japanese at the time. Oh, how sorry everyone had been for him! I had been his favorite grandchild, probably because I was his first granddaughter. Japanese men in those days refrained from show-ing their affection to their sons and grandsons but were generous with their affection toward little girls. He used to take me home with him after playing hours of *Go* with my father, and treated me to *Gyoza*, my favorite Chinese dumplings, and let me sleep next to him in his luxurious futon. This was a privilege granted only to me, the first granddaughter. As I grew, I came to regard him almost as a distinguished-looking but spoiled child whom the whole family pampered, probably because of the way he played *Go* with my father. They would sit at the *Go* table, specially made of heavy wood about six inches thick with lines of one-inch squares drawn on the surface. We would then hold our breath, expecting to hear Grandfather's flustered *"Matta! Matta!* (hold it, hold it)" plea to my father. It always happened when my father declared *atari*, which is an equivalent of declaring "check" in chess. Father would always give in, shaking his head, and move his white pebble one step back, to give Grandfather a few minutes to better adjust to the inevitable ending.

Everyone was waiting for me to bid him farewell so that they could prepare him for the wake service. I could feel them watching me with concern, ready to comfort me. But I could find no words for him. I sat there, staring at him, deeply trapped in my own thoughts. Grandfather had lived to be seventy-two, an eternity to me then, and had died in his own bed, surrounded by his family. Wasn't this an occasion calling for a celebration? Especially at a time when thousands of young men were dying every day in the battlefield, and hardly by their own choice? I thought of my oldest brother Mamoru, who had had to go to war leaving his pregnant bride behind. He might never have a chance to see his young son, born a few months after he had left. I thought of my second-oldest brother Kay, who had toasted Mother before he left. I thought of Kunio, who might be called to war before he finished college. And I thought of myself, realizing that I too had quit thinking of my life after the war, as if my life would end when the war ended. I could not picture myself, or Kunio, or any of my brothers living normal adult lives and surviving to age seventy-two. My entire generation was a sacred sacrifice dedicated to the "divine" war. And this was an ultimate honor. We had been taught over and over that life was meaningless unless it was given up for a cause. "We live in preparation for honorable death." "One's life must not be a mere existence, and death must not be simply an end of existence." "A death must be a glory, an ultimate honor."

I put my hands together and bowed, silent and dry-eyed. Something within me was holding back my tears, the tears for the grandfather I had loved dearly. I was miserable and confused.

"Kazuko has lost a lot of weight, hasn't she?" Aunt Masu whispered to my mother.

"Yes, and she looks tired, worn out," my mother whispered back, "the poor child." They hurried to the kitchen to prepare a meal for the poor, starving young patriot. I was under orders to report back by eight that night. There was no time to waste. They took me to the dining room and urged me to eat, but I had no appetite. I had not had an appetite for a long time.

"You look exhausted, Kazuko. What is the matter?" Mother asked as she stared into my face.

"I don't know, Mama. I just don't know what's wrong with me."

"They're making slaves out of you freshmen, aren't they?" Aunt Masu asked with a touch of anger.

"No, not really." I said defensively. "We do work around the hospital in the mornings, but afternoons are like school."

"Like school, I'll bet! I've heard a lot about how they treat you there." Then she changed her tone, "You don't get along with the upper-class girls and the supervisors, do you?"

"How did you know?" I was astonished.

"I knew it. I knew it from the very beginning. You just don't fit in there."

"Now, now, don't get upset," Mother cut in. "Everything will work out fine once they get to know you. There's something I must tell you before I forget. Your father has been promoted to head the Furanten branch of the Japanese government office and we are moving there as soon as a suitable house is available."

"Furanten? I am not sure where that is."

"It's at the border of the Liaotung Peninsula and Manchukuo," Aunt Masu answered my question. "A small farming town. Nothing much is going on there."

"Is everyone going?" I looked across the room to where Mamoru's wife Hisako was rocking her newborn baby Yukio. Hisako looked up and nodded assurance to me with a soft smile. I returned the smile, satisfied. I loved this gentle sister-in-law who was also my peer, only five years my senior.

"We'll be over to see you before we leave," Mother said, "but after that, your Aunt Masu will keep in touch with you, all right?"

The symptoms my mother and aunt had noticed became more clear to me as the days went by. I couldn't eat, often woke up in a cold sweat, and felt tired and feverish all the time. One evening, the chief nurse walked into the student lounge and noticed my flushed face. She asked me some questions and I finally told her about my loss of weight and the other physical problems I had been having. The chief nurse sent me to the hospital the following day, scolding me for not reporting it sooner. After an extensive examination, my problem was diagnosed as tuberculosis in its early stage, and I was placed in an isolation ward. My family was notified, and my father asked for my immediate release.

CHAPTER 2

Paris in the Far East

MY RED CROSS training had lasted barely six months by the time Aunt Masu came to the Red Cross hospital to pick me up. I was to stay at her house in Dairen, where the medical facilities were far better than those in Furanten, at least until after the severe Manchurian winter was over.

I could hear my aunt's voice long before she came into my room, a pleasantly vibrant alto, full of energy and vitality even when she was holding it down in the hospital. Long-legged Aunt Masu leisurely strode into my room while the chief nurse held the door open for her. She was still talking and smiling and trying her best to apologize for the inconvenience that I had caused the Red Cross, although she did not look very humble. Humility was one quality that my aunt lacked. She was a born queen. The domineering air that caused her employees and business associates to call her *Tai-tai* ("married woman" in Chinese but "boss lady" in this case) followed her everywhere. In the 1940s, when women were not expected to run businesses, Aunt Masu was unique even in the colonial metropolis of Dairen. She ran a scrap iron importing company right along with her husband Hozen.

"Are you ready?" She asked me cheerfully.

I was sitting on the bed, hugging my pillow. Good old Auntie—I smiled to myself. The beige knit suit with mink trimming that hugged her and the brown leather beret that tilted fashionably on top of her bobbed hair were as foreign as she herself in the Red Cross world. But that was my aunt. She never catered to the environment. She created her own.

"I brought you warm clothes." She laid out a colorful sweater, a pair of wool pants, and heavy stockings on my bed and dropped a pair of snow boots to the floor.

"Is it snowing already?" I quickly turned to the window. I loved snow. It was the beginning of October, a little too early for snow, though it could happen in Dairen. But the sky was bright and clear.

"No, silly. I just wanted to keep your feet warm."

I slipped into the clothes quietly while Aunt tugged at my sweater as if dressing a small child.

"We will send someone for her things later," Aunt said to the chief nurse. "We really appreciate all you did for her."

"I—er—thank you very much for everything, Ma'am." I bowed deeply to the chief nurse, the stiff fifteen-degree bow of the Red Cross salute already forgotten.

"You're welcome. Now you mind your aunt, and take good care of yourself." The chief nurse patted my back with unexpected gentleness and then quickly left the room.

"Did you notice that she didn't say 'hurry back?'" I asked as soon as we got into the car.

"You want to come back?" Aunt raised her eyebrows.

I turned away from her and sank deeper into the seat.

"No, I don't think so. I don't belong here."

Aunt Masu's house, which was western style with a few Japanese rooms, was in one of the many scenic residential areas around the hills that enhanced the city of Dairen. It stood on top of the hill called *Mei-kaku-dai* (Singing Crane's Heights), dominating the neighborhood. The house was one of the largest in the area: cream-colored walls with red-tiled roof, as bright as a children's storybook illustration; two-storied at the front with a "Romeo and Juliet" balcony over the main entrance; three-storied at the back with a spacious glassed-in sunroom extending into a rock garden over the sloping hill. The upstairs guest room that Aunt had prepared for me was the only room that had access to this "Romeo and Juliet" balcony which I had named and had always loved. From this balcony, I could see rooftops of all colors stepping down the hill, layer by layer, all the way down to the main street, where busses, cars, and streetcars seemed to be part of a busy world of miniature people.

To the southeast, this street ran as far as the scenic beach of *Roh-ko-tan* (the High Sea of Great Tigers), passing by several swimming resorts separated by capes. The furthest part of *Roh-ko-tan* was a rough beach unsuitable for swimming but known for its scenic beauty, with hundreds of sharp-edged black rocks jutting far out into the blue-green ocean, fighting against the roaring tide, smashing the waves into icy sparkles. To the north, streetcars and busses traveled to the city center, passing by colorful residential areas until they reached the Central Park. A memorial tower for the war dead, *Chu-lei-toh*, stood high above the evergreen forest in the center of the park, two baseball stadiums lay in the sun, playgrounds and ponds hid in the forest, and my old school *Futaba Gakuin*, from which I had graduated only ten months ago, sat quietly in the shadows of tall acacia trees at the edge of the park.

This street, like all main streets in the city of Dairen, extended from one park to another, with all main streets eventually meeting in *Oh-hiro-ba* (Great Field) Park in the center of the downtown area, surrounded by the Japanese government building, the British Embassy, a hotel, banks, and other stately buildings. *Oh-hiro-ba* Park was shaped like a wheel, with spokes of promenades leading toward the center where the tall bronze statue of General Ohshima, the first governor of *Kanto-shu* (Liaotung Peninsula as a Japanese colony), stood, declaring ownership of the colony. The main streets that radiated out from this park were named after the heroes of the Russo-Japanese war, constant reminders of the glorious history of Dairen. The park was also the place where a jubilant parade was held to celebrate Japan's victory over China in 1932, the event that led to the birth of Manchukuo, a country arbitrarily separated from China proper by the force of the Japanese military. As a little girl, I had watched the parade from the balcony of my father's office building near the park. The marching high school students following their school bands waved Japanese flags in the daytime, but at night they held up lighted paper lanterns, which, with big red dots painted on a white background to represent the Japanese flag, lit up the streets like waves of thousands of illuminated red balls flowing into the park.

Dairen had been an insignificant fishing village called Chingniwa, when Great Britain took the Bay of Dalyan from China in 1860. The British renamed the bay Victoria Bay after their queen, and opened Port Arthur (named after the queen's husband) thirty miles west of Chingniwa. Japan took control of the area when she was granted the Liaotung Peninsula and Formosa by the Treaty of Shimonoseki in 1895, after winning the Sino-Japanese War. Shortly afterward, however, Russia, with help from Germany and France, forced Japan to return the Liaotung Peninsula to China. Three years later, in 1898, Russia succeeded in forcing the lease of Liaotung Peninsula from weakening China, and developed Port Arthur into a great naval base as the first step to exert its power over Asia.

Czarist Russia then brought in their finest architects to this insignificant fishing village to build their dream city, a "Paris in the Far East," copying the layout and architecture of Paris. Nicholas II named the city "Dal'nii"—the faraway place—and declared it a tax-free commercial port. At the same time, fortified by their naval power in Port Arthur, the Russians started to exert control over Manchuria, and gradually increased their pressure on Korea.

The Russian expansion in the Far East was a serious threat to Japan, a threat that eventually led to the Russo-Japanese War. On 8 February 1904, the Japanese navy began the war with a surprise attack on Port Arthur, seriously crippling the Russian fleet there, while the Japanese army gained a succession of victories over the czar's garrisons in Manchuria and Vladivostok, succeeding in wresting Korea from Russian control. The Japanese army also invaded the Liaotung Peninsula, cutting off Port Arthur from upper Manchuria. Russian squadrons at both Port Arthur and Vladivostok were forced out of action by August 1904 and Port Arthur surrendered in February 1905. After the destruction of the Russian Far Eastern Navy, the Baltic fleet was dispatched to the war zone. This fleet arrived in the Far East in May 1905 after a six-month voyage halfway around the world, but was completely destroyed before reaching Vladivostok by the Japanese navy which was under General Togo's command in the strait between Korea and Japan. A month later, all of the Russian troops surrendered and the war was over.

Later that year, in the Treaty of Portsmouth, Theodore Roosevelt, then president of the United States, persuaded both Japan and Russia to return Manchuria to China, except for the lease of Liaotung Peninsula which was to be transferred from Russia to Japan. More importantly, the right to set up the Southern Manchurian Railroad Company was to be granted to Japan. *Dal'nii* was renamed *Dairen*, the Great Connection, and Japan took over the construction of the dream city, developing it into a base for the further development of Manchuria. The Japanese government then poured money and manpower into building the railroad, which eventually included some six-thousand miles of railway network, reaching all corners of Manchuria.

The Treaty of Portsmouth, however, left many Japanese feeling that

Roosevelt had tricked Japan into giving up the valuable land of Manchuria, and that it was a power play to hold back Japan from becoming too strong an economic and military power in the Far East. So the Kwantung Army (the Japanese field army in Manchuria), which often defied Tokyo, took it into their own hands to gain what they felt they had been cheated of. On 18 September 1931, a group of Kwantung Army soldiers staged an act of sabotage on a railroad track near Mukden, a city in south central Manchuria, giving the Japanese army enough excuse to move in. This was a well-planned surprise attack to take over the heart of Manchuria. By noon the next day, 19 September, the Kwantung Army occupied both Mukden and Changchun. This well-calculated invasion was undertaken without prior notification of or official approval from the Japanese government in Tokyo, but the field commanders in Manchuria were supported by the General Staff and the War Ministry of the Japanese government. By January 1932, a full-scale invasion of Manchuria had been completed.

Thus Manchuria was cut off from China proper, and Japan arbitrarily set up an independent country, naming it Manchukuo. Henry Pu Yi, the last emperor of the Manchu dynasty that had ruled China since 1644, who had lost his political power in the Chinese revolution of 1911, was selected by Japan to be Manchukuo's puppet ruler.

Manchuria thus became a land of opportunity open exclusively to the Japanese. The Japanese dominated key positions in government, railroads, and all other industries and trades. They poured into Manchuria with dreams of Utopia, in search of a quick fortune, or simply looking for a better life. In 1935, the Japanese government drew up a plan to send five million Japanese farmers into the underdeveloped northern part of Manchuria over the next twenty years. Soon, groups of farmers recruited with promises of cheap and rich land were sent into the remote areas under Japanese military protection. Japan, which for centuries had been confined to four overcrowded islands with few natural resources, was now well on her way to realizing her dream of long-needed expansion in Manchuria. However, in the same way that hostilities broke out between European settlers and Native American tribes during the pioneer days of North America, Japanese on the frontier frequently clashed with the Manchurian natives. Conflicts between anti-Japanese guerrillas and the Japanese army occurred frequently throughout Manchuria.

Dairen was far from the frontier, however. It had been a well-guarded Japanese colony for years, and the native Chinese, White Russians

(Czarist Russians who had escaped the Russian revolution of 1917), and other residents who had lived there before the Japanese took over the city had withdrawn to live in the shadow of the prosperous Japanese. The Japanese, drenched with national hubris after the victory in the Russo-Japanese War of 1905, shamelessly dominated Dairen. Dairen became the frontier symbol of the supreme power of the Rising Sun, forever erasing its Russian name, *Dal'nii*. It was only natural, then, that Japanese of my generation, who had been born in Dairen, grew up taking the Japanese supremacy for granted and were totally unaware of the hardship and true feelings of the others around us. To us, to me, Dairen was Japan—not an extension of Japan, but the representation of its power, the symbol of its international supremacy.

Aunt Masu's doctor was not alarmed by my condition. It was evident that I had been exposed to tuberculosis within the last few months and my body had reacted to it, but, he assured us, nothing serious was in progress. His prescription included relaxation and a nutritious diet, which were easily provided.

Aunt Masu and her husband Hozen usually went to their office in the midmorning when they were in town, leaving my grandmother to run the house with a Korean housemaid and her husband who was a gardener and chauffeur. My cousin Toru, Aunt Masu's son by her first and short-lived teenage marriage, was my age and we shared a private English tutor for some time, but we were never close. While I would prefer to walk in the sun he would often hide behind bushes and watch people go by. He was in the habit of avoiding people's attention, probably because he was noticeably lame as a result of infantile paralysis he had suffered just before he turned three. He especially avoided his stepfather Hozen, who, in turn, made no effort to communicate with him. Uncle Hozen was a man of few words, and when he did talk it was usually in a short, imperative phrases and in an intimidating low voice.

Uncle Hozen was the son of a Zen priest. Although he had not become a Zen priest himself, he kept his head shaven and chanted the Paramita Sutra, the core teaching of Zen Buddhism, whenever his mood called for it, especially when he had a few drinks in him. Although he would confine himself to the Japanese room upstairs when he chanted the sutra, his booming voice would ring through the house, picking up speed and getting louder and louder, accompanied by banging on the wooden gong, as he went on.

"It's too bad that you are not a boy." Toru startled me one evening, silently limping into the library where I was leafing through a book. Aunt Masu had a cozy little library, with hard-covered thick books stacked to the ceiling.

"I know. That's what everybody says," I replied shortly, uninterested in the old comment I had heard all my life. If a girl excelled at school, everyone wished she were a boy in those days.

"Well, what do *you* think? Do you wish you were a boy?"

"What on earth for? I like what I am."

"But isn't that why you joined the Red Cross? Because it's the closest thing to the army that a girl can get into?"

"Maybe."

"You like wars, don't you? You wanted to go to war like your brothers, didn't you?"

"So what's wrong with that?" I was getting irritated.

"Nothing," Toru shrugged. "Nothing is 'wrong' with wars, I suppose. Wars are essential to the progress of mankind. There will always be wars as long as there are men. So, did you get to play soldiers at the Red Cross?"

I closed the book and turned to face his sneer. I remembered the crawling and hiding on the hills, carrying a stretcher with a mock patient in it, much too heavy for young girls. Were we "playing soldier" then? Was that what I wanted?

"Well, did you?" Toru repeated. "Did you learn to march and salute like soldiers too? Show me how you salute."

"A Red Cross salute is different from a soldier's. But we had a sergeant from the regular army to give us drills."

"Drills? Girls doing drills?"

"Why not? You're silly, Toru. Why can't girls do drills?"

Toru shrugged again and changed the subject.

"Do you know, Mother wants us to pick up the English lessons again now that you're back?"

"Hm . . ."

Much to the disapproval of those with broader views of the world, the Japanese government had taken English off the required curriculum in all Japanese high schools shortly after the war in the Pacific had broken out, although Chinese was kept compulsory in all Japanese schools in Manchuria from the fourth grade up through high school. This was meant to discourage any Western influence of individualism on the younger generation and to promote imperialism instead. Aunt Masu was one of those who did not approve of what the government was doing. She accused the government of blindfolding the young people and leading them in the direction that suited their military purpose.

"You know, I prefer Chinese over English, as far as the language learning goes," I said, not really to Toru, but more like thinking out loud to myself. Then I turned to explain my thoughts to him, "Chinese is what's needed here, if we are to be brothers with the Manchurians and fight the war together . . . "

"Oh, come on, Kaz-chan, you're so naive." Toru shook his head with exaggerated disbelief.

"Don't you know that the Manchurians hate our guts?"

"What do you mean? They don't hate us. They can't. Look at all the things that the Japanese have done for them. How can they hate us? I know they appreciate us. They are nice people. I've had Manchurian classmates and I liked them. They liked me too."

Although the schools were segregated, as well as other public facilities such as restaurants, theaters, busses, streetcars, and even the residential areas and shopping areas, some selected Manchurian children were allowed to attend Japanese schools.

"Oh, you are hopeless, Kaz-chan. I'll bet you think Koreans just love us to death too, don't you?"

"Why, Koreans *are* Japanese. Well, almost."

"Yeah, almost," Toru laughed.

In 1910, after five years of military occupation, Japan had officially made Korea her subject state, forcing all Koreans to take Japanese names and educate their children in Japanese. They were now Japanese citizens, but the Japanese in Korea still held top positions in most trades there and remained the upper class of the country. This was very similar to the position that the Japanese held in Manchuria, but the way Japanese felt about Manchurians and the way that they felt about Koreans were interestingly different. While the Japanese, especially my father's age group, tried to reach out to Manchurians, with a touch of a guilty conscience, most Japanese regarded Koreans as somewhat inferior.

Korea had a long history of invasion because of its strategic location between Japan, China, and Russia. At the end of the sixteenth century, China and Japan had fought over Korea over a period of six years. In the end China retained its control over Korea, but Japan never gave up. Korea was strategic because it could serve as a land bridge to Manchuria, where

China and Russia held control. China finally gave up all claim to Korea after being defeated in the Sino-Japanese war of 1894, and granted Korea independence. Russia then tried to take over Korea but was defeated by Japan in the Russo-Japanese war of 1905. Since then Korea had been under Japanese occupation.

Korea had been handed back and forth like some kind of a prize for any winner to take, as if the Koreans had no self-respect or national pride. The Japanese, who were overloaded with national pride, looked down on Koreans and were crudely arrogant toward them as if they were destined to be subservient to all people, especially to the Japanese.

"Think of it this way for a minute, Kaz-chan," said Toru. "Suppose you were stateless, and given a choice of becoming Korean or Manchurian, which would you choose?"

"Manchurian," I said without hesitation.

"Why? Why not Korean?"

"Because—well, because I was born in Dairen. Manchuria. Dairen is my home and I love Dairen. But I have nothing to do with Korea. I've never even been to Korea."

Toru took a long, hard look at me.

"You don't know Japan either. And you've never been to Japan either."

"But I am Japanese. By blood."

"By blood, yes. But do you know what that amounts to? It means only that you think you love Japan, because you've been taught to love Japan, or because the adults around you talk of Japan with such reverence and attachment. And you think you believe in Japan because you've been taught to believe in Japan. You see, Kaz-chan, you are only what you've been taught to be."

I was amazed. I had never known Toru to talk at any length, let alone with such passion.

"You're sick. You've got a twisted mind," I mumbled a weak protest, and averted my eyes from his sharply narrowed gaze.

"You will spend the rest of your life in Dairen and you will be speaking Chinese," he said, as if handing down a life sentence.

"So? I don't want to go anywhere else. I'll live and die here like Grandfather did. And I'll be happy. Very happy. But getting back to the English lessons, I don't mind having English as my third language since Dairen is an international city and I can certainly use it here."

Mrs. Hayakawa, the widow from whom Uncle Hozen and Aunt Masu had bought their house, agreed to resume my English lessons. Toru

25

declined the offer, using his college work as an excuse. Mrs. Hayakawa had spent most of her adult life abroad, as her late husband had worked for the Ministry of Foreign Affairs in the Japanese government. She came two afternoons a week, and the lessons were more like pleasant visits now that Toru was out of my way. Since we always met at the library, the conversation usually centered around books. I was rather surprised to find that Aunt Masu collected Japanese classics, of which Mrs. Hayakawa highly approved. Because Aunt Masu always dressed in Western clothes— hat, gloves, and business suits in the mornings when she went to the office with uncle Hozen—and because of her bold articulacy, which in my mind was more closely associated with Western culture than with Japanese tradition, especially for women, I had expected her to be reading something like translations of Tolstoi, Dostoevsky, or Turgenev, who were quite popular among the young intellectuals in Dairen at that time. Mrs. Hayakawa, in spite of spending most of her adult life abroad, always dressed in kimono of elegant taste, even when I saw her in her own home. Then I noticed that Aunt Masu had started to wear kimono the afternoons that Mrs. Hayakawa was expected. They exchanged compliments on each other's taste in kimono, which they seemed to share. When in kimono Aunt Masu transformed herself into quite an attractive Japanese lady: her voice toned down, her smile softened (she never laughed with her head thrown back, as she did with me), and she was even coquettish with Uncle Hozen in those evenings in kimono. Seeing the two ladies in kimono of shared elegance, exchanging gentle compliments, I could see that they shared the same taste in books. This was the hidden side of Aunt Masu.

Aunt Masu owned a complete set of *Tales of Genji* by Murasaki Shikibu, the world's first novel written by a female author, depicting a court romance of eleventh-century Japan. It had been beautifully translated into modern Japanese by the famous author Junichiro Tanizaki. At Mrs. Hayakawa's recommendation, I started to read it, and soon lost myself in the magical power of the book. With the help of Mrs. Hayakawa, I translated some of the poems exchanged between Genji and his lovers into English.

Thus the winter days went by uneventfully and I had almost forgotten that a war was still going on until one day Akiko from the Red Cross came to visit me. Akiko had also been my high school classmate. We had been on the school volleyball team together. I had been only an alternate, but tall and quick Akiko was the captain of the team, guarding the front line and shooting a sharp ball into the opposing team's weak spots.

Sitting up straight, clad in the Red Cross dress uniform, Akiko looked like another person. The pillbox hat over the tightly pulled-back hair made her look much older than her eighteen years. She had also gained an air of authority about her, making her almost intimidating, and I was rather uncomfortable. This was not the "Ako" with whom I had shared laughter and dreams in my high school days. When Aunt Masu brought in a tray of tea and cookies, Akiko stood up and saluted my aunt with the stiff Red Cross bow in the most spontaneous manner. I introduced them formally, then waited for Aunt Masu to leave.

"You look great, Ako. You look like a full-fledged Red Cross nurse already," I said, with genuine admiration. Indeed, she looked like the picture of the nurse I had seen in the poster that had inspired me to join the Red Cross.

"Oh, don't let the uniform fool you, Kaz. I am as dumb as I was last year." She laughed and I felt better. Her laughter hadn't changed.

"You're looking much better, Kaz. Are you getting better?"

"Me? Oh, yes, I am all right." I had almost forgotten that I had dropped out of the Red Cross because of the suspected tuberculosis.

"Yes, I am doing fine. My fever is gone and my appetite is back. I will probably be fat before I know it."

"You need to exercise to regain your strength. Do you take a walk regularly?"

"No, but I will when the weather gets better. How is everybody at school?"

"Fine. Everybody is just fine. We were all worried about you. Why didn't you write me back? I wrote you twice, you know."

"I know. I am sorry."

But I had nothing to say, I thought to myself. What was a drop-out supposed to say? Sorry that I couldn't keep up with you? Sorry that I let you down? But then I was not really sorry. I did not feel that I had failed the Red Cross—it could even have been the other way around. In any case, it was the wrong place for me. I had knocked on the wrong door. So our conversation was awkward. We did not belong to the same world anymore. We no longer shared the same dream. I was not interested in what went on in Red Cross any more than Akiko would have been in the world of *Tales of Genji*.

Akiko looked out of the glass door to the snow-covered rock garden and paid her compliments. I thanked her—Gosh, weren't we being polite. It was obvious to me that Akiko was not really impressed with the beauty of the garden.

"Those poor soldiers . . . " Akiko said, proving me right. All she saw was the snow, the icy snow, not the carefully selected and arranged rocks underneath, or the surrounding evergreens humbly holding out layers of sparkling snow.

"You know, it's below zero around the Manchurian-Siberian border," she continued. "I am glad that I am healthy. I can take cold weather."

"Are you expecting to be sent there someday?"

"Most likely. We can handle the cold weather better than the mainland nurses can."

"You remember my oldest brother, Mamoru, don't you?"

"Yes, he is in the Kwantung Army, isn't he?"

"Yes, he is stationed in one of the outposts north of Harbin, right by the Amur River. He can see Siberia across the river, he said."

"Well, he'll be safe there, at least. The Russians won't invade Manchuria because of the nonaggression treaty with Japan."

"I know. And he is used to the cold weather. But my second oldest brother, Kay, is in the Pacific."

"Oh, where?"

"We don't know. All we know is his mailing code. But we think he is somewhere in the southern Pacific because he sent us a postcard with a drawing. You know how he always drew cartoons. Well, he drew a cartoon figure of himself with big drops of sweat dropping out from under his helmet and captioned it, 'For the first time in my life, I am having a hot new year's day. A Happy New Year.'"

I laughed, remembering the miserable expression of the cartoon soldier, sweltering under a huge sun. Akiko smiled politely but did not laugh. There was nothing funny about war—Akiko was sending me a silent reproach.

I was becoming more and more uncomfortable and was relieved when Akiko got up to leave. I followed her to the door and was going out to walk her to the gate, but she stopped me at the door.

"The air is too cold for you, Kaz. Let's say good-bye here. I'll be back to see you soon. And you hurry up and get well, won't you?"

Akiko gave me a quick hug and swiftly stepped outside, shutting the door tightly behind herself. I stood by the closed door, listening to her footsteps squeak in the snow, fading away step by step—*My God! Will I ever see her again?* I flung the door open.

"Ako!"

Akiko turned around.

"Take care! Please take care of yourself!"

"Yes, I will. Thanks. And you too, Kaz."

Our eyes locked and for a fleeting moment I imagined myself running out to hold her and cry with her as we had done many times when we had lost or won a game of volleyball. But instead, I stood there helplessly, looking at my proud friend, a picture of a young patriot in navy blue uniform, the Red Cross emblem on her cap reflecting the afternoon sun. She took a deep breath, then sharply turned around on the heel of her ankle-high laced boots and walked away without another word.

I felt a pang. I envied her, my beautiful friend. I feared for her life, but still I envied her for her unwavering faith in Japan, for her innocent pride, and for her passionate dedication, all of which seemed to be slipping through my hands.

In a Forgotten Spot on Earth

CHAPTER 3

IN MARCH 1945, when the weather was warmer, my father came to Dairen to take me to our new home in Furanten. I could have traveled there on my own, but my father considered it his parental duty to thank Uncle Hozen and Aunt Masu in person for taking care of me. My father did everything properly.

He brought a supply of fresh eggs, chickens, and top-grade rice, all of which were becoming harder to obtain in Dairen but were still plentiful in a farm town like Furanten.

"Sumi sends her best regards to you and Hozen," Father said as he bowed to Aunt Masu. "And how is your mother?"

"She is doing very well, thank you. She went to the temple this afternoon. It's her day to visit my father's grave."

Since my grandfather had passed away my grandmother had been visiting his grave every month. According to his wish, part of his ashes had been sent to his family grave in Japan and the remainder had been buried in the cemetery in a Jodo Shinshu temple in Dairen. Grandfather had died with no doubt in his mind that Dairen would continue to prosper as a part of Japan and he wanted to be there with his children, grandchildren, and all the descendants to follow. To this day, I cannot totally deny the feeling that he may still be there waiting for us to come back.

Furanten, where my father had been transferred to head the Japanese government office for the area, was a farm town of about ten thousand native Chinese and four to five hundred Japanese, located at the border

31

of Manchukuo and the Liaotung Peninsula. It was only about seventy miles north of Dairen, but the local train took about two hours to get there because it stopped at every small town on the way, picking up Chinese farm laborers, who rode in separate coaches, and Japanese passengers, who rode with us. I was content sitting next to my father, enjoying the slow ride. After leaving the outskirts of Dairen, the scene outside the window was an endless flat field with scattered snow mounds, a reminder of the past winter, each like a doughnut with a large hole, about to give in to the dawn of spring.

"Look, Father, look how wet and shiny the snow is now, like diamond chips have been sprinkled on."

Father looked out, nodding with a smile. We watched in silence for a long time. Then he pulled out the small notebook that he always carried with him. I knew he was going to write down a Haiku or two. He was a poet. He belonged to a group of amateur Haiku poets. As a small child I used to watch him go through hundreds of Haiku poems sent to him for his approval. He carefully selected those suitable for publication for the monthly booklets for the members. When the printed booklets were delivered to our house, I helped him fold them in half and wrapped a brown envelope around each one, then watched Father write an address and a name on each in his bold penmanship. Later we would carry the bulk to a nearby mailbox which was painted fire-engine red. I used to love to stretch out to feed the booklets into the mouth of the red "monster" while Father patiently handed them to me a few at a time.

It seemed a lifetime ago since I had felt his warmth next to me, and I savored every minute of it because I knew once I reached home I would have to share him with everybody else. My mother, my brother's wife, Hisako, her little boy Yukio, and my youngest sister, Toshiko, were waiting for us at home. My other sister, Michiko, who was thirteen then, had to remain in Dairen with my Aunt Sadako's family since there was no Japanese high school in Furanten.

When we finally reached Furanten, the train stopped barely long enough to let us off. As Father and I stepped down to the one and only concrete platform, there wasn't anybody to get onto the car, or waiting for another train. All I could see was a small brick building in front of us which seemed vacant.

"Is this a railway station?"

"Yes, this is it." Father smiled at my puzzled look.

"So this is Furanten," I whispered, awed by the tranquillity that seemed to dominate the town. In the open space in front of the station there were a few rickshaws (carriages pulled by men) and one *mache* (a carriage pulled by a horse), but the drivers were not with their carriages. They were sitting cross-legged on the ground in a sunny spot, leisurely smoking long, narrow pipes. No taxi, no bus, no streetcar, and most of all, no bustling crowd, as I had expected at a railway station.

"That's my office there."

Father pointed out a two-storied gray building across the open space. A police station, fire station, dispensary, a few stores, and a small hotel were all in this one area, but I did not see a living soul on the street. No pedestrians, no running children, not even a stray dog. Everything was standing still, like a faded sepia photograph from a timeless era. The *mache* into which my Father and I stepped was the only thing that was in motion, the only evidence of life.

"It's Sunday afternoon, Kazuko. Everybody is resting, getting ready for tomorrow," Father said, somewhat apologetically.

My father's two-storied office building was the tallest in town. All of the others were single-level buildings, almost parallel to the height of the *mache* in which we were riding. Even the poplars planted on sidewalk were not tall enough to tower over our *mache*. They stood awkwardly, too young to shade the town, helplessly leaving the whole town exposed to the glare of the harsh Manchurian sun. Off the main street, the *mache* led us through a neatly kept residential area, obviously reserved for Japanese. In the middle of the area was a Japanese elementary school with a large Japanese flag on top of a tall pole, hanging limp in the windless air. A few blocks from the school, I saw a tennis court protected by a tall chain-link fence.

"There's our house," Father said pointing to a red brick house with a large picture window, sitting at the foot of a mountain. The white picket fence that surrounded the house was low enough for any child to walk over, quite a contrast to the houses in Dairen, which usually were surrounded by tall concrete walls or hedges tall and thick enough to discourage an intruder.

"Everything here is so different from Dairen, isn't it?" I exclaimed.

"I know. It's a peaceful town. I hope you'll like it here."

"I already do, Father."

This was a forgotten spot on the war-filled Earth, a lagoon at the mouth of the Manchurian subcontinent, far away from hatred, power struggle, prejudice, and bloodshed.

On the other side of the mountain behind our house there was a Shinto shrine. Shinto, a form of ancestor worship, was Japan's indigenous religion before Buddhism, and Japanese pioneers always built a shrine wherever they settled, believing that the spirit of their ancestors would watch over them and protect them. The Furanten shrine was much smaller than the Dairen shrine, of course, but it had all the makings of a Shinto shrine—a Torii gate and a long walk from the Torii gate to the main shrine, with a line of cherry trees on both sides. The cherry trees were still young, as were the poplars in town, but by the time I started to take my daily walk to the shrine at the end of April, the young trees were in full bloom, doing their best to adorn the shrine.

I walked to this shrine in midmornings, taking a roundabout route through town, passing by coolies taking naps in the sun, and street venders sitting cross-legged on the ground by their meager shops of candied plums, shooing flies occasionally. The plums were coated with shiny, red-colored honey, however, forever inviting the flies back to them. The candied plums were on bamboo skewers, which were stuck in all directions into a straw-bed on a pole. They were quite appetizing, as well as pretty to look at, and I was always tempted to try them, but the sight of the flies discouraged me.

Once in a while I met a parade of schoolchildren heading toward the shrine in an orderly march like miniature soldiers, which was how they were trained at that time. It was mandatory that students of all grades pay a visit to the shrine on the first day of every month to dedicate a one-minute silent prayer to the war casualties and to pray for Japan's victory in the Pacific. My father, being a loyal Japanese subject, accompanied me to the shrine on those first-day-of-the-month visits.

One day when he was with me, a small incident happened. On our way home we saw a group of Manchurian high school students marching toward us. When the teacher recognized my father, he suddenly ordered a loud "Atten-tion!" followed by "Eyes Right!" all in clear Japanese military terms. My father was astounded, to say the least. He quickly looked around to see if this formal military group salute was meant for someone near us, but saw no one. He straightened himself up and returned the salute, imitating military fashion as best he could manage. I remained next to him, dumbfounded.

"Wow, what a surprise . . . " I said afterward, catching up to his suddenly quickened steps, and saw that he was terribly embarrassed.

"It's this *kokumin-huku*," he said somewhat curtly. Only then did I realize that he was wearing *kokumin-huku*, the government ordered "national clothes." The father I remembered had always worn a suit and tie, but now he wore khaki clothing closely resembling a military uniform. It had become a requirement for all Japanese men to wear *kokumin-huku* after I had left home for Red Cross.

"So the teacher took you for some military person?" I ventured consolingly.

"No, he knows me. He knows who I am."

"Oh, well, you are one of the highest ranking people in town."

"I am only a civil servant," he cut me off.

"Yeah, but . . . " I swallowed the rest of the sentence—*but we are Japanese.*

I knew that the Japanese supremacy that my generation of Japanese in Dairen were taking for granted had always made my father uneasy. The Japanese government in the Manchurian colony was the frontier symbol of Japan's international power, the power of "the Rising Sun," its officials bigger than life. But this was exactly what frightened my father—our blind faith in military propaganda, our innocent acceptance of Japanese supremacy. I often sensed it in him like a hidden guilt he didn't want to see himself. When I first announced my decision to join the Red Cross and boldly displayed my unquestioning faith in Japan's "divine" mission as the leader of all Asian countries, he winced as if I had touched his hidden scar. And his promptness in requesting my immediate release from the Red Cross when the symptoms of tuberculosis were noted in me made me feel as if he had been waiting for a reasonable excuse to rescue me from a trap. Yet he was one of the proudest and the most faithful Japanese men I knew. This was the complexity that my father's generation lived through and died with: a combined sense of guilt and pride.

Japan had been losing ground in the Pacific steadily for more than a year now. Since the United States Navy had won their first major victory at Midway, the Allies had gained initiative and the movement in the Pacific had been westward—through Guadalcanal, the Solomons, the Philippines, the Marshall Islands, Saipan, and Guam. These losses were skillfully underplayed, however, by the loud propaganda extolling the heroism of Japan's servicemen. The newspapers were full of stories of brave soldiers, especially those of the suicide attacks—*Kami-kaze*—as if they were the promises of tomorrow's victory. Such propaganda fooled no one in his right mind, and yet it fed the emotional need of the public. We needed to believe in something.

It was about this time that the Japanese government sent a Shinto priest to the Furanten shrine to reassure us of Japan's ultimate victory. Shinto was the power behind the Japanese concept of loyalty to the emperor. According to Shinto dogma, the emperor was the direct descendant of the Sun Goddess, who had chosen the islands of Japan to which to send her grandson to establish a divine country in 660 B.C. The Sun Goddess had since protected Japan against all foreign invasions, helped the country expand, and was to help Japan rise to become the world's leading power. Having exhausted all other resources, the Japanese government was now using Shintoism to hold the people together. The priest was carrying an Imperial plea to the enshrined ancestral spirit to enlist all the divine power from every shrine, even from those in remote towns like Furanten.

As the representative of the Japanese government in Furanten, my father had the responsibility of receiving the Imperial messenger. Formal ceremonial attire was sent to him with detailed instructions for the ceremony. He practiced his walk and bow at home, measuring the length of his steps and degrees of his bow, reminding me of my regulation-bound days with the Red Cross. When the time came, the priest and my father played their roles to perfection, as expected, but it seemed to have no effect on the course of the war.

My mother also was busy heading the women's patriotic organization. She cut her kimonos at blouse length, making loose-fitting pants with the remaining material, a more suitable outfit for the wartime lifestyle. She did not, however, cut any of my kimonos. They were stored away in a chest with mothballs, waiting for the end of the war. My mother was sure that the day would come when her daughters would dress up in kimono again.

Across the tennis court in front of our house lived the Furanten police chief, Mr. Kawano, and his wife. Mrs. Kawano came to visit my mother almost daily, and she always brought her Chinese housemaid, May-Min. Mrs. Kawano was a motherly, fortyish, plump lady who treated May-Min like her own daughter, perhaps because they were childless.

May-Min was one of nine children of the janitor who worked for the Japanese police force in Furanten. When the Kawanos had first come to Furanten four years ago, May-Min's father had offered May-Min to be their housemaid. May-Min had been fourteen then, pale, skinny, and shy.

Mrs. Kawano had happily taken May-Min under her wing, feeding and clothing her well and teaching her everything that she thought a girl of her age should know. May-Min had become deeply attached to the Kawanos, going home only when Mrs. Kawano sent her home with groceries and clothes for her family.

Since May-Min and I were the same age, we quickly became good friends. I followed her to town on her errands and made friends with the native Chinese at the shops where May-Min would stop to visit. For the first time in my life, I was exposed to the part of town set aside exclusively for the Manchurians, and I was pleasantly surprised that everybody in the area knew my father and spoke of him with respect and genuine affection. For one thing, my father was fluent in Chinese, both Mandarin and local Manchurian, and had many Manchurian friends and acquaintances, both officially and personally. He also had a reputation for being fair and courteous to all his subordinates, Japanese and Manchurians alike.

I knew I was treated well because of my father, but gradually I started making friends on my own merit. They made me try their Chinese cookies and laughed when I made a face because I didn't like the sesame oil flavor. They also laughed at the stiff textbook Mandarin that I had studied since fourth grade and taught me their local dialect. I was a good mimic and a fast learner, and they enjoyed teaching me their language.

There was a woman whom May-Min called A'yi, who May-Min said was almost like her aunt. A'yi had soft round face with the eternal smile of Mona Lisa, and right away I started calling her A'yi also. She was a seamstress and had a small shop of her own, and we stopped by there often. She showed me how a Chinese dress was made. The everyday dress that the local Chinese women wore then was a loose-fitting, straight-cut, cotton dress with a Mandarin collar. A'yi cut them without patterns. The process was simple enough for me to learn right away, but the button making was hard. The small, fabric buttons were used to close the opening of the dress. A'yi first made a long, narrow string, and then knotted it with her delicate fingertips in such a way that each ended up looking like a tiny cauliflower head. She could make one in a few seconds, and this fascinated me to no end.

Every time we stopped by A'yi's shop, her son, Lien-Chuan, who was a few years older than May-Min and I, appeared from nowhere, his dog faithfully at his heels. He never talked to either one of us, but corrected my Chinese rather bluntly, and unlike May-Min, never mixed Japanese in the process. I wondered if he knew any Japanese at all. Other than that, he just stood there and watched us visit with his mother.

One day, A'yi sang a song for us. The slow and shrill melody sounded sad, so sad that I thought A'yi might be crying. The song was supposed to be a long love story, but I didn't quite understand. When May-Min failed to explain it to me, Lien-Chuan walked over and wrote it all out for me in a beautiful handwriting. He was obviously better educated than May-Min was. Since Chinese characters are used in Japanese also, I was able to get the gist of the long and complicated story, and I thanked him in my best Mandarin. He smiled for the first time, showing his pearly white teeth. Then I felt like singing something in Chinese to please him. The only Chinese song I knew was the national anthem of Manchukuo, which I had learned at elementary school. I started to sing it with all sincerity and motioned to Lien-Chuan and May-Min to join me. To my surprise, however, May-Min became upset and tried to stop me. It was too late. Lien-Chuan stood up abruptly, his face tense and pale, and stalked out of the shop, almost kicking his faithful dog. I was stunned.

"What did I do wrong, May-Min? Tell me!" I ran after May-Min, who had also left the shop, leaving me behind.

"Nothing! You did nothing wrong. You are just stupid! That's all. Just stupid!"

I walked home alone, deeply hurt and perplexed. I knew that they knew what I was singing. If the national anthem of Manchukuo had been taught in Japanese elementary schools, I was sure that it had been taught in the schools of the native Chinese also, the Manchurians. *After all*, I argued with myself angrily, *they are the true Manchurians, aren't they? Don't they feel the national pride and that close-to-your-heart emotion that I always feel whenever I sing the Japanese national anthem? Aren't they proud of being Manchurians? What's the matter with them?* I was innocently perplexed and hurt. Then I remembered Kunio's words: that Manchukuo was a puppet country set up by the Japanese military as a stronghold to invade China proper, and that Japan was not "helping" Manchukuo but was an exploiter and invader. Hadn't Kunio further stated that what really existed between Japan and Manchukuo was not brotherhood but mere military coercion? *Oh, God, could it be true?* I also remembered my cousin Toru's sneer: "Oh, you are so hopelessly naive, Kaz-chan."

My question, however, had to be put on hold because of a sudden turn in the course of war.

On 9 August 1945, Russian tank columns, accompanied by their air force, broke through the southern border of Siberia at the northeast end of Manchuria. This was totally unexpected by the Kwantung Army. Only four years earlier, in 1941, Japan and the Soviet Union had signed a nonaggression pact, agreeing that Japan would stay out of Mongolia and the Soviets would stay out of Manchuria. Because of this pact, and because of the desperate need for manpower in the Pacific, the Kwantung Army on the Manchurian-Siberian border had been drastically reduced. The Russians had waited for this crucial moment to break the pact. (Years later I learned that this was the day after the atomic bomb was dropped on Hiroshima, Japan.) It took only a matter of hours for the Russians to crush the surprised Japanese garrisons at the border. There was no time to warn the civilians. The Japanese pioneer farmers near the border fled in all directions on foot, hiding in the mountains during the day, running for their lives at night, carrying small children on their backs, feeding on whatever they could pick in the field, or aided by those Manchurians who remained humane. The Russian armies were not the only thing the Japanese were running from, however. The anti-Japanese guerrillas who had been suppressed by the Kwantung Army for years were now surfacing all over Manchuria, taking savage revenge on all Japanese.

My oldest brother, Mamoru, had been stationed in one of the outposts at the northeastern border, exactly where Russian troops broke through. When we heard of the Russian invasion at the border where Mamoru was stationed, Mother and Hisako turned chalk-white, squeezing each other's hands in silence. Hisako was visibly trembling and breathing hard. We tried our best not to give in and to keep hoping, yet there really was no word to comfort one another. We knew that the chance of Mamoru's survival was slim.

My uncle Hideo, my mother's younger brother, was in Mukden, where the Kwantung Army's Headquarters was located, the most likely target of the Russian army. It was in the center of southern Manchuria, approximately 650 miles from the Manchurian-Siberian border and about 300 miles north of Dairen. As was customary among many executives of the Manchurian Railway Company, Uncle Hideo had left his family in Dairen, where living conditions and schools were better, coming home once or twice a month.

Uncle Hideo's wife, Sadako, frantically tried to contact him by phone and telegram from Dairen without any success. My mother also tried from Furanten and my father tried using the official phone from his office, but all communications were completely cut off north of Furanten.

Then we found out that there had been another invasion from the southwest. The Nationalist Chinese Army of Chiang Kai-shek had broken through the southwest border of Manchuria at the same time that the Russians invaded from the north, heading northeast to link with the Russians.

No one knew what really was going on. The only information we had was the vague and unconfirmed news that my father gathered at his office. Communication between Manchuria and Japan was cut off at this point. We did hear that some powerful bombs had been dropped somewhere in Japan around the same time as the Russian and Chinese invasion of Manchuria. There was also a rumor that the Japanese government had decided to abandon Manchuria. Japan was about to give up the fight.

Suddenly, we, the Japanese in Manchuria—pioneer farmers, employees of the Manchurian Railway and numerous other industrial companies, government officials, doctors, teachers, people of all trades and their families, almost two million in all—found ourselves trapped in the midst of our enemies, without any contact from Japan.

Six days of fear and uncertainty passed. On the morning of August 15, my father called home to tell us that we were to listen to the radio at noon. There was going to be a message from the emperor. Father had to stay at his office to listen to it with the other officials.

Father had told us the night before, after Yukio and Toshiko had gone to bed, that he had heard that Japan was facing a choice between a suicidal fight to the end or surrender, perhaps an unconditional surrender. As most Japanese men did then, my father did not think that Japan would choose to surrender. It was unthinkable that Japan would surrender to any country. Japan had never bowed to another country and never would. Japan would choose to fight to the last man and die with honor. It seemed that Father had already accepted the idea that the time had come for all Japanese to end their own lives. He was merely wondering what method the emperor would choose to execute this mass suicide: would each man have to kill his family members and then shoot himself, or would the government distribute potassium cyanide pills to all Japanese?

I was still hopeful, however. I wasn't exactly expecting the emperor to send us the *Kami-kaze*, the divine wind, the famous timely typhoon that wrecked the invasion fleet of Kublai Khan twice in the thirteenth century, to blow the Russian troops out of Manchuria, but I was hopeful. I believed in Japan's deity and the emperor's divine power. *Surely the emperor must have some kind of last measure to pull us out of this crisis,* I thought.

At noon we turned on the radio. The reception was so poor that we had to strain our ears to catch the emperor's high-pitched, somewhat childlike voice, which faltered often.

"In order to avoid further bloodshed, perhaps even the total extinction of human civilization, we shall have to endure the unendurable, to suffer the insufferable. . . . "

Mother, Hisako, and I looked at each other in confusion. Had we heard it right? Did he mean that Japan would surrender? Only when the halting and sobbing announcer started talking after the emperor's speech was done were we able to confirm what we thought we had heard—Japan had decided to surrender, unconditionally.

We were stunned, looking at each other in disbelief. Had that really been the emperor? Could this be some kind of a horrible mistake? Maybe I should call Father and ask him. Confused thoughts raced through my mind. Then the phone rang. I dashed out to answer it. It was Mrs. Kawano. She was crying hysterically into the phone.

"Yes, we heard it, Mrs. Kawano. Yes, we'll see you tonight." I answered her briefly and then went back to the dining room.

Mother was quietly weeping into a handkerchief. Hisako was also weeping, hugging my mother. I sat down by the table in a daze. I didn't want to join the weeping. The stupid weeping! There was something violent churning within me, like a high fever. I held on to the edge of the table, breathing hard. I knew this was not a nightmare. This was for real. But the reality somehow failed to touch me. It whirled around me. As if sitting in the vacuum eye of a tornado, I felt untouched.

Toshiko came home. School had been closed and the children were sent home early.

"Were you crying, Mama?" Toshiko asked, looking at Mother in surprise.

"I was, but I am all right now." Mother pulled Toshiko gently into her arms. Just a few minutes ago, she had been ready to die, if it were the emperor's wish. And take this innocent child with me? She shuddered at the thought.

"Why, Mama? Why were you crying?" Toshiko looked around. "Why was everybody crying?"

"Because Japan lost the war!" I hissed at her sharply.

Toshiko cringed in Mother's arms. I suddenly realized that I was shaking with anger. I was furious. I felt betrayed: betrayed by Japan, the God-chosen country with a noble mission, the country that could do no wrong.

CHAPTER 4

For the Sake of Our Children

THE KAWANOS CAME over that night. May-Min was with them, as usual. May-Min was genuinely concerned about the Kawanos, especially about Mrs. Kawano, as if Mrs. Kawano had suddenly aged and needed May-Min's help for every move she made. Mr. Kawano, a black-belt Judo expert, was a heavy-set, jolly man who talked loudly and laughed even more loudly. But he was a different man that night. He and my father had always played *Go* for hours when they got together, but that night they slipped into my father's study and did not come out until almost midnight. The safety of all Japanese in Furanten was on their shoulders.

The war was over. Japan was defeated. I had no idea what an "unconditional surrender" really meant, but I knew Japan had surrendered. Japan had surrendered, Japan had surrendered—the dull bell rang idly in my blank head as I watched, rather than listened to, the conversation that was taking place between my mother, Mrs. Kawano, and Hisako.

My mother's main concern was my three older brothers, but it seemed that she flatly refused to believe that anything could have happened to any of them. Somehow she just knew that all three of them were alive and safe somewhere. She kept repeating it to Hisako and Mrs. Kawano, who were more than eager to agree with her. As if in a delirium, Mother talked about the time when she had been in bed with high fever a long time previously. Mamoru, a preschooler then, had pressed his little hands against the ice-cold window, then had run back to put his cold hands on his mother's flushed cheeks, to "chase the fever away."

"Mamoru is, and has always been, such a sweet boy."

She said it with the conviction that it would be for this virtue that Mamoru would be saved and would come back to her sooner or later. Moreover, Mamoru simply could not die without seeing his infant son, Yukio. As for Kay, her second son, who had promised to call to her with his last breath, she hadn't heard his "call" yet. She knew he was not dead.

"Kay is resourceful. He has a strong sense of survival. He is too much of a devil to die so easily." Mrs. Kawano and Hisako agreed with her, nodding their heads eagerly.

My younger sister Michiko came home from Dairen a few days later. Schools in Dairen had been closed temporarily and the students whose homes were not in Dairen had been told to go home and stay with their families until further notice. But, Michiko said, Dairen seemed to be functioning as if nothing had happened. Except, she said, everybody was "sad." Aunt Sadako, Uncle Hideo's wife, had sent a suitcaseful of valuables with Michiko. She and my mother had decided over the telephone that Furanten would be safer than Dairen because of its insignificance, and she wanted us to keep some of her jewelry and expensive kimonos in a safe place. My father stored them in the ceiling inside the closet, along with some of our valuables.

We knew it was only a matter of time before the Russians would race down south to take over Dairen and Port Arthur, but these cities were hundreds of miles from the border. Also, we believed in the Kwantung Army's resistance. They might be able to stop them somewhere, we thought, or at least slow them down. What we didn't know then was that the Russian Army was 1.8 million strong, while the Kwantung Army had only seven-hundred thousand men.

Days went by without incident. We stayed home most of the time, having May-Min do our daily marketing for us. May-Min told us that the main street where only the Japanese had shopped was now crowded with native Chinese. The Chinese were not shopping, but were just standing around watching the Japanese, sometimes snatching the purses away from Japanese women's hands.

On August 24, nine days after the Japanese surrender, the Furanten police force was officially disarmed by order of their headquarters in Dairen. The first Russian troops had reached Dairen the day before and had taken over the city. The Japanese garrison and police force in Liaotung Peninsula had now officially been disarmed.

My parents had decided that we should store away as much food as possible, so Mother and I went downtown. We bought bags of rice, oil, flour, sugar, and canned goods and hired a *mache* to take us home. As we loaded our groceries and climbed onto the seats, a crowd of native Chinese started to form around us. The crowd quickly grew larger and noisier. It was frightening. When the driver tried to start the horse, the frightened animal backed up, rattling the whole carriage. The crowd jeered, coming closer. I looked around over their heads, desperately searching for a familiar face. Please, one friendly face! But they were strangers, boldly glaring back at me. I felt their intense hostility and braced myself.

It was then that I caught a sight of a tank, clanking down the street toward us. A Soviet flag was flapping on top!

"Mama!" I cried out, "A Russian tank!"

The crowd turned their heads to where I was pointing. The street was suddenly hushed. Everyone watched the tank in dead silence. The tank came to a stop near the crowd around us. While we watched with horror, the tank's top was pushed open from inside and a soldier jumped out. I gasped. It was a woman! She was in a khaki uniform, but unmistakably a woman. Her incredibly large bosom bounced with each heavy boot step. She walked like a fat general and then spat on the street like a peasant man, totally ignoring the crowd.

"Look, Mama, it's a woman. A woman soldier," I whispered to Mother.

Then, at the same time, the driver of our carriage rose halfway to give the horse a good whip and shouted, "*Dzou ba! Dzou ba!* (go! go!)" Through the middle of the surprised crowd, which was now backing off, the horse pulled us into the clear.

So the Russians were in town! We had hoped that the Russians, the Chinese army, or the guerrillas would bypass this insignificant little town on their way to Dairen or Port Arthur. There was nothing that any of them could gain in this little town, unless they wanted to kill every Japanese in Manchuria.

I called my father as soon as we reached home safely to let him know of the Russian tank in town, but he already knew about it, and said that there might be guerrillas or the Chinese army following the Russians.

The minute I put the telephone down, it rang. I thought it was my father, wanting to tell me something more, but it was Mrs. Kawano. She was so agitated that she was almost incoherent.

"May-Min went home! Can you believe it? She has never done that before. Her little brother came after her and she said she had to go home. Her father wanted her home right away, she said. And then she closed every window in the house and locked them all. Can you believe it? She even locked the back door and told me to lock the front door when she was gone, and not to open it for anybody except for Mr. Kawano. Isn't that strange?"

I sensed that this might have something to do with the Russian tank in town and tried to tell her about it, but she was too upset. She said that May-Min had gotten angry with her when she had protested about shutting all the windows and had made her promise not to open them and had pleaded with her to stay in the house until she could come back herself to check on the Kawanos. Did May-Min know about the Russian tank? Or did she know about something more than a Russian tank? I wondered.

It became a long, hot afternoon for all of us. At the end of August Furanten was still as hot as at midsummer during the afternoons, although it would get cold at night. The Russian tank seemed to have left the town after a while, but the town remained strangely hushed. It was holding its breath with the terror of the unknown.

Father came home early. In the silence of fearful anticipation, all of us went to bed in one room in the back of the house, our clothes neatly folded right by the bed, like firemen on duty.

"Remember, if anything happens, get out of the house through the back door and run to the mountain," Father told us.

"Tsunami?!" Something like the roaring echo of tsunami woke me up violently. Father was already dressed.

"It's a riot! Run! They are at the police chief's house now. Hurry up and run!"

Somebody was banging on our back door, shouting. A riot! We had to run! I rushed into my clothes. Thank goodness, our house was right by the mountain. But, hey, the warning was in Chinese! It suddenly dawned on me. Whoever it was that came to bang on our back door shouted the warning in local Chinese. A Chinese came to warn us! I felt encouraged. We still had friends among the local Chinese! We dashed out to the backyard. In the moonlight I saw the Kawanos' house across the tennis court, surrounded by the huge waving shadow of the mob, which, from the distance, looked like a giant serpent coiled around its prey, twisting and roaring.

"Run! Run to the mountain!" Father hissed sharply to us while helping Mother run. Hisako, who had been known for her athletic talent in her high school days, was already running ahead of us toward the mountain, holding Yukio tightly against herself, with Michiko closely behind her. I was pulling on Toshiko, who was trying to tell me something but gave in to run with me.

We ran until we were deep in the coolness of the woods, where the threatening sound of the mob was swallowed by the trees. The air in the woods was pleasantly cold on my flushed face. Mother, who had always been in delicate health, was almost out of breath, sitting on a rock that Father had found for her. Hisako sat down on the grass by Mother, checking on Yukio. Michiko came to sit by Hisako, breathing hard. Toshiko was breathing hard too, still clutching my hand. I tried to make her sit down, but she wouldn't let go of my hand. Then I noticed that Toshiko was barefooted, clenching her shoes in her other hand. I realized then that that was what she had been trying to tell me when we started to run, that she didn't have her shoes on. Now she seemed to have forgotten about her shoes. I pulled my hand out of hers and got down on my knees to help her with her shoes, but she was unable to let go of them.

"Here, give me your shoes!" I had to force the shoes out of her hand, peeling off her numb fingers one by one while she watched helplessly, in a daze.

"Let me have your foot," I said, grabbing her foot. It was stiff and ice cold. Father came over to hold her steady, rubbing her back, whispering, "It'll be all right, it'll be all right."

"I am cold," Toshiko whimpered.

"I know. Let's go sit with everybody. It'll be warmer."

Mother held out her arms to take her. We all sat close together, except Father. He was looking around into the darkness, trying to determine exactly where we were. Then he told us to stay put while he went back to town to see what was happening.

Every time he came back he brought back another group of Japanese families. He told them not to make a large group, but to scatter in the woods and hide by the bushes. He also brought back bits of information. The Chinese guerrillas had slipped into town the night before and had stirred the local Chinese into a vengeful riot against the Japanese in town. They knew that the Japanese police force would have been disarmed as soon as the first Russians reached Dairen. The mob first raided the armory and armed themselves. Then they attacked the police chief's house. Chief Kawano might be dead, or dying. Our house, or my father, would have been the next target. But somebody had saved us. *A local Chinese*, I thought to myself, *had saved us.*

Also, a group of Japanese *Gakuto* (college student draftees), who had been disarmed and dispersed at the end of war and were heading for Dairen on foot, were caught in the middle of this riot. They were either captured or killed, Father did not know for sure. Kuni-chan! My thoughts ran to Kunio. He could very well have been one of the *Gakuto* boys, if not in Manchuria, then somewhere in the ruins of a battlefield, running for his life.

Hisako was whispering softly to Yukio, "Nice boy, Yukio, you're a nice boy." Yukio was wide awake, looking around from the safety of his mother's steady arms. Mother joined Hisako and touched Yukio's soft cheeks gently. Then I noticed that Hisako had a bag of diapers sitting beside her.

"You brought his diapers!" I whispered in amazement. Hisako looked at the bag in surprise. "So I did. . . "

"Shh . . . " Someone hissed from the darkness. Everyone was on edge. The moon had disappeared behind a dark cloud, making the darkness in the forest almost pitch black. All we could do was listen for any sound of movement. We listened intensely to the darkness around us. There were thirty or forty of us in this area, mostly women and children. The men had gone back to town in search of more Japanese, and only a few of them had stayed behind with us.

"Look, it's raining, Mama." Toshiko snuggled against Mother. The summer rains always came suddenly and were heavy, although they did not last long. Hisako tried to cover Yukio with her body, then with the diaper bag, but the rain was falling harder. Yukio was annoyed and started to whimper.

"Don't let the baby cry!" Again, someone hissed from the darkness.

I got up to help Hisako cover Yukio. Then Michiko and Toshiko joined me. Three of us bent over Yukio like a human umbrella, trying to keep him from the rain. The rain hit our backs hard, draining over our soaked clothes. Yukio took this as a game and tried to reach us, smiling happily. We tickled him and kept him entertained while keeping him dry. By the time the rain finally stopped and the moon reappeared, Yukio was fast asleep.

Then we heard an eerie hissing sound flying over our heads, like the sound of fireworks shooting into the sky. Instinctively, we flattened ourselves to the ground. The hissing kept coming, one after another, although we could not tell which direction they were coming or going. They came from the darkness and flew into the darkness.

"Scatter and take cover!" someone hissed.

We scattered to the bushes or behind the trees. Toshiko and I sat low by a large bush, half hidden. The hissing sound continued. I held Toshiko tightly against me. She was stiff with terror. After what seemed an eternity, the hissing sound stopped as suddenly as it had started. No one moved. We were frozen with terror, glued to the ground, waiting for it to start again, straining our ears and holding our breath.

Then, without any sound at all, a tall Chinese man appeared in the moonlight right in front of me and Toshiko. I gasped and instinctively pushed Toshiko behind me. For a fleeting moment I thought it was Lien-Chuan, though I could not tell for sure. The moonlight was on his back. From the way he was dressed, however, I decided that he was a local Chinese, about Lien-Chuan's age, not one of the guerrillas. He was even followed by a dog like Lien-Chuan always was, but it wasn't Lien-Chuan's dog. The man was armed with a rifle, but the rifle was slung on his shoulder, pointing upward. It seemed that he was as surprised and frightened to find us as we were to see him.

No one stirred. The man and I stared at each other in frozen silence. The dog's quick, short huffing dominated the silence. Then, from the corner of my eye, I caught a glimpse of the dog wagging his tail. The stupid dog! He wanted to play with us! I turned to the dog, almost with a smile. The young Chinese man followed my eyes and looked down at his dog. The dog looked up at his master and then back to us, wagging his tail even more vigorously. A long moment passed. Then the young man nudged his dog gently with his knee and silently walked away.

We listened to his soft footsteps on the wet grass until they could no longer be heard. Would he bring back his friends to kill us all? No, he wouldn't. I was sure. Somehow I knew that he wouldn't. He was too much like Lien-Chuan. I refused to believe that anyone like Lien-Chuan would come to kill a Japanese family hiding in the woods. Still we waited and listened. We strained our ears in the excruciating silence, expecting the hissing of the bullets to begin again any moment.

We were still glued to the silence when my father and his small group of men appeared from another direction, whispering, "It's us, is everyone all right?"

It was almost dawn. I could see my father's face from the distance, extremely intense and alert. *Like a soldier in the battlefield*, I thought. He told us that he and his men had met with other groups of Japanese in hiding and it had been decided that he would go down the mountain to meet with the leader of the mob and work out some kind of a truce. Sharp anxiety crossed my mother's face, but she remained silent. Somebody had to do it, and she knew it had to be Father.

Father took off the white shirt that he was wearing underneath the *kokumin-huku*, and tied it to a stick. Waving this white flag, my father and another man started down the mountain.

It was a long wait. Mother was sitting up straight on the wet grass, eyes half closed, hands tightly clasped on her lap. I knew she was praying. I was praying, too. I knew my father was well liked and respected among the local Chinese, but it was the guerrillas that he had to deal with. And what did we have to offer them? That we would abandon all our properties in town? Our properties were already in their hands and ruined. What about the wounded and the dead? Were we to abandon them? How and where were we to go anyway? I was choked with intense apprehension.

"Mama! They are coming back!" Michiko shouted. She had been standing up, anxiously watching for any sign of Father and his man. I turned and saw the top of a white flag bobbing up and down in the woods, then recognized my father and the other man walking toward us.

Father called for everyone in hiding to come out. He told us what he had accomplished with the guerrillas. We were to go down the mountain to the Japanese elementary school, where he would contact Dairen to ask for transportation to rescue us, and we were to abandon all of our properties in town to their disposal, but we must leave the town before dark. The leader of the mob, who, as we had suspected, was the leader of the anti-Japanese guerrillas, did not guarantee our safety if it took us too long.

There was no time to lose. My father told everyone to form a column, with men on the outside, guarding the women and children. He also told us not to respond to any kind of agitation on our way to the Japanese elementary school, just to keep our heads up, looking straight ahead, and to march in silence. Some were apprehensive and reluctant to make a move toward town. My father and some of the men nearly had to herd them like frightened animals. After all, how long could we stay in hiding on the mountain?

Hisako was holding Yukio tightly against herself, shielding his tiny head with her tensely spread hand. Yukio must have sensed the urgency.

He buried his face in his mother's blouse without protest. I was close by her, clutching the diaper bag in one hand, holding Toshiko's hand in the other. Michiko and Mother were holding on to each other. No one spoke. Father led this silent, hesitant march from the mountain, a few steps at a time, waving the white flag high in the air.

The town was deathly silent, deserted. Since our house was at the foot of the mountain, it was the first thing we encountered. Our house, or what had been our house ten or twelve hours ago, was now a skeleton. From the roof tiles to the tatami floor mats, the looters had stripped the house to its bare frame. Not a piece of furniture, not a shred of rag was left. The knocked out doorways, hollow windows, crushed roof, trampled yard made it a ghost of a house, cursed by hatred. No one uttered a sound. This was a shock, a terror that was far more direct and real than the emperor's announcement had been. This was the physical manifestation of the unconditional surrender.

We marched through the deserted streets without turning our heads to look at another destroyed house or broken fence. The mob, however, had not destroyed the school or public buildings. Obviously, they had been under orders to save those buildings for later use. They had destroyed only our private properties. We reached the school and assembled in the auditorium. Most of us could hardly wait to sit down, and crumpled to the bare wooden floor. Hisako was already sitting down, getting ready to breast-feed Yukio, who was now tired and hungry. Father and some men went to the office to contact Dairen. The wounded and the sick were taken to the school nurse's station, where simple first-aid was available. Most of the children were wearily lying down on the bare floor, their heads resting on their mother's laps. Toshiko did the same, her eyes half closed, as Mother stroked her hair.

A large crowd of native Chinese formed outside the open windows, noisily making comments among themselves or fighting for a better view of the once-invincible but now-defeated Japanese. Since the building's floor was higher than ground level, the shorter ones had to jump up to take a quick look at this show of the century.

"Excuse me! Let me through, please!"

A young Chinese woman was frantically weaving through the crowd, hopping from one window to another, obviously looking for someone. It was May-Min. Her usually calm, pretty eyes were now bloodshot, desperately looking for her mistress, Mrs. Kawano. She had locked all the windows and doors at the Kawanos' yesterday, hoping it would keep the mob out. Little did she know the enormity of what was to happen only a few hours later. She saw the wildly excited mob, including her neighbors and even her own father, running all over the Japanese section of the town. She heard the shouts and screams of the hunters and the hunted. When the mob was finally dispersed at dawn, she ran to the Kawanos', to find only the bloodstained ruins.

She was beside herself. When she spotted me, she waved at me frantically, jumping up and down, until I finally focused my attention on her. My mind was hazy from exhaustion.

"May-Min!"

I stood up. What was May-Min doing here? I walked slowly to the window, weaving through the children lying on the floor. May-Min's eyes were enormous with anxiety.

"*Oku-san* (mistress)! Where is my *oku-san?*"

I turned back to see where the Kawanos might be, but they were nowhere in sight. I forced my tired and hazy brain to search through the nightmare of the night before. I remembered the mob storming the Kawanos' house across the tennis court, the giant serpent coiled around its prey, twisting and roaring. I remembered the inhuman and hollow echo of the frenzied mob. Then I remembered my father telling us that the police chief had been killed, or was dying. Did he say that he had been beaten to death? I wasn't sure.

"They killed Mr. Kawano," I blurted out, but May-Min did not seem to have heard me.

"They killed Mr. Kawano," I repeated, staring into the whitened, small face. Still no response. I raised my voice.

"The mob has beaten him to death! The Chinese style, you know!"

"Ai-eeya!" May-Min shrieked and wavered, her raised hands blindly groping for support.

"May-Min! Watch out!" I leaned out the window, but she was too far away. Someone caught her. May-Min let out another shriek and ran through the crowd into the street. I stood there watching her until the small running figure became a dot and then finally disappeared into the dust. Slowly I walked back to sit by my mother. Mother had been watching us.

"She was looking for the Kawanos, wasn't she?"

"Yes."

"The poor girl . . . "

"I know."

Suddenly, I was tired. So tired that I didn't care what had happened or what was going to happen.

"Would you like to lie down? You look tired." Mother offered her lap for me to rest my head. I looked at her as if I were seeing her for the first time. If this fragile little lady, who didn't even weigh a hundred pounds, could hold her own after this ordeal, I sure could do better than lying down on the floor.

"I think, maybe, I can help the ladies in the kitchen."

I forced myself to get up. Mother nodded silently.

I went around to the back of the school cafeteria where some women had been cooking rice in a huge pot. They were standing around, waiting for it to cool off so that they could make it into hundreds of rice balls to distribute to all the hungry people in the auditorium. It was getting close to noon. No one was saying much. Each was struggling through the slow process of accepting this nightmare as reality. I looked out the window and saw a number of men digging in the corner of the schoolyard. I was about to ask one of the women what they were doing when it dawned on me that they were digging graves, for the dead from last night's riot. The bodies were in military uniform.

"*Gakuto?*" I turned to a woman standing nearby. She nodded.

A group of *Gakuto*—college students drafted and shipped to the front lines toward the end of the war—were disarmed and dispersed at Japan's surrender and were running for their lives a few steps ahead of the Russians. They had been caught in the middle of the riot. All had been slain mercilessly.

"They fought to the last minute with their bare hands," the women said hoarsely.

A man was kneeling down among the bodies, cleaning the boys' faces with a rag, buttoning up their bloodstained jackets, dusting off their pants, his own tear-streaked face dirtier than those of the boys. It was my father. He then went through their pockets and wallets, looking for their identities, recording them and putting them away, impatiently brushing away his tears with the back of his clenched fist. I knew this was tearing his heart apart. He had three sons of his own, the youngest about the same age as these boys. They lowered each body carefully into the crude grave, shielding it with old newspapers before covering it with dirt.

"Here, here, sit down."

The woman sat me down on a chair. I was unaware that broken sobs were escaping through my hands, which were clasped tightly over my mouth.

After a few minutes, I pulled myself together and went to help the group of women making rice balls. Somehow, I knew that this was only the beginning of the tragedy I would have to live through. The luxury of tears would have to wait. (Years later, my father told me that they buried twelve *Gakuto* boys, two fellow workers from his office, and one man from town.)

We took plain rice balls and water to the auditorium. This was all we had to offer to the people lying in exhaustion there. This was likely to be our last meal until we reached Dairen, if we were lucky enough to get there.

Then my father walked into the auditorium and announced that an arrangement was being made by the Dairen station to send a train to rescue us. He was not sure exactly when it would arrive, but it would be here, and we would reach Dairen sometime before dark. I noticed that he was deliberately calm and assuring. I wondered if he were telling us the truth or just trying to keep us calm.

Just as he was leaving the auditorium, a man stood up, calling after my father.

"Forget Dairen!" he shouted hysterically, shaking a fist in the air. His other arm was in a makeshift sling.

"We have no idea what's waiting for us in Dairen. Dairen is already occupied by the Russians. Why run to Dairen? It's only a matter of whether we die here or die in Dairen. We should all have died the day Japan surrendered. Japan is crushed and has given up Manchuria. We are abandoned. We are on our own in the middle of the enemies. We are trapped in a no-man's land! What's the use of running? Let's finish ourselves here and now! You can get us enough arms to kill ourselves, can't you?"

A heavy silence filled the auditorium. We knew that the man was speaking the truth. We had nowhere to run. We were in the middle of our enemies in a land where no one was in control. Yes, the man was right. What was the use of running? And yet, we all looked to my father, waiting for him to give us something for which to live, a reason to keep running.

My father took a few deliberate steps back to stand in the center of the stage, alone, listening to the man's demand. He waited for the turbulence to subside and then quietly but firmly spoke his words.

54

"Let's not make a hasty decision." Father looked at each one of us, taking his time. "Decisions must not be made by emotions," he went on, weighing each word. "Let us take a few minutes to think of our children. Are they to pay with their lives for what we have brought on? Don't we owe it to them to rebuild their country, from the ashes if that's all that's left of Japan? I agree with you that we have only a slim chance of escaping this situation, but at least let us try. We must try. For the sake of our children. We have to get our children back to Japan. It's their only country, their only future, for whatever we can salvage."

He paused, making sure that we were reasonably calmed down. Then he raised his voice, shaking his fist high in the air, "Let's pull together! I am sure we can make it!"

Someone clapped his hands and then we all clapped our hands. Father nodded gravely and walked off the stage.

"Father is right. We'll be all right once we get to Dairen." I turned to Mother.

"Let's hope so."

"But, Mama, where will we go? We don't have a house in Dairen anymore," Michiko said.

"We will probably go to Aunt Sadako's place. It's my brother's place. And Aunt Masu's place is in the vicinity. There are a lot of Japanese living in that area, away from downtown or the Chinese section. We'll be safe there." Then she turned to Hisako. "We'll contact your family as soon as possible. But don't worry. There are a lot of Japanese in Dairen."

"Do you really think a train will come from Dairen?" Hisako's concern was on a more immediate matter. "They will have to risk their own lives."

"Sure they will," I said with conviction.

"How do you know?" asked Michiko.

"Because they are Japanese. They wouldn't leave us here to die." I said again with conviction.

Just then Father walked into the auditorium and calmly announced that the Dairen station master had confirmed that a freight train had been dispatched an hour ago, and we should get to the railway station right away. He instructed all of us to go out into the schoolyard and form a column as we had done earlier, coming down from the mountain. There was no sign of the rescue train at the station yet, but we started our silent march toward the railway station. The town was deathly silent. No one was around, nothing moved. We walked close to the hedge around the schoolyard, keeping our heads low. Then we walked in the shadows of the school building, and the office buildings, until we reached the corner of my father's office, across from the railway station. There, we had to cross an open space to get to the railway station. The small open space where rickshaws usually waited to pick up customers off the train now seemed dangerously spacious and bare. We huddled in the shadow of the office building while the men gathered to decide what to do. We didn't trust the hushed street. We felt countless eyes watching and waiting for us to walk into the open space.

My father and his men finally decided to crawl across the open space to the station, closely hugging the black asphalt. Men went around showing women and children how to crawl.

"Lie flat on your stomach, pull yourself with your elbows, pushing ahead with your knees at the same time. And keep your heads down, no matter what! If you hear anything, anything at all, lie flat on the ground and don't move!"

Hisako held Yukio beneath her, supporting herself with one elbow. I held the diaper bag like some important possession. We inched our way, crawling awkwardly on the warm, dust-covered black asphalt. I knew, somehow, that the guerrillas were watching us from somewhere, savoring this humiliation of the once-proud Japanese.

Just as I expected, as we were about to reach the railway station, a handful of armed guerrillas jumped out from hiding, shouting wildly, their rifles at the ready.

"We are not armed!" My father shouted in local Chinese. Then he turned to us. "Hold up your hands. Show them we are not armed!"

Toshiko and the other children screamed in terror. Father came running, hissing at Toshiko, "Stop it! Or they'll kill you!"

Mother held Toshiko tightly for a second, then helped her hold up her trembling hands. The guerrillas slowly walked around us, shifting their rifles to point at each of us as they walked by. Hisako held Yukio in one arm and held up the other hand, grateful that Yukio was quiet. I looked straight ahead, avoiding their eyes. Still I saw them. I saw how they were dressed, or rather how they were not dressed. They were all half naked, except one or two who had torn shirts hanging loose. Some wore old caps or worn-out felt hats, but all of them had a strip of red rag tied around their necks or upper arms or around their heads, to indicate that they were communist. This was one of many anti-Japanese guerrilla bands in Manchuria that had been suppressed by Japan's Kwantung Army for many years.

They walked around us ever so slowly, their half-naked bodies glistening with sweat under the high noon sun. They herded us around the flag pole in the center of the platform where a Japanese flag was still flying.

"Take that dirty flag down!" The guerrilla leader ordered.

Yelling and shouting, his men pulled down the Japanese flag, rolled it into a ball, and threw it to one of the Japanese men, who quickly hid it under his shirt. Then with an air of ceremony, they replaced it with a plain old red cloth and hauled it to the top of the staff with screams of delight.

Then the guerrilla leader shouted some kind of an order to my father, who sharply turned to him in disbelief. The leader repeated his order louder, pointing his rifle straight at my father.

"I want the *Banzai* cheers from all of you!" The leader repeated.

Banzai, literally meaning ten thousand years, was a salutation reserved for the Japanese flag, along with "long live the emperor" cheers for the Japanese emperors. It was also a cheer of victory. Japanese soldiers cried out *Banzai* with their last breath as they gave their lives to their country on the battlefield. It was at the heart of the Japanese pride. The guerrillas were well aware of the sacred meaning of the *Banzai* cheers, and they demanded it for the meaningless red cloth in order to strip the last piece of dignity from the Japanese.

His face burning red with anger, my father glared at the guerrilla. The guerrilla glared back, gripping his rifle, which was still pointing straight at my father. A painful, long moment passed. Finally my father turned to us and shouted a heart-wrenching order, as loud as the guerrilla leader's had been.

"Three cheers of *Banzai!*"

There was a moment of tense hesitation, then with tears of humiliation streaming down our faces, we shouted, *"Banzai! Banzai! Banzai!"* holding up our hands in salutation to the red cloth hanging limply at the top of the staff. I felt hot tears trickling down my flushed face, but I ignored them. I wasn't about to give in and cry, and wished those who were sobbing would stop it. The half naked guerrillas were quietly watching us, savoring their victory, the revenge that they had waited for so many years.

Then we heard the whistle of a locomotive. Far down the track was an engine, hauling a string of cars. Slowly it approached, blowing its whistle in warning as it came closer. A Japanese crew had risked their lives to rescue us, their fellow Japanese. I had known they would come! I was filled with pride. I took a deep breath. Staring at the welcome sight of the train, I straightened myself and pulled my shoulders back with tremendous pride.

The train was made up of roofless freight cars, the kind normally used to haul coal. As the guerrillas watched in silence, we scrambled aboard the bare boxcars, jamming into them so that there was barely room to sit down. Then we had to wait while the engine turned around and was hooked to the other end of the train.

Finally the engine started and the train began its journey back to Dairen. When the engine blew a whistle, the guerrillas suddenly resumed their yelling and screaming, and shot their rifles into the air, scaring us to the floor. As if this was a signal, a crowd of local Chinese appeared from nowhere onto the platform and started throwing rocks at us. Hisako shrieked and bent over Yukio, making herself a shield over him. We covered our heads with our bare hands and waited for the train to pull us out of the station.

It seemed forever before the train picked up speed. Only then did we dare to look up, one by one, looking at each other in relief. We were finally out of danger. The open air felt clean and assuring, although it was hot under the naked August sun. The train ran smoothly for a while. Then it jolted to a sudden stop.

"Chinese! The Chinese are sitting on the track! They are holding us up," a man who was standing at the side of the first boxcar shouted. Father stood up to see the trouble. Then, as suddenly as it had stopped, the train started up again with determination.

"Get down!" the men shouted, covering their heads with their hands. The Chinese who had stopped the train were now throwing rocks at us. The train plowed through the shower of missiles and was on its way again.

After this incident, the men took turns watching, but all they could do was to give us warning of trouble ahead. There was nothing we could do to fight back or avoid it. The word had spread that a group of escaping Japanese were on the roofless freight train, and here and there hostile local Chinese were waiting for us with piles of rocks.

None of us was seriously hurt from these rock attacks, but they slowed the trip down considerably, causing small children and the elderly to suffer from the August heat in the crowded, roofless freight cars.

A group of people with first-aid and stretchers met us at the Dairen station. The wounded and the sick were carried away. The rest of us walked to the closest elementary school, where a temporary shelter had been set up for us, one of the first groups of refugees to reach Dairen from the north, the first of countless more to follow.

CHAPTER 5

The Unfinished Dreams

ON THE SURFACE, Dairen did not seem to have changed at all. There was no trace of Russian soldiers, and none of the urgency and confusion of the defeated country. At least, not around the Dairen Railway Station in the broad daylight. The area was still dominated by bustling crowd, mostly well-dressed Japanese, mixed with some Chinese. People walked by us as busily as ever. No one paid any attention to us, a group of disheveled and exhausted men, women, and children of all ages. But this was Dairen, a metropolis. People were strangers to one another, engrossed in their own busy lives, with no time for others. We walked in silence, like the aimless families of refugees that we were. We assembled in the auditorium of the nearest elementary school. It was decided then that those who had relatives or friends in Dairen were free to go, and that those who did not have anyplace to go would have to make a temporary shelter in the auditorium. My family was one of the very lucky few that had family in Dairen.

We bid farewell to the neighbors and friends who had shared the life-threatening experience of the night before, my father promising everyone that he would come every day and do all he could to help them. I knew that he would.

We went out to catch a streetcar. We were heading for my uncle Hideo's house. A few Japanese who were waiting for the streetcar turned to us with curiosity. Separated from the group, people paid more personal attention to us now, especially on the platform still reserved for the Japanese. A man about my father's age approached my father.

"Excuse me. Did anything happen to you?"

"Well, yes, as a matter of fact, something terrible has happened."

As if this were a signal, everyone on the platform came to surround us—What? A riot? Where was it? Was the whole town destroyed? Was anyone killed? If something like that is happening in Liaotung Peninsula, then there's no telling what's happening to all the Japanese in Manchuria. What do you mean all the Japanese in Manchuria? We don't know what's going to happen to us in Dairen. Yes, the Russians took over Dairen a few days ago and they are the wildest, most undisciplined bunch of soldiers, pillaging and raping. Isn't there a military police in the Russian army? Well, if there is, they aren't here yet. So what is the Japanese government going to do about this? Everyone talked at the same time, letting out their anxieties, fear, and anger.

"Excuse me, but do you have streetcar tickets?" the middle-aged gentleman asked my father politely. My father automatically looked for them in his pocket, but of course he did not have any.

"Please use these." The man handed him a book of streetcar tickets. My father thanked him and took out the exact number of tickets we would need, then tried to return the remainder to the man.

"Oh, no, please keep them." The man looked embarrassed and pushed it back to my father. "You will need them later."

Thus we started our first step of survival in Dairen, with a book of streetcar tickets given to us by a charitable stranger.

Uncle Hideo's house was located on the hill called *Toh-ghen-dai*, Heavenly Heights, across the main street from *Mei-kaku-dai*, Singing Crane's Heights, the hill on top of which Aunt Masu's house stood. These hills were all in the same vicinity, reserved as the Japanese residential areas. The area was always quiet, far away from the city center. Yet I noticed that it was unusually hushed now. All the windows and gates were shut tight. No children were seen in the playgrounds or in the yards around the houses.

The gate at Uncle Hideo's house was also locked and the curtains in the windows closed, as if no one was at home. These gates and fences around the private homes in this area were not seriously tall. The houses around here had been built after Dairen had become well controlled by the Japanese army and the police. The fences were nothing more than property lines, ornamenting the houses. Anyone could climb over them if they wanted to, but still they were locked and barred. I pressed the button on the gate post.

Responding to the bell, Aunt Sadako peeked from a small crack between the curtains, took in the urgent situation in a glance, and ran out to open the gate for us.

"What is this? Oh, my dear. It's terrible. Are you all right? Is anyone hurt?"

Raising her high-pitched voice yet another octave, Aunt Sadako almost pushed us into the house, locking the gate and door securely behind us. My cousins, one boy and three girls, ran out to the hallway to meet us. They stopped short and stared at us in shock. All of us just stood there looking at one another, not knowing what to say.

My father started to tell Aunt Sadako what had happened, but when he opened his mouth, he suddenly found himself choked. He stood there speechless, rubbing his face, breathing hard, trying to regain his composure. Then my mother, who was standing in front of me, crumpled to the floor like a puppet that had suddenly lost its controlling strings. Hisako got down on the floor also, gently hugging my mother's shoulder. We stood there, my father, Aunt Sadako, and all of us children, helplessly looking down at the quiet sobbing of Mother and Hisako.

"Let's go to the dining room, anyway. We can talk later. I'll fix you something to eat and then you can take a bath."

Aunt Sadako took charge of the situation and led everyone to the dining room. I took Yukio from Hisako's arm and followed.

There had been no word from Uncle Hideo, Aunt Sadako was telling my father.

"If only he survived the first crisis, I am sure he will find a way to escape to Dairen someday. But, I don't know. Mukden has been occupied by the Russians, I understand, and the Chinese mobs have been attacking Japanese homes and destroying the city."

Uncle Shoji, Aunt Sadako's younger brother, who also worked for Manchurian Railway, had been supplying her with information.

"But what about the Kwantung Army? Couldn't they have at least gathered all the Japanese civilians to safety?" Father asked.

"I don't know. I suppose there was no time. It happened so fast, so unexpectedly. I, er, oh, dear, I'm sorry, I didn't mean to cry. You've been through a terrible ordeal yourselves. I'm sorry."

"How about the Japanese in Dairen?" My father changed the subject. "I've heard that the Russian soldiers are pretty rough."

The Russian soldiers seldom came this far, Aunt Sadako said. They did most of their wild carousing downtown, although there had been a few incidents in some residential areas. The soldiers would walk into a house and help themselves to whatever caught their fancy, mostly wristwatches.

"They take your watch at gunpoint," Takeshi, my cousin, said, "just to add to their collection. They can't even read time, those ignorant peasants! But they want them. Take a few watches home, they'll be millionaires, I understand." Takeshi, a sixteen-year-old boy, continued with contempt, "They say that some of them wear watches clear up to their armpits!"

"Uncle Shoji told us that they are uneducated morons, but that is why they are dangerous," said another cousin, fourteen-year-old Masako. "A Russian soldier shot and killed a Japanese man who was taking his picture. You see, he thought the camera was some kind of a weapon aiming at him. Can you believe it? It happened downtown in broad daylight."

Thanks to the distance, the area had been safe from the chaos of downtown. The front part of Aunt Masu's house had been requisitioned by the Russians for one of their high-ranking officers, Aunt Sadako told us. This officer, however, was not at all like the Russian soldiers described by others. From all descriptions, he was a gentleman. He was always accompanied by an orderly, who was also well mannered. He would come out to the sunroom once in a while, but mostly stayed in the front room, a spacious living room with a fireplace. He never came out to meet the family, nor did any of the family make an effort to meet him, but because of his presence, Aunt Masu's neighborhood was safe from the wrongdoing of the Russian soldiers.

This whole vicinity was like the outskirts of the city, and we were fairly safe. We were hardly ever bothered by the Russian soldiers or the local Chinese. But the men in our neighborhood decided to form a self-defense unit, and my father was asked to join them. They called it a self-defense unit, but none of them owned a gun. Most of them probably would not have known how to handle a gun even if someone had had one. They were professors, company executives, doctors, and lawyers. All they did as members of the self-defense unit was to take turns standing on guard near the foot of the hill and to blow a whistle like that of a boy scout, when they saw a suspicious figure coming up the hill. Then we, in turn, would bang on pots and pans in our yard, to spread the warning to the whole neighborhood. The noisier the better, we were told. This would let the intruder know that the neighborhood was aware of his presence, and he usually would run away.

The banging was also a signal for all girls to go into hiding. Hisako would carry Yukio, I would gather up my sisters and three cousins, even little six-year-old Taeko, and rush to the storage room in the back of the house while sixteen-year-old Takeshi, Aunt Sadako, and my mother stayed inside the locked house. The storage area in which we hid was a sturdy brick-built coal bin in which my father had installed two locks inside the door. It had two windows, but they were small. No man could come through those windows. I made a peeping hole at the corner of the dirty window with a wet fingertip and waited for Takeshi to give us the signal to come out.

We only needed to do this twice, neither time with any incident. Our self-defense unit was dissolved around the middle of September. By that time the Russian military police, the G.P.U., had finally started to control their soldiers, although they had no authority over the anti-Japanese local Chinese, who continued to skirmish with Japanese residents in some areas.

My father went to see the Furanten refugees at the elementary school every day, as he had promised. He turned in an official report on the Furanten riot and asked for help, but the Japanese government in Dairen at that point was in turmoil. The refugees were thus, more or less, left on their own. Men went out looking for any kind of work while women, disguised in men's clothing, set up a makeshift "shop" of empty crates on the sidewalk and sold inexpensive items such as cigarettes, candies, and cheap jewelry.

One day my father decided that my younger sister Michiko and I should cut our hair short and dress as boys. He had heard about too many rape cases. Michiko was hesitant and was excused for the time being, but I was delighted. Now I could walk around the neighborhood, at least. It was getting to be pretty boring staying home with my younger sisters and little cousins. Also, I was thinking about going out to look for some kind of work to help support the family. I knew we had no funds. All Japanese assets were frozen. Whatever savings my parents had had were now as good as old newspapers. I once told my father that I wouldn't mind working as a shoe shine girl, which would not require any capital and seemed to be something that I could handle. My father turned away from me, rubbing his nose, and did not answer me, and I never mentioned it again.

Aunt Sadako brought out a pair of Takeshi's black serge pants and a white sport shirt, which fit me just right. This was the way all Japanese high school boys dressed during the summer. When I put on his student's cap, tucking in my hair, I looked like one of the high school boys, I thought. Everyone agreed, encouragingly.

Dressed in Takeshi's clothes, I went to a small barbershop at the foot of the hill, behind an elementary school. As I walked in through the glass door, a man was just getting off the one and only revolving chair. An elderly man was sitting by the window, basking in the soft September sun with an old magazine spread in front of him. The barber, the elderly man, and the man who had just got off the chair all turned to me in surprise. Obviously, I had not fooled any of them. I was embarrassed. I did not know whether I should smile at them or turn around and run home.

"Hi!" The barber rescued me. "Need a hair cut?"

"Yes, I do."

"I have one customer before you. So please have a seat. It won't be long."

Then the elderly gentleman still staring at me, told the barber, "Go ahead and do this young lady first. I have plenty of time." He went back to his magazine.

"That's nice of you, thank you," the barber said and motioned for me to sit in the revolving chair. I sat in the chair, took off my cap, and let my hair fall to my shoulders.

"How short do you want it cut?" he asked.

"Short, like a boy's."

"Like me?" The barber grinned. He had a crew cut.

"No! Not like that!" I giggled.

The elderly man looked at us over his magazine, unsmiling.

"Well, let's see," the barber brushed out my hair, holding it in his hand as if weighing it.

"Are you sure, now. . . ?"

"Yes, I am sure."

The elderly man looked up.

"You know that you don't have to cut your hair off and dress like a boy if you just stay home. The Russians won't come this far. Just stay out of downtown."

I looked at him in the mirror and said, "But I don't want to stay home. I want to go out and do something."

"All right, all right," the barber cut in. "You are not the first girl to cut her hair off. Besides, the hair will grow back. Otherwise, I'll be out of work, won't I?"

The barber first cut off most of my hair with a pair of scissors, then worked his way up with a clipper. The hair piled on the floor moved like living creatures as the barber moved around me.

"Do you want me to save some of your hair?"

"Oh, no. I don't want any of it."

I was excited, expecting myself to come out looking like one of my brothers. I remembered an incident when I was in the first grade. Coeducation was not commonly practiced when I was growing up, but there was one coed class in each grade up to the third grade, perhaps as an experiment. I was in one of the coed classes and was "the smartest" by everyone's admission, especially by my own, well deserving to be the class leader. When the new term started, however, I found that I was denied the privilege and had to settle for the position of assistant class leader because I was a girl. When I protested this to my teacher, he lectured me on the "virtue" of a girl taking second place to a boy, which made no sense to me. I had always been "special" to my parents, especially to my mother, because I was the long-awaited girl after three boys. The most valuable virtues in a woman, the teacher went on, are humility and modesty. I gave up and settled for assistant class leader not only for the first grade, but for the second and third-grade years as well because the co-ed class continued up to the third grade.

The result of the haircut was, however, not quite as I had anticipated. I did not instantly become a boy. I did not even look like any of my brothers. In fact, I looked more fragile, in a strange way. My neck seemed helplessly delicate without the shadow of my hair around it, my suddenly exposed ears looked almost transparent, like a couple of seashells held against the sunlight, and my round eyes looked larger than ever. At best, I looked like a fragile twelve-year-old boy.

"It will grow back in no time, Miss," the barber said, misunderstanding my disappointment.

"That's all right. Thank you."

As I got off the chair I met the elderly gentleman's eyes. I smiled at him weakly, or rather apologetically. He did not smile back. He shook his head sadly and sat in the revolving chair without looking at me again.

I decided to stretch my venture a little further. I wanted to walk around. It was a clear day without a trace of cloud in the sky, the kind of day that the Japanese called *Nihon-balle* (Japan clear), my favorite kind of autumn day. The sky seemed higher and further away from the earth in those days, making us feel lighter and freer, like Peter Pan.

I walked across the deserted schoolyard to get to the main street. I wanted to watch the traffic. There were about fifteen or twenty people on the small platform, waiting for the streetcar. It was unusual for this area to have a platform full of people waiting for a streetcar. Then, adding to my amazement, I noticed that the streetcars were passing them by. They were already jam-packed, with some people hanging on to the handrails at the door like spillover stuffing. The jam-packed streetcars stopped only when someone wanted to get off. If three people got off, ten people fought to get on. It was a frightening sight. The streetcars that I remembered had always been comfortably roomy, with a conductor in each car to help the passengers. It had been only one month since I had ridden a streetcar with my family to come to Uncle Hideo's house. It hadn't been crowded then.

Then, to my utmost surprise, I noticed that the local Chinese were mixed with the Japanese passengers, fighting their way as impatiently as the Japanese. Oh, yes, Father had told me that the segregation had been lifted, I remembered, but it was something else to see it myself. The bright orange cars that once were set aside for the local Chinese had disappeared and now they were riding "our" cars. I felt invaded. One by one, I was losing my Japanese privileges. Eventually we would be chased out of this quiet residential area reserved for Japanese too. Then I remembered the uncomfortable feeling I had experienced while riding a streetcar with my Manchurian classmates one afternoon. Manchurian children who were allowed to attend Japanese schools had special passes that allowed them to ride the streetcars reserved for Japanese. When I got on a streetcar one afternoon, I saw two of my Manchurian classmates seated in the car, neatly dressed in our school uniform. I automatically greeted them with a broad smile, seated myself next to them, and started a conversation. Both girls were very pretty and well-mannered, but had a strong Chinese accent in speaking Japanese and faltered often in the course of simple conversation. It was a dead giveaway. The Japanese passengers around us suddenly turned their heads and rudely viewed the two girls from head to toe, almost accusingly. I was embarrassed and wished that the girls could speak better Japanese, at least well enough to hide their racial identities. I also felt guilty, as if associating with native Chinese was a treason to my fellow Japanese.

I had become so accustomed to the segregated life of colonial Dairen that I had never thought it strange not to have Chinese friends or neighbors. And yet, they were an inseparable part of my childhood memories. Our days used to begin with a tall Chinese "tofu" vendor who came around blowing a squeaky bugle every morning around six. He would briskly come in to our kitchen with a broad smile, greeting the entire household in his loud and clear Japanese, "*Samui neh?* (cold, eh?)" He would mark the small credit book hanging by the door with a stub of pencil—a square for a tofu, an oblong for a *kon-nyaku* (arum root pastry), a triangle for an *abura-ghe* (deep fried tofu), and so forth. We shared a great communication made up of smiles and pictographs. Fresh fish and vegetable vendors who came around the Japanese residential areas were also local Chinese. My mother, who had never taken up the study of the language, had no problem in dealing with them, between her broken Chinese and their broken Japanese. And then there were Chinese men whom we called *bolo neeya* (scrap buyer). Instead of blowing squeaky bugles, like the tofu vendors did, they called out, or sang out, "Bolo—ye, bo—lo—,"in a plaintive tune as they zigzagged through the residential area, swinging two baskets hanging from a bamboo pole over the shoulder in front and back. There was a unique serenity and calmness in the way they "sang" the *bolo* calls. They bought all kinds of scraps—old clothes, old newspapers, old magazines, old shoes, old anything, which would then end up in a flea market. Then there was a Chinese woman we called *syi fu* (wash woman), who came to our house to do the laundry by hand twice a week. I could always detect her presence when I came home from school by the odor of laundry detergent from our washroom. If Mother was out, *syi fu* would yell from the washroom, "*Oku-san nai-yoh!* (no mistress)."

Our parents were careful in our relationship with the local Chinese. For instance, we were taught to pay more than the asking price when we rode rickshaws, which were always pulled by local Chinese. (I never saw Japanese men doing manual work in Dairen while I was growing up.) When we lived in the government quarters designated for the higher ranking officials, the rickshaw runner would never tell us how much we owed. He would fan his hand in front of his smiling face and say, "*Bu yau, bu yau* (no need, no need)." So we always paid more than the usual asking price. But we were not always so gracious. I remember, with shame, that my brother cheated the lion dancers one day during the new year holiday season. My second-oldest brother, Kay, had always been the most mischievous of the clan. One day, two of my brothers and I were home while Mother was out with my sisters. Kay was in charge of us. The unfortunate lion dancers, an older man who banged and shook the tambourine and a younger man dressed in a gold-painted lion's head and long green cape, came knocking at our door. We were not supposed to let anybody in, but Kay suddenly had a bright inspiration and invited them in. They started the dance immediately. I was frightened because I knew that we did not have enough money to pay for it. The lion danced with comical quick movements while the older man shrieked and groaned some kind of a song which was indecipherable to us. Then Kay suddenly yelled at them, frantically motioning them to leave, "*Dzou ba! Dzou ba! Kwai kwai de!* (go! go! quickly!)." Kay, a teenage boy, pushed the two grown men out of the door and locked it noisily. Kay was flushed with excitement. After listening to their footsteps receding from the door, Kay fell on the floor, roaring with laughter. "Did you see them? Did you see how they ran? Scared of me! The goddamn yellow-bellies!" The incident never reached my father's ears, or so we thought at the time. Kay had made us promise never to tell our parents, but I told my mother, who paled and severely reprimanded Kay, and told us not to tell Father. I have a feeling, however, that Mother did tell Father, and that they decided to leave it a "secret" lesson. It was more effective than any of Father's thirty-minute lectures.

Another memory of the local Chinese that is not quite pleasant to me is my experience of watching a Chinese funeral procession. The Chinese funeral procession, to me, seemed more like a parade of festivity because of their colorful papier-mâché furniture, toys, and animals, which were to accompany the dead to heaven. The procession was followed by a troupe of professional mourners, wailing and lamenting. The wailers were covered by white sheets from head to toe, tied at the waist by a rough straw rope. I had often wondered if the wailers were really crying, and one day my curiosity got the best of me. I ran after the wailers, trying to see their faces, but their faces were deep inside the drape of the sheet. I went around to the front of one of the wailing women and squatted down halfway to take a peek. The wailer growled at me and spat sharply to the asphalt close enough to my foot to scare me away. I ran home in tears.

Above all the native Chinese who surrounded my early life, however, there is one Chinese man who still stands out in my heart. He literally saved my life. It happened when I was four or five. Our house was then near a large pond called *Kagami-ga ike* (mirror pond). In the winter when the pond froze, my brothers used to change into their skates at home and walk across the street on their tiptoes to get to the pond. One afternoon I followed them to the pond in my boots. I was standing at the shore, waiting for one of them to skate around the rink toward me so that I could wave to him. When none of them appeared, however, I began to entertain myself by "skating" in my boots close to the shore. Nobody was aware that I was getting close to the section where the ice was thin and a red warning flag had been put up. I slid into that area and instantly fell through the thin ice. The water was shallow, but I was wearing a heavy winter coat and could not move. I felt the water pulling me down. People tried to reach me, but the thin ice prevented them from getting close. Then a big, tall coolie walked right into the freezing water, holding onto the handrail of the deck with one hand, pulling me out of the water with the other, and handed me to another coolie. The coolie rushed me home, pushed me inside the door, and walked away without a word. By the time my family understood the whole story and dashed out to thank him, he was long gone.

Standing under the clear blue sky on that autumn day, watching the Chinese passengers fighting their way just as impatiently as the Japanese, I came face to face with the new world, a world where Japanese supremacy was a big joke, where Japanese privileges no longer existed. I did not, however, think of this new situation as disappointing or discouraging. Instead, I felt that I now could become a true resident of Dairen, as if by losing my Japanese privileges I had now earned the right to join the natives—to become a native Dairenian. I now knew what I wanted to do with my life.

The next day, I went to see Professor Hayashi, a renowned scholar of the Chinese language, whom I knew only by name. I had decided to pursue the study of the language that I had always loved as the first step toward becoming a true citizen of Dairen. I looked up his address in the phone book and left home without talking it over with anyone.

As I waited for my turn to get on the jam-packed streetcar, I noticed that farm carts drawn by two horses were now being used to transport people instead of hay or firewood. The passengers on those carts were mostly coolies. I waved down one of the carts and jumped on it, squeezing in between the garlic-breathed coolies. Dressed as a boy, I wanted to behave like one, and I also wanted to prove to myself that I could indeed mingle with native Chinese of all classes. As I hung onto the slow and rickety cart, I became aware of a fellow passenger's curious glances— *What's this girl doing here dressed like a boy?* he was probably wondering. I turned to him and smiled a sheepish smile—*Keep my secret, would you?*

The coolie blinked and looked away as if I did not exist. I felt safe sitting next to him.

I got off at the Central Park and started to walk through the long blocks of the quiet residential area toward the huge Dairen Hospital compound. The area was said to have been reserved for the residence of Nicholas II when Dairen was under the control of czarist Russia. The compound was set on top of the slope not far from the *Oh-hiro-ba* Park. I was at home in this area. Often, while attending *Futaba Gakuin,* a private junior college for girls near the Central Park, I had walked this street with my friends on Saturday afternoons instead of taking a streetcar home. My house was then several blocks north of Dairen Hospital, directly behind a *Mantetsu* Park, where I had watched many of my Aunt Kiku's ballet performances at the performing arts theater in the park.

Professor Hayashi was supposed to live across the wide asphalt street that surrounded the hospital compound. I strolled gingerly from house to house, checking each nameplate on the gatepost along the seemingly abandoned street until I found what I was looking for. The wrought iron gate of Professor Hayashi's house was securely barred from the inside and the tall concrete wall around the house had glass shards embedded on top. I was rather surprised to see the fortlike wall, but then I had seen other old homes with this same kind of "protection." It was a telltale sign of the early days of the pioneer Japanese. I pressed the button on the gatepost, but there was no response. I looked through the gate, afraid that the silent house might have been vacated, but the neatly trimmed shrubs in the front yard assured me that someone still lived here. Taking advantage of being dressed as a boy, I climbed the wrought iron gate and jumped into the front yard. *Nobody's watching me, anyway,* I thought. As I walked to the door and proceeded to press the doorbell, however, I realized that a man had been watching me from a small window by the front door. Oops! I squirmed. But the man smiled and opened the door for me.

I introduced myself and found out that this was Professor Hayashi himself. He was a slightly built man with horn-rimmed glasses, about my father's age. The air of tranquillity about him reminded me of my father, which helped me feel at ease with him. As soon as he showed me into his study, I told him that I wanted to be his private student to further my study of Chinese. He nodded. This wasn't anything unusual. Most students who knocked on his door must have expressed the same desire. I felt the urgency of explaining my reasons and wished I had prepared a speech of some kind, but it was too late.

I took a deep breath and blurted out, "You see, I love the Chinese language. I always have. I think the language is important. It's the key to communication. If you don't know the language, it causes misunderstanding. And how can you build a good relationship among people of different cultures without close communication? The Japanese in Dairen should take up the study of Chinese more seriously and get into the Chinese world. We, the Chinese and Japanese in Dairen, should get to know each other better. A lot better. We should work together. Dairen belongs to all of us. I want to study Chinese so that I can be a true citizen of Dairen."

"I see. Is your family planning to remain in Dairen?"

"Pardon me?"

"All Japanese in Manchuria will be shipped back to Japan sooner or later, I suppose, unless you have a special reason."

Shipped back to Japan? The thought had never occurred to me. Even during the escape from Furanten, my destination was Dairen, not Japan.

"But why? Why Japan? I don't want to go to Japan."

"I don't think you have a choice in this matter, my dear. I am sure that all Japanese will have to go back to Japan."

"I don't believe it. Why can't we stay here?"

"Why?" The professor bent over the table, looking deep into my eyes.

"Because Japan has lost Manchuria and the Liaotung Peninsula." Narrowing his eyes, he whispered slowly, "We have lost the right to live here."

Lost the right to live here?

"But Professor, I was born here!" I whispered back in agony and pursed my quivering lips. *I was born here. I am a native of Dairen. The native Chinese didn't have to leave here when Japan took over Dairen, or when czarist Russia had it before Japan. Why do I have to go? Why?*

The professor reached for a cigarette and lit it, his hands unsteady. As he inhaled deeply, the amber glow at the end of the cigarette flickered like a traffic signal. Slowly blowing out a silky line of smoke, he leaned back in his chair, looking over my head with unfocused, half-closed eyes. He was deep in his own thoughts. For all I knew, he belonged to my father's generation, which had come to Manchuria with the ideals of Manchurian development, of opening a new road, of creating a new world, a new nation. How could they walk out on their unfinished dream, their disrupted lifework?

"I must commend you, though," the professor said calmly, sitting up straight to face me, "that you want to study Chinese in order to be a true citizen of Dairen. For all these years, that is exactly what I've been telling people; study their language so that you can work with them rather than act as their rulers; respect their culture, their way of life, then they will respect yours. I am sure some Japanese have understood me, but they were in a hurry. They were impatient, especially the Japanese military. They wanted to rule the Chinese instead of coexisting with them. They pushed their way. And they created a country without nation, without people, to justify their actions."

His forgotten cigarette was about to drop ashes. He gently put it out in the ashtray and played with the ashes without saying another word. I waited, chewing on every word he had said. His sadness, his disappointment, his regret, and his poignant anger sank into me drop by drop, like the slow drops of intravenous fluid.

"Have you ever studied English?" he asked, looking up.

"English?" I was taken aback. "Yes, I have. After it was banned I kept it up with a private tutor."

"That's good. This is only my personal opinion, but for what it's worth, I think you should keep up with your study of English instead of Chinese. It will help you in the future."

"But Professor, what we need here is Chinese, not English."

Professor Hayashi nodded his agreement, then, shifting in his chair, he looked straight into my eyes.

"Go back to Japan with your family, my dear. I know how deeply you feel about Dairen, and how much it hurts to give up and leave this beautiful city. You are not alone in this, believe me. It hurts me a great deal also, a great deal. As things stand now, however, there's nothing you or anyone else can do except to go along with the tide. There's no telling what lies ahead of us, but as I understand it, Japan is now under American occupation. It would be to your advantage to keep up with your English, I am sure. You understand, don't you?"

As I nodded in silence, a few teardrops trickled over my flushed cheeks. I brushed them aside impatiently. I did not want to cry.

The professor walked me to the gate.

"Good-bye, my dear, and take care."

I felt his warm hands gripping my shoulders as I looked up to bid him a silent, tearful farewell.

The author (in front of her mother) with her parents and older brothers in 1931.

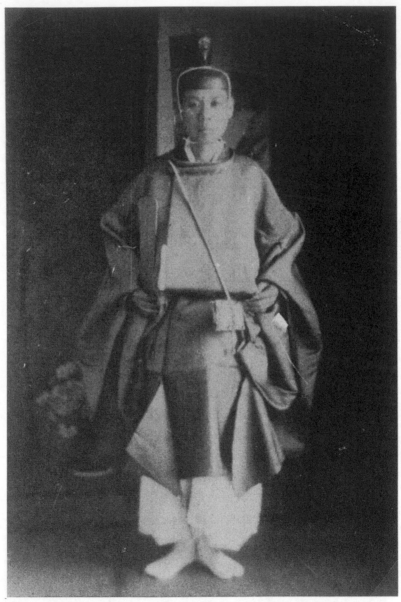

The author's father in formal Shinto attire to receive the Imperial messenger at Furanten shrine. 8 June 1945.

The author's mother (front row right) pictured with her parents, her brother, and her sisters.

The author (front row, third from the right) with her Red Cross classmates in the spring of 1944.

Oh-hiro-ba Park (Central Square) at the center of downtown Dairen before 1945. After 1945 the statue of General Ohshima was removed, and the shrubs went untrimmed.

The front entrance of Dairen Hospital, built in 1926.

Shopping street in Downtown Dairen before 1945.

The Dairen Railway Station built in 1936. Departure gates were on the upper level, and arrival gates were on the ground level.

Asia was the air-conditioned super-express of the South Manchurian Railway (1906–45).

The pier at Dairen.

The author in Col. Tippin's backyard, Beppu, Japan, in 1950.

This portrait of June Marie was taken in 1959 when she was six years old.

The author in Ontario, Oregon in 1996.

CHAPTER 6

My Brother Mamoru

THE SITUATION IN Dairen became more relaxed as a security police force consisting of local Chinese men was organized in late September. The hastily organized Chinese police force went through a short but strict training program and took their responsibilities seriously. The khaki-uniformed, proud policemen patrolled even the suburban residential areas. Stores opened, classes resumed, and I started my English lessons. I did not go back to Mrs. Hayakawa's conversational English program because I wanted to take up English as a grammar-oriented course study so that I could pass the entrance exam at a Japanese college.

I did not discuss my visit to Professor Hayashi with my family or anyone else. I kept it deep within myself, like a wound still bleeding. But I had decided to follow his advice and tried to focus my future plans on Japan, or rather on anywhere other than Dairen. It was not easy, but I knew I had no choice, as the professor had pointed out. Japan was the country my grandparents had come from, a country to which I had been taught to be loyal. Yet I had no physical attachment to Japan. My hometown was Dairen, and it would remain so for the rest of my life, no matter where I might live. But Dairen did not belong to me any longer and I had to come to terms with this.

The Russians released Aunt Masu's house at the beginning of October. Then Aunt Masu's family was ordered to take in five homeless Japanese from Port Arthur. As soon as they had taken over Port Arthur, the Russians had started an extensive renovation program to reinforce the port's military capacity and had ordered all Japanese—over forty-thousand of them—out of the city, keeping only a handful of engineers for their own use. The Japanese had abandoned their homes and properties and had come to Dairen with only what they could carry.

No Port Arthur refugees were assigned to Uncle Hideo's house because we, as Furanten refugees, were there already, although I was staying at Aunt Masu's place half of the time.

Three college boys and two girls about my age came to live at Aunt Masu's house. The boys had come from Japan to attend the engineering college in Port Arthur a few months prior to the end of the war. The two girls had also come from Japan, to work in a factory in Port Arthur. I tried to make friends with the two girls but gave up after a few days. They kept their conversations to themselves, shutting me out with meaningless giggles whenever I attempted to join in. I did not quite understand their local dialect and suspected that my Japanese might have sounded somewhat unfamiliar to them as well.

The girls automatically put themselves in the rank of housemaids, working in the kitchen with Aunt Masu's Korean maid. I soon found out, however, that these girls were surprisingly arrogant to the maid and her husband simply because they were Korean. Every time the maid or her husband spoke Japanese with a strong Korean accent they giggled shamelessly. The Korean couple did their best to ignore them, but I knew they were hurt.

"If that's the way the mainland Japanese are, I don't think I'd be comfortable in Japan," I complained to Aunt Masu one day. I had begun to separate myself from "the mainland Japanese" after my unpleasant experiences with the upper-class girls in the Red Cross. The two girls were definitely mainland Japanese. Aunt Masu understood my annoyance and came up with a new house rule. Until then the Korean couple had eaten in the kitchen while the family and our "guests" ate in the dining room, but the new rule called for everyone to eat in the dining room, so that the two girls had to sit next to the Korean couple and had to be on their best behavior.

This did not matter to Uncle Hozen, since meals had become just a matter of survival, although he still had a before-dinner drink. Why not enjoy it while it lasts, was Aunt Masu's philosophy, and she joined her husband in his before-dinner drink occasionally.

Whiskey was not the only thing that was becoming scarce. Rice, the most important food item for most Japanese, had become scarce. We now ate rice mixed with *kaolian*, a pinkish, round grain produced abundantly in Manchuria. It was dry and of a coarse texture, unpalatable to the Japanese tongue. I remember that my brother Kay used to cook it with whale meat for his dogs. Cooked together with rice, however, it looked rather pretty, and we ate it with pickles or various kinds of vegetables and a small amount of meat. Once in a while we were able to get some fish, fresh or cured. We also ate what was called *paomee*, ground millet resembling flour, only it was coarse and bright yellow. We mixed it with water to make it into patties and then pan-fried them. I did not mind this strange diet, but really felt sorry for my grandmother. Aunt Masu had had regular rice cooked for her separately at first, but as the price of rice went up, grandmother insisted on eating the same thing as we did.

"This is like eating sand," Uncle Hozen commented loudly one evening, shocking everyone at the table. No one had ever complained or made any comment about what was served at the table.

"This is for dogs and horses," he went on, ignoring our shocked silence, "but it suits us fine at this point. We are no better than dogs and horses, since surviving from day to day is all that we are doing."

Then, as if he had just noticed us sitting at the table with him, he looked up, glaring at us one by one. We automatically avoided meeting his glare. His eyes revealed that he had had a few drinks in him and would welcome any challenge.

"Listen!"

He suddenly stood up from his chair, with the swiftness of an athlete.

"Listen, everybody. Just because you're eating *kaolian* rice, don't degrade yourselves to the level of a dog! Don't you dare settle for surviving from day to day. Keep your dreams and hopes up. This is not the end of the world. Certainly not the end of Japan. You'll see. Japan will get back on her feet in no time. This is the only war that we've ever lost. The hell with it! Japan will rise again. You just wait and see. Don't you ever doubt that. Keep your chins up! Hold your heads high! And work. Go out and work. Work with all your might. If you can't find work, then read books. There are plenty of books in my library. Feed your brains, if not your stomachs!"

He would have gone on all night if Aunt Masu had not made him sit down.

"You know, your grandfather was a lucky man," Grandmother said after we went to bed. Since the room I had always used when I stayed at Aunt Masu's house was now occupied by the three college boys, I slept in my grandmother's room downstairs, next to the dining room.

"He was lucky to have died before all this happened. I envy him, really."

Grandmother murmured to herself. I could hear Uncle Hozen's sutra chanting from upstairs. It was always the Paramita Sutra, the core teaching of Zen Buddhism—*Shiki soku ze kuu, kuu soku ze shiki* . . . The tangible is the emptiness, the emptiness is the tangible, the whole universe is a continuous flux, nothing is permanent, all things arise and subside, appear and disappear, according to direct and indirect causes and results.*—Uncle Hozen's resonant voice shook the whole house.

"They say that a woman's *goh* (karma, the accumulated causes for one's suffering, in this case) is deeper than a man's *goh*," Grandmother sighed. "I suppose my *goh* was deeper than his."

"Oh, Grandma, your karma has nothing to do with the war."

"You don't think so?"

"Of course not, Grandma. Your individual karma has nothing to do with the wars between countries." Then a thought came to me. "But, then again," I said, more or less talking to myself now, "there could be something like a national karma. A nation could build its own karma by the way it has been established, by the way it has interacted with other countries, or by the characteristics of its people and things like that."

"That's it, that's it." Grandmother took my words in her own way.

"That's *Inga oh-ho* (causes and effects), you see. The Japanese army has committed many sinful acts. That's why Japan has lost the war. It's a divine punishment."

"That's not right, Grandma." I sat up to face her in the semidarkness of the room.

"Japan was defeated because she ran out of military resources. The Japanese military caused its own defeat. It's not a divine punishment. I am not saying that the Japanese military did nothing wrong or sinful. I am sure they did, but then what about the armies of other countries? Look at the Russians and the Chinese, right here, right now in Manchuria, murdering unarmed civilians and raping women. Why are they allowed to keep doing wrong? Why is there no divine punishment on them? There is no right war or wrong war. No war can be totally justified. It's just that each country believes in its own cause, condemning the other, so they clash. And the winner takes it all, justification and all. The loser becomes the criminal and everyone throws rocks at you."

Heart of the Great Wisdom Paramita Sutra by Rev. Gyomay Kubose.

I stopped abruptly, remembering the rocks showered on us during our escape from Furanten in the roofless freight train. Grandmother was quiet, but I knew she was taking in every word I had uttered, or had not uttered.

"Poor child," she said, "and you were at the beginning of your life."

I lay back on my bed, looking at the dark ceiling.

"I still am, Grandma. I still am."

The Korean couple's room was on the other side of the kitchen. The first thing the maid did every morning was to start a pot of hot water. I always listened for the sound of the running water, then the hushed "pooh!" as she lit the gas range from the pilot, followed by the oceanlike sound of the heavy drapes opening in the dining room.

One morning, I missed all of these familiar sounds. How had I slept through all that noise? I got out of my bed and went into the kitchen. The kitchen was dark and so was the dining room. I looked around and noticed that the door to the Korean couple's room was ajar. I peeked in. The room was empty, as was the closet, which was left open. Futons, their clothes, and all their belongings had been cleaned out of the room.

I ran upstairs to report this to Aunt Masu. Aunt Masu and Uncle Hozen hurried downstairs in their nightgowns to look over the ransacked room.

"Strange people. They didn't have to sneak out like this. They were free to go anytime," Aunt Masu said, shaking her head.

"Well, that's two fewer mouths to feed," Uncle Hozen commented dryly.

Then Toru ran in to tell us that our car was gone. Aunt Masu and I followed Toru to the garage. The car was gone and the garage door had been left wide open.

"Shall we report this to the police?" I asked, looking around in disbelief.

"We could, but I doubt if it'll do us any good," Aunt Masu said, shaking her head.

"If they are on their way to Korea, the police should be able to apprehend them." Toru was quite agitated.

"Oh, no, they won't be heading for Korea. It's too dangerous up north. And there hasn't been much gas in that car for a long time. I am surprised that it moved at all," Aunt Masu said. "They probably took it somewhere to dismantle it and then sold the parts."

The theft was never reported to the authorities simply because no definite authority existed in Dairen at that time.

Aunt Masu was about three months pregnant then. Despite the uncertain situation we were in, and the more uncertain future we faced, Aunt Masu was ecstatic that she was carrying her first baby by Uncle Hozen. She moved about more cautiously now, which made her even more suited to her nickname, *"tai-tai,"* the mistress of the clan. The war and its chaotic ending did not seem to have affected her private joy in having another child.

One day, when I was again at Aunt Masu's house, Takeshi came running, out of breath and beside himself with excitement.

"Kazuko-chan! Hurry! You've got to come home! It's Mamoru, your brother! He came home! He was alive! He came home alive!"

A sharp chill ran through me. I grabbed Takeshi by his shoulders and looked into his face. The next thing I knew, I was running down the hill at full speed. I ran across the main street, through the elementary schoolyard, and up the hill to the house.

"Where is he?" I shouted to Toshiko in the hallway.

"He just went out to the backyard," she shouted back, still flushed with excitement.

I ran out to the backyard and found a tall and gaunt figure standing there. It was Mamoru, my brother. He was alive. I flew into his arms.

Toshiko had been the first to see Mamoru walking up to the house. She had stood still in shock, staring at the gaunt, filthy coolie who was smiling at her through tears. She had screamed the news into the house and jumped into his arms. Mother had come out of the house, crying out his name. Then everyone had poured out of the house, screaming and laughing hysterically. Mamoru had panicked when he did not see his wife Hisako among the tear-streaked faces surrounding him.

"Where is Hisako?"

Everybody had turned around to look for her. She was standing, holding onto the door, her face chalk-white, just short of fainting.

"Hisako." Mamoru had walked over to her as if in a dream, letting her scream into his open arms. Mother had run into the house to bring out Yukio.

"So this is Yukio." He had held out his hands to hold the son he was meeting for the first time, then had realized how dirty he was.

"I guess I am too dirty for him."

"Yeah, you are dirtier than the real coolies." Everyone had laughed. Hysterical.

"And you smell! Phewee!"

80

So he had been sent to the backyard to strip off everything he was wearing before he was allowed to come in to take a bath.

Hisako and I stood there in silence, waiting for him to take off his dirty clothes. After he went into the house, wrapped in a big bath towel, Hisako and I made a small pile of the dirty clothes. Using old newspapers, we started a fire underneath the pile, poking it with a stick. As the rags smoldered, Hisako started sobbing. I held her and we sobbed together.

"I am so happy for you, *Onay-san* (big sister)," I whispered.

"Thank you. You know, I had always thought my wedding day was the happiest day in my life. But today, oh, Kaz-chan, today is much, much better than my wedding day." She smiled through her tears.

By the time Father came home, Mamoru was clean-shaven and relaxed.

"So you have survived." Father gripped the shoulder of his first-born son, whom he had almost given up hope of ever seeing again. The two men, father and son, stood there without a word, staring into one another's tearful eyes.

"You have lost a lot of weight, haven't you?" Father asked hoarsely then walked off, rubbing his face.

With his treasured bottle of Johnny Walker whisky, Uncle Hozen and Aunt Masu came over to help us celebrate this joyful miracle.

Mamoru had been a cryptographer stationed at Songo, one of the outposts along the Amur River, the Manchurian-Siberian border. As fate would have it, he was in the Harbin Headquarters on official business on the day of the Russian invasion. The first news of the Soviet attack shocked everyone at the headquarters. Then, almost simultaneously, Mamoru received another message from his unit, reading, "Burning cryptograph book," which meant that they were going out for *Gyoku-sai*, a suicide battle. That was the last he heard from his unit. The Japanese field army in Manchuria had been totally unprepared for the invasion. It had taken only a few hours for the Soviet tank troops to crush the Japanese garrison at the border.

Losing the unit to which he had belonged, Mamoru had remained at the Harbin headquarters, preparing to face the south-bound Soviet Army. In the middle of the chaos, however, they had learned of Japan's unconditional surrender.

That Japan would surrender had never crossed anybody's mind. They had been prepared to fight to the last man. But instead, they were disarmed by the Russians without a chance to fight. They were taken to the Harbin railway station, on their way to the Siberian prisoner of war camps. At the station, a Russian officer proceeded to spot-check the Japanese soldiers in line and discovered a jackknife that Mamoru had hidden inside his boot. He was immediately taken to a jail courtyard for execution. A young officer and an interpreter came in with an order to carry out the execution. The interpreter came over to blindfold Mamoru.

"I don't need to be blindfolded, sir."

Mamoru's refusal to be blindfolded was an expression of his last shred of pride. The young officer understood it. He stood in front of him and held up his pistol, aiming straight at Mamoru, who was glaring at him. Then the young officer said something. Through the interpreter he was asking Mamoru if he had any last words. Then Mamoru thought of his family. He wanted to let his family know where he had died. He looked for a piece of paper and found that the only thing he had in his pocket was Yukio's picture and his small foot and handprint, which Hisako had sent him. He wrote down our registered home address in Japan on the back of Yukio's picture and handed it to the Russian officer.

"I would appreciate it, sir, if you'd let my wife know at this address that I died here."

The Russian officer looked at the picture of the chubby little baby boy.

"Is this your son?"

"Yes, sir. He was born right after I was drafted."

"Oh, that's exactly what happened to me. I also have a son I have not seen yet."

"I am sorry, sir."

"You want to see your son, don't you?" The officer looked into Mamoru's eyes and waited. Mamoru gritted his teeth and kept his silence.

"Run!" The Russian officer motioned. "And run fast." Then he turned and walked away.

Mamoru had worked for a bank before he was drafted. He knew there was a branch office of his bank in Harbin. He ran to the bank. The local Chinese employee took him in and hid him in a small storage room upstairs, while waiting for an opportunity to get him into a group of migrating coolies heading south.

Having been born and raised in Dairen, he could handle smalltalk in local Chinese. No one around him suspected him of being a former Japanese army officer. Everything was working out all right until a few Russian soldiers got onboard the train in search of escaped Japanese prisoners of war. Mamoru's own panic revealed his identity. He was chased from one car to another until he reached the last car. He either had to jump off the speeding train or to climb up to the roof. He chose to climb up, and remained there until he reached Mukden. In Mukden he hid and lived on streets until he had a chance to mingle with a crowd of Japanese refugees from northern Manchuria who were heading south.

Mamoru's escape story kept the family awake deep into the night.

"So you heard the emperor's broadcast in Harbin then," Uncle Hozen said.

"Yes, we were stunned, to say the least. Unconditional surrender. How could Japan even consider surrendering? I still can't believe it. We just didn't know what to think or what was going on. Everything was happening so fast. And, my God, all these refugees. Had we been forewarned, we could at least have held the Russians back long enough to let the civilians get away to safety. We could have fought, you know. In fact, we were better dressed and better equipped than the Russians who came to disarm us. They had been fighting on the European front. They were tattered and exhausted. One of them asked us why we weren't fighting, when we still had all the ammunition."

"Yeah, why didn't you?" I asked abruptly, and Mother turned to me in horror.

"It was the emperor's wish that we lay down our arms." Mamoru sighed, shaking his head.

"The emperor wanted to save what was left of Japan and the Japanese people," Father said quietly.

"Yes, what's left of Japan," Uncle Hozen said, holding up his glass.

"To what's left of Japan!" Then he emptied his glass.

CHAPTER 7

Winter of 1945

TWO DAYS LATER Uncle Hideo came home. He was also disguised as Chinese, but not as a coolie as Mamoru had been. He was warmly dressed in black Chinese clothes of quilted silk, complete with a small round cap and a matching jacket. He even had a false identification paper with him.

The Russians had reached Mukden on August 19, four days after the Japanese surrender, and had requisitioned the hotel where Uncle Hideo and other out-of-town executives of the Manchurian Railway Company and its relative companies were staying. All residents had been ordered to move out of the hotel within four hours. Uncle Hideo had moved in with a friend's family and had waited for the chance to slip out of the city.

"Mukden is a living hell now," Uncle Hideo said darkly. His voice had always been extremely low, but now it was almost inaudible. He was a man of very few words and he'd never repeat those few, so when he opened his mouth, we all strained our ears to catch those precious few words.

His short, clear-cut description—"living hell"—was not followed by any explanation. We held our breath and waited. A picture of a city engulfed in flaring red flames and black clouds of smoke, with thousands of people running in all directions crossed my mind. I shuddered at the thought and anxiously waited for Uncle Hideo to give us a more feasible and acceptable picture of "living hell." It was a dreadfully long moment before Aunt Sadako finally broke the silence. She showered him with questions that we all wanted to ask—What do you mean by "living hell"?

How did the Russians reach Mukden, by tank, by air, or by train? Is Mukden now under the occupation of the Russians, the Nationalist Chinese, or the Communist Chinese?

Uncle Hideo waited for Aunt Sadako to stop and catch her breath. Then he proceeded in his own way, one sentence at a time.

"Mukden is overflowing with Japanese refugees from northern Manchuria. They are living in vacant shacks, or on the streets, in the parks, just anywhere. The Chinese, who have raided Japanese homes, stores, and factories, are further victimizing those poor, helpless refugees on the streets. Something must be done in a hurry. They won't be able to survive much longer."

"I know. I mingled with them in Mukden," Mamoru said. "Most of them were women and children. Men had been drafted just before the end of war." He paused to let out a long sigh. "The ones who made it to Mukden were the lucky ones. Many didn't make it to Mukden, not even to Harbin."

"How did you manage to get on the train with the refugees?" Uncle Hideo asked Mamoru. We all turned to Mamoru. That was one part of his miraculous escape about which no one had thought to ask.

"I ran into an old high school classmate who happened to be working at the Mukden railway station. He made me carry an old, sick lady on my back. One of the refugees from the north. She was near exhaustion." Mamoru shook his head.

"So what did you do with the old lady when you reached Dairen?" I asked.

"The old lady? I left her with her family. They were taken to a school or somewhere."

The first Russian troops to reach Mukden, as I understood, were made up of ex-convicts, not of professionally trained or disciplined soldiers. They had treated their pistols like toys, shooting at random, helping themselves to whatever caught their fancy, and raping women, Japanese and Chinese alike. It did not matter to them. When the G.P.U. (the Russian military police) finally had reached the city, this had subsided to some extent, but not entirely.

"So, are they trying to restore order now?" Father's voice was shaky.

"They are trying. They just don't have enough G.P.U. to cover the whole city. Dairen is a heaven, compared to Mukden."

"A heaven!" Aunt Sadako cried out. "Don't you know we've been through the same horror here too?"

"It's getting better," Father said calmly. "The Russians and Chinese are working things out. It will be all right."

Now that there were three men in the house, we felt more secure. Survival seemed possible. So far, the main source of income had been Aunt Sadako's kimonos, which my father sold to the Russian soldiers on the street. All Japanese assets were frozen. The only currency we could use were the Russian military notes, which were pink and looked like play money. The Russians loved the colorful Japanese kimonos and paid generously for them. For most Japanese, selling such possessions as kimonos, watches, dishes, dolls, and jewelry was the only means of making a living.

To accommodate the need for an appropriate place for the Japanese to sell their possessions, department stores rented out spaces by the showcase. My brother Mamoru rented one of those spaces with two showcases and asked me to be his salesgirl while he collected salable items from relatives and friends. Since the merchandise was accepted on consignment based on mutual trust, the only capital my brother needed was the daily rent. We would sell the merchandise for them for whatever we could get for it and charged them ten percent for handling it. It was the most suitable new business for my family, who had lived in Dairen for nearly forty years. We had many relatives and friends who would trust us with their valuables.

The basement of most Japanese department stores were reserved for grocery items and a delicatessen. Since there were no longer any normal grocery items, the department stores rented the booths to Japanese, who sold homemade French fries, steamed sweet potatoes, or steamed buns concocted with *paomee* or whatever grain powder was available.

My father and Uncle Hideo rented a booth in the basement of the same department store where my brother and I had the consignment business on the ground floor, and opened a *tempura* shop. *Tempura* is Japanese-style deep-fried seafood, mainly shrimp, mixed with various vegetables that have been dipped in batter. My mother and Aunt Sadako gave my father and uncle a quick cooking lesson and prepared the ingredients for them every morning. A former major company executive and a former government official were now learning to be chefs. Of course, there were no shrimp in their *tempura*. It was all vegetables, whatever ones were available. Still, people loved it. They came not just to eat, but also to meet with other people and to exchange information. This took the place of newspapers.

After a while, my mother began to come to the store to help. When she came she brought what were called *kan-kollo-mochi*, a popular new food among the Japanese then. They were dark brown steamed buns, a little smaller than hamburger buns. She and Hisako would make them the night before and Mother would take them down to the *tempura* shop. She served them with *tempura* in place of rice, which was too expensive.

We were excited about this new way of life. By then my hair was long enough and the city was safe enough for me to go back to being a girl. Aunt Masu's clothes fit me perfectly. I got up early every morning, went to my English teacher's place, which was on my way downtown, then went to the department store to open my little shop. Kimonos were hung in the back. They made a colorful background. Watches, cameras, and jewelry were laid out on the top shelf of the showcase. Little purses, pretty scarves, blouses, and sweaters were on the next shelf. Dishes, silverware, and dolls were at the bottom of the showcase. Japanese dolls brought in more money than silverware.

The best customers were, of course, the Russian soldiers. I found them to be simpleminded and easy to handle. They carried the pink Russian military notes in bundles and either bought things as I priced them or just walked away. They did not bargain as Chinese customers did. The Chinese were sharp bargain hunters. They checked the items carefully and compared the prices with those of other stores. When they decided to buy something at my shop they would start their bargaining. I soon learned to deal with them and enjoyed the bargaining. I made friends easily and gained many steady customers. The trick was to go along with their bargaining as if a few cents really mattered, and when it reached close to the price I had in mind, I'd let go of the item with my best act of regret and hesitation. The Chinese loved this game.

Once we had adjusted, this life was not totally intolerable for us children. We had grown up within the economic restrictions of wartime, which had been reinforced by the classic Japanese emphasis on valuing one's perseverance and accomplishment over material luxury. My dogged effort to study English was respected and encouraged. The piano lessons for my sisters and cousins were continued even when we lived on *kaolian*-rice and leftover *tempura*. If the adult members of the family were fighting the battle of everyday survival, they made sure that we children were spared the burden. If the meals were tasteless, this was compensated for by pleasant conversation. We entertained ourselves by remembering every little incident that we considered funny. We laughed a lot. Old jokes were repeated again and again, just so we could laugh. We made ourselves laugh.

We also had many visitors at night. They came to exchange news and information. No one talked about the war and its consequences. All we talked about was how we could make more money, where we could buy food cheaper, or in what we could best invest for the future. The visitor whom I most enjoyed was Aunt Sadako's high-spirited younger brother, Shoji. He had worked for the Manchurian Railway Company's Bureau of Research and excelled in Chinese. He was a brilliant young scientist, a fast and witty talker. He could tell jokes with a straight face as if he didn't know why people were laughing. He was also a chain smoker, the kind who would light another cigarette from the one he still had in his mouth. Holding a cigarette between his first two fingers, he'd write a *kanji* (Chinese character) in the air between puffs while he talked. He often paused to add a line or a dot to the invisible *kanji*. I used to sit right next to him so that I could try to guess what *kanji* he had just written. Often the *kanji* had nothing to do with what he was saying. He would be thinking about something else while carrying on a conversation or making people laugh.

It was on one of those fairly uneventful November days that Aunt Masu gave birth to a healthy boy at the Dairen Hospital. One day, I went to meet my newborn cousin.

The first thing that caught my attention as I entered Aunt Masu's private room was a large sheet of calligraphy on the wall. Two *kanji* characters that showed powerful brush strokes completely covered the white rice paper, crying out for more space. The top character was *katsu*, a shout that Zen priests use to call one's wandering mind back to meditation. The bottom character was Zen Buddhism's *zen*.

"What do you think of it?" Aunt Masu asked, smiling proudly.

"Powerful strokes. Uncle Hozen, isn't it? I can't think of anyone else who uses a brush like this. But what is it? What does it mean?"

"Why, it's his name. The baby's name."

"Oh." I looked down at my tiny new cousin, fast asleep in his little crib decorated with a big baby-blue ribbon. "Katsu-zen" would make an impressive name for a Zen priest, tall and muscular, with shaven head and thick eyebrows, glaring at you fiercely.

"Isn't it a great name?" Aunt Masu was quite contented.

"It sounds—well, great, yes," I said with an effort. I didn't want to hurt my aunt's feelings. "But, what do we call him? He is not a Zen priest."

"I've been thinking about that. How about Katsu-boh for the time being?"

Adding "boh" to a little boy's name is something like adding "boy" to make "John-boy" or "Danny-boy."

"I like that. Hey, Katsu-boh, you are quite handsome, aren't you?" I bent over the sleeping baby.

"Isn't he? He's got Hozen's features. Look at his strong jaw line and straight nose. He looks like he's got his own mind already."

"Yes. I am sure he'll grow up to be as strong as Uncle Hozen." I said exactly what Aunt Masu wanted to hear and she laughed happily. I understood her prayer for him. Katsu-boh had to grow up to be a willful and resourceful man if he were to survive the difficult years ahead of him. Aunt Masu and I admired the little fellow in silence. Then Aunt Masu whispered, "Do you know there are a lot of girls and women in this ward having abortions?"

"Abortions?" I was puzzled.

"Yes, abortions. They are the rape victims of the Russians, you see? It's terrible. But what else can they do?"

I winced and looked away. Rape, abortion—the kind of vocabulary that would not have reached the ears of a teenage girl in peacetime had now become everyday vocabulary in postwar Dairen. It had been whispered at first, behind my back. Now my aunt was whispering the words to my face. Did I grow up, maybe ten years in ten weeks? Sudden tears welled in my eyes.

"I'll be back." I got up quietly and left the room.

Winter came. Since coal was in short supply, the heat in the house was reduced to the minimum. We kept only the dining room warm. The nightly bath that we had always taken had dwindled from every other day to twice a week and finally to once a week. We simply ran out of wood to make hot water. The use of gas and electricity had long been minimized to cooking. We burned wood furniture piece by piece. We could not take them back to Japan anyway, no matter how valuable they might be. We cut down the trees in the yard also.

One day my father was cutting branches off the peach tree in the front yard of Uncle Hideo's house when a couple of Chinese patrolmen walked by. They stopped and watched my father.

"Hi, how are you? It's getting pretty cold, isn't it?" My father greeted them.

90

The two patrolmen came closer to the fence and asked my father what he was doing. My father told them that he was in the process of cutting the tree down to heat the bath. The two patrolmen consulted with each other and then one of them told my father that we could keep the branches that had already been cut down, but that we could not cut any more. He explained to my father that not only the trees around the house but the house and the land too now belonged to the Chinese government. They were now public properties. The Japanese no longer owned any personal property.

"You are lucky that my government lets you live in this house for the time being," the patrolman said graciously. Father apologized for his ignorance.

"Guess what?" He came in to report the incident. "I was just told by the Chinese patrolmen not to cut down the trees in the yard. All Japanese properties belong to the Chinese government now, he said. They are all public property. He also said that we ought to be grateful that his government is so gracious as to let us live here."

The idea of public property was a new revelation to us.

"Is this communism?" I asked, "The idea of public property?"

"I suppose." Father was not sure what communism was all about.

"But they can't just take away people's private property, can they? Without payment?"

"They did, apparently." Takeshi, my cousin, laughed.

"Yeah, apparently," I agreed. "So we live in a house that's not ours, but is paid for by us." We all laughed, uncomfortably but good-naturedly. And we were indeed grateful that we had a roof over our heads when thousands of Japanese lived on the streets.

The winter in Dairen always came in a hurry. It did not give us enough time to enjoy the autumn, which made autumn more precious. Aunt Masu gave me one of her fur coats to keep me warm for my early morning English lessons. The fur on the coat was short, smooth, gray mink, but the trimming on the hood was white and fluffy. I loved the way the fluffy white fur framed my face. I wore it every day, until one day an incident happened that scared all of us.

I was walking down the street one evening after closing our shop when I heard someone running behind me. I did not pay much attention until the running figure came around to stop right in front of me. I looked up in surprise. A tall, young Russian soldier with cherubic red cheeks was bending over to look into my face under the fluffy fur trimming. His clear, blue eyes studied me earnestly and searchingly, as he panted from running. It was a long moment. Then, as suddenly as he came, he turned around on his heel and walked away, leaving behind a sense of disappointment and a touch of embarrassment. Had he taken me for someone he knew and then been disappointed? Or had he thought I was a Russian girl? Maybe he hadn't been able to decide whether I was a woman or a child. When I told my family about this incident, everyone became frightened for me, and they blamed it all on the white fur coat. My father was alarmed and made me return the coat to Aunt Masu immediately.

My sister-in-law Hisako made a coat for me out of a camel's-hair blanket. Hisako was an expert dressmaker and the coat was perfectly tailored to my size. Everyone, of course, praised it readily. Aunt Sadako gave me a fringed wool scarf of dark brown plaid to drape around the shoulders, which made a significant improvement on the blanket-turned-to-coat look. I honestly appreciated Hisako's effort and everyone's support. I had a loving family, enough to eat, and a job. What more could one want?

In Dairen, the snow usually came toward the end of November. Once it covered the whole city, it would not melt until the spring. The snow would pile up and be pressed hard as people walked on it. Then the whole city would be as slippery as a wet mirror and the trees along the sidewalk would turn into finely sculptured ice flowers. I had always loved the winter scenes in Dairen. But the winter of 1945 was not a winter of lovely scenes. It was a winter of death. It claimed hundreds of lives among the homeless Japanese refugees. They died of cold, hunger, and lack of sanitation. They also died of desperation. Many hung themselves in the parks, some leaving poetry of despair. There were a number of deaths among the Furanten refugees. As my father told us years later, he took it as a part of his responsibility to carry the bodies in a cart to a mountain for disposal. The hills behind the evergreen forest in the Central Park, where a memorial tower for the war dead still stood tall, were now covered by piles of abandoned bodies. Wild dogs fed on them and multiplied fast. The baseball stadiums that once had attracted thousands of spectators, the lanes around the ponds where lovers once had strolled, and the sunny playgrounds where children once had played were now at the mercy of the wild dogs. It was a winter of death.

But it was also the winter that Yukio took his first steps. One evening, as the family gathered around after supper, Hisako helped Yukio to stand up.

"He's been trying to stand up by himself lately," Hisako announced proudly.

"Then he may be ready to walk now."

Everyone excitedly gathered around Yukio. My mother called him, holding out her hands. Instead of crawling, the brave little boy tried to walk to her, waving both of his arms in the air like a bird. He did take a few wobbly steps, but then landed on his bottom.

"Oh, no!"

Everyone was disappointed. But Yukio was in a good mood. When his mother helped him up, he started walking, again waving both of his arms like a bird. When he took a few steps and fell into my mother's waiting arms, we all cheered.

"Hey! Yukio walked. Did you see it? Yukio walked!"

I was moved to tears. It was evidence of the eternal strength of life, which continued on even when we were faced with a totally uncertain future.

By the time the winter was almost over, I had become interested in reviving contact with my old classmates, from my high school, *Futaba Gakuin* and from the Red Cross.

The first classmate from my Red Cross days whom I encountered was *Ninjin*. I had nicknamed her *Ninjin* (carrot) because of her red hair, which was extremely unusual for Japanese. She was pale, small, and pensive, fitting the description of the little redheaded boy in a French novel, *The Carrot Head,* that I had just read. Ninjin was one of my roommates at the Red Cross training school dormitory. The four of us who shared a room at the time had put on a skit at the welcome party in our honor. I had written the skit overnight, depicting my own family's reaction when I had first expressed my wish to join the Red Cross Nurses Corps. I had played myself, Ninjin had played my little sister, and the other two had played my parents, whose feeble attempt to stop me had failed in the end. It was a shared expression of our youthful patriotism.

If it hadn't been for her red head, I would have missed her. She was about to pass by my showcase when I happened to look up from the book I was reading.

"Ninjin!" I yelled, startling the people around us. Reaching across the showcase, we celebrated this unexpected reunion with tearful laughter.

The Red Cross training school in Dairen had been closed in December 1945, four months after the Russian occupation, Ninjin said. The girls from Dairen had gone home, but the girls from out of town who had lost contact with their families had remained at the hospital.

Ninjin and her family were now in the jewelry business. Many people, mostly Japanese, were trying to hoard valuable jewelry, since we all knew that the current currency, the Russian military notes, would be worthless in Japan, or even in Dairen once the Russians pulled out. So the Japanese and Chinese had resorted to collecting valuable gems. Ninjin's mother, who had always had an eye for jewelry, had taught Ninjin and her sisters to be her scouts for their business.

"It's a lucrative business if you know what you are doing." Ninjin smiled with a touch of self-deprecation.

"But I couldn't find any bargains in your showcase. You must have someone who knows jewelry."

"Yeah, my aunt. I have one aunt who was a jewelry collector and another who was a kimono collector. So they price those items for me."

"You'd also have a good supply, then, wouldn't you?"

"Well, if we didn't have to do this too long. I hate to see them stripped of the things they had loved so much."

"I know. But what else can we do?"

From Ninjin I learned the latest news of Akiko and another one of my high school classmates, Mari, who had also joined the Red Cross. Akiko was now working at a Chinese beauty shop only four or five blocks away from my department store. Mari had joined a medical volunteer group to nurse the wounded soldiers in the Red Chinese army hospital in the north.

"It looks like Mari found her niche after all," Ninjin said, not without admiration.

The next day, I went looking for Akiko's beauty shop. Akiko and a beauty shop, a Chinese beauty shop at that, did not quite connect in my mind. The image of Akiko, the picture of a young patriot in her navy blue Red Cross uniform, proudly standing against the background of the sparkling afternoon snow at the front gate of Aunt Masu's house was still vivid in my mind. It had been barely a year since her visit. Her intimidating air of pride, her unwavering faith in Japan, and her youthful and passionate dedication, I remembered, had made me envious of her then. It was hard for me to picture her life in the Chinese section of town, a world where the Japanese were no more than unwelcome guests.

I was surprised that the Chinese section of town was only four or five blocks away from my department store in the center of the Japanese downtown. So close and yet so far. After asking a few Chinese passersby, I found the beauty shop that Ninjin had described. It was a run-down, two-story building, distinctively Chinese, with a bright green dragon crudely painted on the dingy white front wall. It did not look like a beauty shop at all. I peeked in. A customer was sitting in a big revolving chair with numerous electrical cords hooked onto her rolled hair. Akiko was nowhere to be seen. A young Chinese man came out of the adjacent barber shop. I introduced myself and asked for Akiko. As the man yelled her name, Akiko came out of the back room, carrying a bucket of water. Wearing a faded blue smock, her hair covered by a scarf, she looked like another person.

"Oh, Kaz," she murmured, as if in a dream. The young man took the bucket of water from her and told her to take a break upstairs. The upstairs was a restaurant, but no one was there at this late afternoon hour.

"How are you, Ako? How have you been?" I was genuinely concerned. She did not look like herself at all. She looked like a faded shadow of the Akiko I once had known.

"Oh, I'll live, I guess." She shrugged her shoulders.

A middle-aged Chinese woman came out from behind the counter with a tray containing two cups of tea and placed it in front of us. I smiled my thanks and bowed to her. She smiled back vaguely and disappeared.

"That's Wing's aunt. She owns the restaurant," Akiko said. Wing was the young barber I had just met downstairs. Wing's family owned the whole business in this building, Akiko told me in a monotone.

"There's a beauty shop, a barber shop, this restaurant, and a game room behind the barber shop. They've been helping me and my mother."

"How is your mother?" I asked. Her mother was a kimono seamstress and had made some kimonos for my family.

"She is all right, thank you," Akiko answered wearily.

Akiko's father had been an artist, although not very well known to the public. He had left Akiko and her mother for no obvious reason when Akiko was still in an elementary school. Some said he had committed suicide, but no one knew for sure.

"Ninjin told me about Mari. Have you heard from her?"

"No, I haven't. I am not sure if I ever will. Of course the Red Chinese guaranteed their safe return after six months, but who knows? Broken promises are nothing new these days."

"Why did she go? I mean, risking her life for the Red Chinese."

"I tried to reason with her, but she wouldn't listen. She turned philanthropist overnight. No, I take it back. She didn't turn idealist overnight. I guess we were all idealistic once, weren't we?" She laughed a short, dry laugh. "But Mari is still holding on to it. Gosh, I miss those days, don't you? Everything was clear-cut then. We knew, or we thought we knew, what was right and what was wrong. But that's a lifetime ago now, isn't it?" She took a sip of tea and looked out the window.

"We had quite an argument before she left. Mari just could not let go of her ideal of dedication and saving lives and all that. I told her no one would appreciate her, but she said she didn't care. It angers me to think that some people are taking advantage of her, of her pureness. But you know, in a way I envy her. I envy her for having that much passion left in her."

I remembered the envy I once had felt toward Akiko for her passion and dedication. Then she suddenly remembered the riot in Furanten.

"Oh, I heard about Furanten incident. That was terrible. Did everyone escape unharmed?"

"Well, everyone in my family is all right. We are living with my uncle's family.

"Was it the Russians or Chinese?"

"It was the local Chinese mob, but they were agitated by the guerrillas."

"How did it happen? And why Furanten? What did they want?"

"I don't know. It was just a part of war, I guess."

I did not really want to talk about Furanten. It had been a traumatic experience and I knew I would never forget it, but at the same time, I could not help feeling defensive about the local Chinese. They had been agitated by the guerrillas and it had been a time of war. It had just happened. I remembered the banging on our back door that saved our lives. I remembered the young man with rifle who did not use it on us. And oh, the agony of May-Min. No, I could never blame those people. It was a tragedy, a tragedy for all of us, Japanese and Chinese alike. It was just the high price of war that we common people had to pay.

"Were there any casualties?" Akiko asked.

"Yes. Mostly the *Gakuto* boys who happened to be there at the wrong time. Maybe twenty or thirty, I am not sure."

I remembered the crude graves at the corner of the schoolyard. I remembered them only too well. But I did not want to talk about it.

"They were unarmed, weren't they?" Akiko cried out in anger.

"Yes, of course. But Ako, it wasn't the local Chinese who killed the *Gakuto* boys. It was the guerrillas. The local Chinese in Furanten didn't do it."

Akiko nodded, looking somewhat puzzled. "So what's the difference? The boys were killed, the unarmed college boys, they were slaughtered, weren't they?"

"The local Chinese in Furanten didn't do it," I repeated to myself.

CHAPTER 8

Last Days in Dairen

"GOOD MORNING!"

I looked up. I had been working on my English homework between customers. It was Liu, a Chinese man in his twenties, one of my regular customers.

"Aiya, Liu-san, Good Morning." I smiled.

Liu was different from any other local Chinese I had known. He did not speak a word of Japanese except what I had taught him and he always wore a long Chinese robe obviously not meant for physical work, which was also unusual. The local Chinese men who worked at offices or stores wore shirts and ties, or sport shirts and pants, like most Japanese men did. Other than that, most Chinese men wore Mandarin-collared tops with loose-fitting pants, both of which were quilted in winter. Liu's lightly quilted long winter robe stood out in the crowd. It must have been quite warm. He always walked leisurely, like a prince strolling in his own courtyard in the spring sun, even on the frozen streets of Dairen. Neither adverse weather nor the boisterous downtown crowd seemed to bother him at all. He kept himself completely detached from it all.

At first, he had bought a few small items at my shop. He did not bargain like the other Chinese. Sometimes he came in the morning, sometimes late in the afternoon. Then one day he started a conversation, somewhat hesitantly, his perfect Mandarin not really surprising me. Now he came just to visit me. He would stay away from my shop when I had other customers, so as not to interrupt my business. But it was obvious that he wanted to visit with me.

"Doing your homework?" He asked in English. Once he found out that I was studying English, he spoke in English sometimes. He was well versed in the language and seemed to enjoy helping me with my homework.

"Yes, but I have just finished it."

He nodded and switched to Chinese.

"Tell me, what's 'kai-lu?'"

"'Kai-lu?' Is it a Japanese word?"

"I think so. I think, maybe, it's written this way." He wrote down two Chinese characters, one meaning to open and another a route.

"I don't know. Is it the name of a street?"

"I don't think so. I think it has something to do with Japan."

Then it dawned on me.

"Oh, you must mean 'ka-eh-lu,' going home, or to return to where you came from."

"Yes, that must be it. It makes sense."

"Where did you hear it?"

"Everywhere. All the Japanese are talking about 'kai-lu.' That's all they talk about nowadays."

"I know."

"Are you going back to Japan too?"

"I suppose so. Sooner or later."

Only it won't be 'kai-lu' for me, I thought to myself. To me, repatriation to Japan meant deportation from Dairen, my hometown, rather than a return to Japan. I had not come from Japan.

"When do you think you'll be going?"

"I don't know. I have no idea."

I looked up and met his eyes. His intelligent, sensitive dark eyes and the way he looked deep into my eyes, as if trying to read my thoughts behind them, reminded me of Kunio, who had always read my mind this way. Had Kunio survived the war? A sharp pain ran through me. It had been two years since Kunio had come to bid me farewell at the Red Cross training school. I had not heard from him since. Communication between Japan and Manchuria had been completely cut off. For all I knew, it was most likely that Kunio had been drafted as one of the *Gakuto* and shipped to the front just before the Japanese surrender.

"Have you ever been to Japan?" Liu was asking me.

"No, I haven't. I know Japan only through books and movies. My family has lived here for three generations."

100

What life in Japan would be like was never discussed at home. If we had asked our parents, they probably wouldn't have known what to say. Parents, as much as children, were in the dark as to the condition of postwar Japan. We knew that Japan had been severely bombed, but just how badly was for us to find out when we got there.

I turned away from Liu and saw my brother Mamoru approaching our shop.

"Here comes my brother," I warned Liu.

Liu was uncomfortable in Mamoru's presence. I blamed it on Mamoru's towering height. He was six feet tall, unusual for a Japanese man, and he carried himself with military precision and swiftness. He was suspicious of Liu's identity and was rather inquisitive. He kept himself polite and subtle, but threw in too many questions in the course of conversation. Liu left silently, a sense of unfinished conversation lingering behind.

After a short spring, the summer brought more people downtown. Our consignment business faced increasing competition. Mamoru started taking some of our less valuable items out to the street for quick sale. When rumors of repatriation became more serious, the Japanese started buying expensive kimonos as an investment, so the expensive kimonos were treated like jewelry and were kept inside. Only the cheaper ones were taken outside.

Sometimes I went out instead of Mamoru. The streets were swarming with people—Chinese, Japanese, and Russians—selling, buying, eating, shouting, and fighting. Full of life and energy. Weaving through the crowd with colorful kimonos draped over my shoulder, I enjoyed the excitement of the streets. I was good at bargaining with the Chinese. I'd let the customer name the price, which always started at the bottom. I would smile and continue walking, knowing that he would follow me. I would let him follow me, his price going up little by little. When his price came close to what I had in mind, I'd turn around and give him my final price. I usually got what I intended to get.

One such afternoon, I was heading back to the department store with one kimono left on my shoulder when I passed by a group of Japanese refugees. It was not unusual to see a group of refugees. They were everywhere on the streets, with their own 'shops' made up of empty crates. They sold bags of peanuts, candies, and souvenirs. Some had small boxes to sit on behind their shops, some sat on the ground, but they were isolated from the boisterous surroundings. They were the forgotten people in the middle of the crowd, a silent discordance in the maddening crescendo.

As I was passing them, something caught my attention. A man was sitting cross-legged on the ground trying to peel the burned skin off a baked sweet potato. It was his abnormal concentration that caught my attention. He was holding the sweet potato in his left hand so close to his tilted head that it almost touched his nose. Obviously, he wanted to peel the skin off the potato with his right hand, which shook out of control. He could bring his right hand to the potato, but the shaky fingers were not able to catch the skin. He was not about to give up, however. When a string of drool dripped from the corner of his half-opened mouth, he would wipe it off with the back of his left hand, still holding the potato, and would then go back to the painful task of peeling the potato skin. I held back my impulse to run over to help him and was becoming angry at his friends for sitting by him but not helping him when he finally caught the skin and yanked it off. When he saw the moist yellow meat of the sweet potato, he looked up and smiled at me as if he had been aware of my presence all along. He smiled happily and I smiled back. Then I gasped.

The man was Mr. Kawano, the former police chief of Furanten. I almost called out to him, but caught myself. He was blank. He had no idea who I was. I stood there and stared at him, breathing hard. I watched him eat the sweet potato with a child's single-mindedness. The man, who once was a judo black belt and a police chief, was now sitting cross-legged on the ground, eating a sweet potato with vacant intensity.

His right hand, which was resting on his knee, continued to shake. A woman, who was sitting behind a crate-shop set up next to him, turned to him and patted his head gently. He looked up and smiled at her. The woman was Mrs. Kawano. She nodded to him like a mother and Mr. Kawano happily went back to consuming the sweet potato.

I backed into the crowd, staring at them. I pulled the kimono from my shoulder and hurried back to the department store. Instead of going back to my own shop, I went down to the basement, where my mother was sitting alone. Father and Uncle Hideo had been deeply involved with the red tape of applying for repatriation and closed their *tempura* shop often lately.

"Mama . . . " I sat down next to my mother, but was unable to continue. I took a deep breath and held the kimono tightly against me, trying to regain my composure.

"What's the matter?" Mother looked concerned.

"Mama, I. . . I just saw Mr. Kawano and his wife . . . "

"Oh, you did," Mother winced.

"You knew it, didn't you! Why didn't you, at least, tell me they didn't die!"

"We didn't know it until a few months ago. They came to Dairen when the winter was over. May-Min and her family took care of them after we left and nursed Mr. Kawano back to life. He was almost dead, you know."

"Have you seen him? I mean, do you know that he is not . . . normal?"

"Oh yes, we've been to see them. We've been helping them as much as we can, but I am afraid Mr. Kawano doesn't recognize anyone but his wife."

The mob had not harmed Mrs. Kawano. Someone had pushed her into a corner and stood in front of her, shielding her from the sight while the mob beat her husband nearly to death and left with everything they could carry out of the house. Mrs. Kawano thought her husband was dead. He was covered with blood and lay there motionless. For hours she was frozen in the corner of the room in a state of shock. Then a small group of men quietly slipped into the house. They examined Mr. Kawano and gently moved him onto a knocked-down door and tended to his wounds.

"Remember, Mrs. Kawano, he must not be moved," one of them said to her, gently adding, "He'll be all right. He'll make it. You just stay put until someone comes for you." The man spoke in clear Japanese to her, but they spoke Chinese among themselves. Then they disappeared into the darkness as swiftly as they came.

"Listen, Kazuko," Mother said with concern, "Try to forget the Furanten incident, all right? Just think of it as a bad dream."

I nodded and left Mother without a word.

When I got back to our showcase, my brother Mamoru was waiting on a Chinese customer. He was relieved to see me. I was better at waiting on Chinese than my brother. But I was in no mood to talk to anyone just then. I threw the kimono back onto the rack and stood there silently, watching the Chinese man scrutinize a ring.

"That kimono didn't sell, huh? That's all right. Don't worry about it. Somebody will buy it," Mamoru tried to cheer me up. He had no idea what I had just encountered on the street.

"He's been looking at that ring for a long time. He probably has never seen a real gem in his life," Mamoru whispered, keeping a watchful eye on the man. The man was obviously of a working class, not the kind that could afford a "real" ring. He was holding the ring close to his face, almost touching his nose. *The sweet potato. Mr. Kawano was holding the sweet potato just like that.* My heart throbbed.

"That's Aunt Masu's star ruby," Mamoru said, "not the kind that he can afford. But that's all right. He can stare at it until he gets tired of it."

"Oh, is that what he is looking at?"

I was suddenly interested. Ruby was my birthstone, mine and Aunt Masu's. We were both born in July. "When I die you can have this," Aunt Masu had said to me years ago. Aunt Masu's supply of jewelry was running low now.

"What do you call this rock?" The Chinese man asked me.

"It's a ruby, a star ruby. The best of all rubies."

"A star?"

"Yes, a star. You can see the star if you hold it this way."

I held the ring up against the light and turned it around until I could see the five sparkling lines shooting out from the center point. The Chinese man took the ring between his thick, coarse thumb and finger, and turned the ring around until he could locate the five sparkles shooting out from the center of the clear red stone just as I had described.

"Hey! I can see it! I can see the star. It's shining inside the stone!" He cried out like a child, gazing into the ring.

"How much is it?" he finally put it down and asked.

I pushed the price tag toward him without a word. I was not about to bargain the price with him. He was genuinely surprised at the price, as I had expected. He took the price tag in his hand and read the price, moving his lips. He did not attempt to bargain it down. He quietly took another look at the ruby against the light and then put it back into its case with reverence.

"*Buta ni shinju* (pearls for swine)," an old Japanese proverb, crossed my mind as I bent down to place the ring back into the showcase. Then suddenly I was overwhelmed by a surge of emotion. *So this is the kind of man who has ruined a man like Mr. Kawano, has slain Gakuto boys like Kunio, and now is looking at a star ruby while Mr. Kawano is struggling to eat a baked sweet potato. But hey, why not? We are war criminals. So why not a star ruby to this coolie and a baked potato to Mr. Kawano and long live the emperor!* I was choked with mixed emotion.

When I stood up the man was still looking at the ruby, which was now in the showcase, his garlic breath wafting across the showcase.

"Pay for it, and you can have it." I heard myself spitting out the words to his face. The man looked up sharply, turning scarlet to his ears. Before Mamoru could come to cover me, he reached across the showcase and slapped my left cheek.

Everything came to a sudden halt. The Japanese men from the nearby showcases came running out to surround the Chinese, who was now pointing at me and shouting for the whole department store to hear.

"The snob Japanese bitch! She insulted me! She made me hit her! It's not my fault!"

"Get the security guard!" someone shouted from the next block, purposely in Chinese. The Chinese man turned defensive and let the Japanese men surrounding him lead him out of the store.

"Are you all right?"

Mamoru turned to me. I nodded and went into our small resting place behind the hanging kimonos. I slumped onto a hard wooden chair. Because of the showcase between us and because of my quick reaction, the man had only touched my face slightly. But I was deeply wounded. Defeated. *The snob Japanese bitch, yes, the snob Japanese bitch, the man had called me. How dare he!* "Pearls for swine" was exactly how I felt about leaving Dairen in the hands of the Chinese. To me, Dairen was Japan, Dairen was my country, Dairen was a pearl nurtured and cultured with my love and respect. *The man could not afford the star ruby, but he's got Dairen now, my Dairen,* the thought cut through my heart

"Liu is here asking for you," Mamoru said peeking in. "What do you want me to tell him?"

I looked up and took a deep breath.

"Are you all right?"

"Yes, I am all right." I tossed my hair back and pulled myself together.

"Tell him I'll be there in a minute, would you?"

When I came out from behind the curtain of kimonos, Liu was a few showcases away, pretending to be looking at something. I walked over to join him.

"Are you all right?" He looked at me searchingly. I nodded and looked away.

"Would you like to go to a coffee shop?" Liu asked. "There's one across the street." I nodded again, letting him gently guide me toward the door. Liu was different from other Asian men. He never walked ahead of me. He walked with me, protectively.

105

When Liu opened the door of the coffee shop for me, I looked around in disbelief. I could not believe this was a coffee shop. The noise, confusion, and excessively bright light startled me. The coffee shops that I remembered had always been semidark, with classical music softly flowing in the air. But now, people were trying to outtalk one another, in Japanese, in Chinese, in Russian, clattering the cups, ordering out loud, arguing and laughing. Once I got over the initial shock, however, I found it easier to lose myself in the noisy crowd than it would have been in a quiet place where you almost had to whisper your private conversation. So Liu and I settled in a booth in the middle of the crowd, the wall of chaos protecting our privacy.

Liu ordered a glass of cream soda for me and a cup of coffee for himself.

"Is anything wrong?" he asked hesitantly. "You look sad."

"Sad? Yes, I am sad, very sad, Liu-san."

"Did anything happen in your family?"

"No, it's nothing like that."

What would Liu say if I told him that one of our family friends had been beaten nearly to death by his people and had become permanently mentally and physically crippled? What would he say if I told him that I had just now been slapped by one of his people? No, I wouldn't do that to him. Some things are beyond, far beyond, our reach, our control. No one was to be blamed for what was going on. I tossed my hair back and looked at him calmly.

"Don't worry, Liu-san. I am getting used to all kinds of sadness." I smiled, hoping to look brave. But he did not smile back. He looked down at his coffee and changed the subject quietly.

"Do you know when you'll be leaving for Japan?"

"Yes. I understand it won't be long."

Father had told us that the repatriation in Dairen was supposed to begin sometime in the fall and that the refugees would be the first to be shipped out. Mamoru's wife Hisako was making huge backpacks out of *obi* material for each of us to carry to Japan.

"Are you sure you want to go to Japan?" Liu asked, still looking down at his coffee. I stirred the pale green cream soda with the straw. Hundreds of tiny bubbles were suddenly created and fought their way up, bumping into one another.

"Yes, I am. I am sure of it now."

What awaited me in Japan did not matter. It was Dairen, the Dairen that no longer belonged to me, that I wanted to leave.

Dairen, once a beautiful city, was now fast deteriorating. The Chinese government that had taken over Dairen simply did not have the time or funds for the city's maintenance. The roadside trees and shrubs, which once had been manicured lovingly, were now growing wild or dying from negligence. The trash-covered streets were crowded with peddlers, beggars, and thieves. It was now a city of decadence, of hatred, and of revenge. Stripped of ideals, pride, and glory, Dairen was now a mockery of what it once had been. The bronze statue of General Ohshima that had represented the glory of Imperial Japan had been destroyed. So had the memorial tower for the war dead that had stood tall over the ever-green forest in the Central Park. All of the stately buildings, the carefully designed parks, and even the private homes had been taken away from the Japanese. One by one, the evidence of Imperial Japan had been erased, branded with the shame and guilt of "war criminals." Now we, the once-proud Japanese, were fighting to survive from day to day, befit-ting of criminals at the end of the rope.

Softly I touched the left side of my face where the Chinese man had hit me. Dairen had now been returned to him and his people. It had been a long, long wait for the native Chinese. What had they thought of the Russians when they had bulldozed their fishing village and started the construction of Dal'nii? What had they thought of the Japanese when they took over Dal'nii and made Dairen out of it? There must have been thousands of Chinese who had wanted to slap someone like me all their lives.

I reached out and held Liu's hand.

"I don't know where I will end up, Liu-san, but it will be far away from Dairen." Far away from Dairen, the one place that I truly loved, the one place whose further destruction I could not bear to witness. Liu nodded in silence.

He offered to walk me to the streetcar stop. We walked in silence, each deep in our own thoughts. When we reached a street corner where the streetcar stop could be seen in the dusk, we stopped as if it had been planned. He turned me around to face him and kissed my forehead lightly, just as Kunio had done two years before.

"I am leaving town in a few days," he said. I looked up at him ques-tioningly and he shook his head.

"I don't know when, or if, I will come back to Dairen." He squeezed my shoulders as he kissed my forehead once again.

As our second winter in the postwar Dairen approached, I was busy collecting my friend's addresses in Japan. Once in Japan, we would be scattered all over the country. Grandmother had decided to go with Uncle Hideo's family to Kyoto, where Uncle Hideo had attended college and where his wife Sadako's family lived. My family was going to Oita in Kyushu, my father's birthplace, a place that he had left nearly forty years before. This was our registered legal address. All of us children had been taught to memorize this address as soon as we were old enough to read. This was where we might be able to find my two missing brothers if they had survived the war and its aftermath.

One day in late October, I went to see Akiko. Whenever I visited Akiko at work, I was careful to go late on Monday afternoon. There were rarely any customers then. Wing and his aunt were always there to greet me with a smile, although they never talked to me directly. They left Akiko and me to our own chattering and seemed to be satisfied to see Akiko enjoy herself.

I pulled out a small notebook from my coat pocket and pushed it across the table to Akiko.

"You're the last, Ako. But you see, I saved the very first page for you."

Akiko looked at the notebook, but did not take it.

"I've got the address of just about everyone I can think of," I said. "You are collecting addresses too, aren't you? Do you want me write down my address in your notebook?"

"I am not collecting addresses," Akiko said briefly. "We are not going to Japan."

"But, you can't do that. All Japanese have to go, I thought . . . "

"I can stay. You see, I am marrying Wing."

"What? You and Wing? Oh, my word! How stupid of me. I must have been blind, not to see the romance that was right in front of me!" I exclaimed. I was excited. This was the best news I had heard in the last two years. Akiko blushed, but did not smile.

"This is not what you think, Kaz, nothing romantic. My mother and I have no place to go in Japan. You see, my mother doesn't have any family. She was an orphan. Didn't you know?"

Akiko looked out the window, pushing back the strand of hair that had fallen on her forehead. The abundant silky hair that used to be tightly pulled back into a librarian's knot under the Red Cross cap was now waving heavily on her shoulders. She was pretty. I looked at her for the first time as a woman. Her delicate features and porcelain complexion stood out beautifully in contrast to the frame of her jet-black hair. I followed her eyes and looked out the window. From the upstairs window we could see the stretch of crowded street in the dusk. The days were getting shorter. The snow would come soon now. Then the merciless Manchurian winter would claim the homeless people on the street, one by one, as it had last winter, unless the repatriation started soon.

"So Wing has offered to take care of you and your mother."

"Yeah. That's the deal."

We kept our eyes glued to the window. There was nothing more to say. I stood up to leave.

"Good-bye, Kaz. Take care."

"Hey, I'm coming back to see you again. Before we leave."

Akiko nodded without a word, without a smile.

I walked through the noisy, crowded street toward our shop to meet my brother. The food booths set up on the sidewalk were now crowded with hungry people after a long day's work, and the streets were filled with the smell of food, the mixture of oil and steam. They were mostly coolies, but with luck a few Japanese were able to squeeze in sometimes. The pork-based soup with dumplings looked steamy hot and appetizing.

The line of crate-made humble shops of the Japanese was getting ready to close for the day. As I walked by one of the shops I noticed a display of hand-made artificial flowers. I stopped to look at the flowers as the woman behind the crate put them away. There were many left. She had not sold many. I picked up a bouquet of tiny red roses.

"How pretty," I murmured. The woman looked up.

"They are beautiful. So exquisite. Where did you get them?"

"I made them myself." The woman had a cultivated, soft voice.

"But this material, it's such a fine silk."

"It used to be my blouse," she laughed softly. "I can't sell my clothes because they are too small for the Russians and too impractical for the Chinese."

I nodded in agreement. I was familiar with the problem. Women's clothes were hard to sell. The Russian women had thick, broad shoulders and huge bosoms compared to Japanese women, and the Chinese women preferred durable cotton clothes.

The woman then pulled out a package wrapped in white tissue.

"I have a sweater here, about your size. One of my most impractical possessions."

It was a white angora sweater with a beaded scoop neckline.

"How beautiful!" I exclaimed, letting my fingertips run through the fluffy warmth of the angora.

"My husband brought it back from Europe a long time ago, before we were married."

"Oh, then you should keep it. You might want to wear it for him someday."

"I don't think so. And I have two small children to support."

I turned to her sharply with a question, and then quickly looked away. I knew the answer.

"He never had a chance to see the youngest," the woman said quietly, as if she had heard my stupid question.

"I am sorry," I whispered.

I bought the white angora sweater and the woman pinned a bouquet of delicate red roses close to the neckline.

"There! This dresses it up, doesn't it?"

"Yes, thank you. It's perfect for the occasion now. You see, I am giving this to my friend as a wedding gift."

"Oh, that's wonderful! I hope she will be happy." The woman smiled happily.

"Yes, I hope so too. She deserves it," I said, but I could not return the smile.

CHAPTER 9

Land of the Rising Sun

As I LEARNED years later, Japan had started the repatriation of all Japanese abroad, including those in the military, immediately after its surrender, but the repatriation of the Japanese survivors in Manchuria did not start until May 1946. U.S. military ships called LSTs, which were normally used to transport troops and heavy equipment, came to Koro Island Port in southwest Manchuria to pick up the Japanese survivors in Manchuria. Through this route, close to a million Japanese survivors were rescued before October 1946. Then, and only then, did the long-awaited repatriation of the Japanese in Dairen finally start, in November 1946. We had been left to somehow survive on our own in a hostile land for over a year. Why? Some say that the government was misinformed about the condition we were in, while others say that there was an international conflict as to the new ownership of Manchuria, all at the cost of the lives of thousands of Japanese men, women, and children. The exact death toll among the Japanese in Manchuria at that time will probably never be known.

Thus, one freezing morning in February 1947, my parents, my two younger sisters, and I left Uncle Hideo's house to join a group of repatriates at Dairen Port. My brother Mamoru, his wife Hisako, and their little son Yukio had left a month earlier. We were to meet at my father's birthplace, Oita, Kyushu, where we might be able to find out the whereabouts of my other two brothers, Kay and Takashi.

The personal belongings that one could carry, one-thousand yen (approximately thirty U.S. dollars then) each, and a bag of bedding per family were all that each repatriate was allowed to take back to Japan. We were warned that if anyone in the group was found guilty of smuggling extra money or jewels, the entire group's departure would be canceled.

When my brother's family left, Hisako was seven months pregnant. She carried Yukio on her back, a big bag of diapers in one hand, and rubber sheets and medical supplies in the other, in case of an emergency. Mamoru carried a huge backpack filled with personal items on his back and dragged another huge bag of bedding. When we left, I helped my father drag our family bedding bag, trying to handle the weight of the huge backpack at the same time. Both my younger sisters were carrying backpacks as well and carryalls in both hands.

It took us all day to go through the long line for strict inspection of our luggage as well as a physical search in an individual booth. I did not have to strip, but a Russian female soldier ordered me to take my coat off and touched all parts of my body over my heavy sweaters and wool pants. She inspected the inside of my shoes also. She was looking for extra money or jewels, as we had been warned.

After going through the long inspection line, we spent a night on the concrete floor of a warehouse at the Dairen Port, each family huddling under their pile of blankets, munching on crackers and biscuits. The lofty warehouse had no heating of any kind, and February was the coldest month in Manchuria. We dozed off now and then, sitting and hugging each other under the blankets. The next morning, we were herded into the bottom of a large cargo ship. There were tiers of metal shelves in the hold, spaced about four feet apart. Reduced to unwanted cargo, we were crammed onto those metal shelves. The naked light bulbs that were hanging here and there barely gave out enough light to distinguish the slippery metal stepladder that led us from one shelf to another. We spread a blanket on the shelf to claim our space and walled it off with our backpacks and bags, a futile attempt for a little privacy. Then Mother, who would usually see to it that everyone else was comfortable first, suddenly whispered, "Please, I must lie down." Father turned to her sharply and noted her flushed cheeks and watery eyes in the semidarkness of the hold and motioned to me. We hurriedly made a bed for her with the rest of the blankets. I went around looking for some ice to cool her burning forehead, but the best I could manage was a bowl of cold water. Father and I kept her head cool by changing the wet towels, all the while assuring my little sisters that Mother was all right and that she would soon get up. I spent the next two, three—or was it four, five?—days wiping her hot face and body with a cold towel, force-feeding her as much liquid as she could take. When she was finally able to sit up, I went up to the deck for fresh air for the first time since we had left Dairen Port. It was dawn. I still remember the moment clearly. I looked up at the sky with a tremendous sense of gratitude and saw the shadows of clouds floating like thin black strips in the foggy orange luminance of the morning sun, like the heralds of God ascending at the edge of the sky. I had no idea where we were, what day it was. I only knew that Mother had survived a close call. She survived the ordeal and all of us reached Japan safely.

Japan, at last. I watched everyone, especially my parents, crying and trembling at the first sight of Japan's shore. I was glad that they were finally home, but what I felt was far from a sentiment of homecoming. I was lost. I remember standing on the deck of the tugboat, captivated by the strange sensation of untimely picnic. Green mountains! In February? And so close to the shore. The port of Sasebo was so small that the cargo ship that had transported us from Dairen could not go in. We had to change into a tugboat to get into the Sasebo Port. In contrast to the numerous concrete buildings of Dairen Port, and the four piers that extended far into the bay, boasting its capacity to handle more than forty of the four-thousand-ton class ships all at once, Sasebo Port had green hills close to the shore. It seemed to me like a picnic spot!

"Welcome home, my fellow repatriates, welcome home!" Standing on a crate, a man greeted us, shouting at the top of his lungs through a megaphone.

"I know how it is to leave everything behind." The man was agitated by his own emotion. "Everything. Your business, your property, your friends, your life that you've built, and maybe your hometown for those younger ones who were born there. I know what it is like. Believe me, I know how you feel, for I, too, have left my lifework and come home empty-handed."

The man stopped, sobbing openly. My father, who was standing next to me, was busily rubbing his face and clearing his throat, and I wished to God that the man would stop agitating us. We were already a bundle of raw nerves. I watched the back of my mother's small shoulders as she panted under the weight of the huge backpack, and was afraid that she might collapse any moment.

We walked protectively, surrounding Mother—my two little sisters at her sides, Father and I directly behind, watching her struggling steps. We were walking on Japanese soil. Japan, the country that I had been taught to love and honor; the country for which I had once been ready to dedicate myself. *Look! I am walking on it, walking on the soil of my country, Japan. Why, then, do I feel like a stranger?*

At the entrance to the temporary barracks set up for the repatriates, we were met by a group of white-jacketed sanitation people. They pulled open each of our collars and stuck in a hose to douse us with a pungent white powder called DDT.

"This is by the order of the occupation forces," they told us, silencing our feeble protest. *The occupation forces! Of course, Japan was occupied by the United States, remember? So why not dunk us, the unwanted cargo kicked out of communist-occupied Manchuria, in DDT? Welcome home, you miserable maggots! Welcome home to the Land of the Rising Sun!* The pungent white powder hissed, crawling down my spine.

Part Two

Postwar Japan

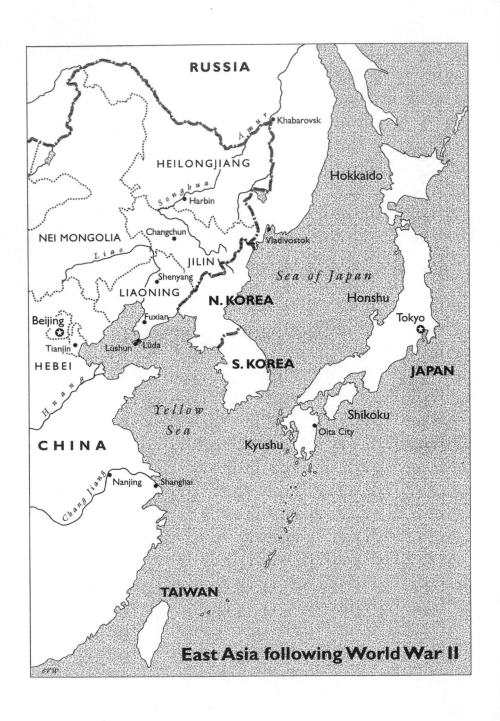

East Asia following World War II

CHAPTER 10

Homecoming

"After all," my cousin Taro said with the irritating drawl of south-ern Japan, "You people overseas didn't experience the horror of the bombshells raining on you." I turned to him sharply, but checked myself from speaking up. I knew Taro, who was almost as old as my father, would not even look at me. He would ignore me completely, sending me the silent message that he was talking to my father, not to me, and that he was not interested in what was on my mind anyway. I was only a woman. Worse yet, a young and opinionated woman who always looked straight into his eyes, instead of casting her eyes modestly, like a "real" Japanese woman—in his mind—should . It took only a few days for me to realize how unfit I was in my father's old home. For one thing, I did not wear a kimono-like top and baggy pants tied at the ankle, which had been a sort of national uniform for women during the war and contin-ued to be their way of dressing for a long time afterward. Also, I talked and smiled freely, a strange habit.

"Yes, I know," my father agreed with Taro, "It must have been terrible for you. There isn't much of Oita left, is there? This is terrible. Lucky that you still have your farm."

We had walked through the ruins of Oita, or what was left of the main street of the city, when we had first arrived here. As with most cities in Japan, Oita had been bombed severely. The evidences of war were still plainly visible, even after a year and half. Debris had been cleared, leav-ing the blackened skeletons of many buildings standing naked. Hovels, or huts, had been built in their places. Streetcars had been restored, but the reconstruction was taking time. This was due to a lack of material, obviously.

"Lucky were the repatriates. Manchuria was too far for all the B-29s." Taro nodded to himself, smug in the idea that the Japanese in Japan had suffered more from the war than had the overseas Japanese. Sure, I said to myself bitterly, we were having a picnic while you fought the war. Taro always referred to us as "repatriates," as if we were of another race, not "real" Japanese. I had first heard this term, *hiki-age-sha* (the repatriates), at the Sasebo Port when we had arrived in Japan. The man who welcomed us had said, "Welcome home, my fellow repatriates." He had not said "welcome home, my fellow Japanese." When we had arrived at Taro's place, my father's old home, a few days earlier, the first comment that Taro had made was about our backpacks, which my sister-in-law Hisako had made out of our *obi*, the heavy sash tied over a kimono, made of closely woven silk brocade with intricate designs. Hisako had used them because they were as sturdy as canvas, and because the Russian soldiers in Dairen had bought kimonos from us but not *obi*, and *obi* were useless to us without kimonos. Taro had caressed the silk with his thick farmer's fingers, and had declared, "What luxury! You repatriates had it all, didn't you?" The fact that we had abandoned all our worldly possessions and had escaped to Japan with only what we could carry in those "luxurious" backpacks was totally ignored and forgotten.

"But, Father, after the war, for almost two years, we had to survive among the enemies without any protection," I ventured.

Tell him, Father, tell him! Tell him about all the terrorizing, pillaging, and murdering of the defenseless Japanese settlers in Manchuria by the Russian soldiers, the Chinese soldiers, and the native Manchurian guerrillas. Tell him how many thousands of unarmed Japanese men, women, and children were slaughtered at random, or left to die of hunger and freezing weather on the streets.

"It was a long two years, wasn't it?" Father nodded to me with a resigned smile. It had been thirty-eight years since he had left his home in Oita, Japan, his birthplace. He was the youngest of six brothers. His oldest brother and his wife, who had raised him, had died in his absence, and their oldest son, Taro, was now the head of the family. Taro vaguely remembered my father, but the rest of us were total strangers to him, as well as to his family, just as they were to us. We could have gone to any other place in Japan, but Father had wanted to come home. He had wanted to bring us back home, to his home. But was this really a homecoming?

"You know, B-29s did fly over Dairen and the vicinity once or twice," Father said to Taro, "but I think it was only for the purpose of reconnaissance. No, they didn't drop any bombs on us."

It was true that we had not experienced "the horror of the bombshells raining on us." Stalin and Chiang Kai-shek had agreed to preserve the valuable Manchurian railroad network, which was six-thousand miles long, along with the facilities of the numerous factories and mines. In fact, the Russians had dismantled the technically advanced key machinery of the Japanese factories in Manchuria, and had shipped them home. Most of all, however, both Stalin and Chiang Kai-shek were after the naval base of Port Arthur and the neighboring commercial port of Dairen, at the south end of Manchurian subcontinent. We had thus never experienced the air raids, as Taro pointed out, but was war all about air raids? I thought of the thousands of farmers and their families at the Manchurian-Siberian border, running for their lives on foot, a few steps ahead of the Russian tanks, some even leaving their small children in the hands of merciful Manchurian friends; and I thought of the hundreds of homeless refugees dying on the streets of hunger and of desperation. A war is not all about air raids, is it? But what was the point of arguing about it?

"Yes, it was a long two years," I mumbled. Taro shrugged it off and looked away. People in Japan had no idea, and seemed to have no interest in knowing, what had happened in Manchuria. The communication between Japan and Manchuria had been completely cut off for the two years following the war. The Japanese in Japan had no inkling of our horror stories, no more than we knew about their horror stories of Hiroshima and Nagasaki.

We did not stay very long at Taro's large house in the country. We soon moved to the city of Oita, or more precisely, to a slum of what was left of Oita. A run-down apartment that had electricity but no running water became our new home. There was a well in front of the apartment, which we shared with other families in the building. Still, we were happy, very happy, because Mother was happy. It had been years since we had heard Mother laugh like she used to—like a girl. In this humble abode in the slum of Oita, we relaxed, laughed, and talked about everything cheerfully. We decided that the well water tasted better than the city water. We marveled at the mild weather of southern Japan. Green mountains and fields in February! And we laughed about my youngest sister Toshiko's innocent exclamation—"Look! There's a great big chicken coop!"—

pointing at a straw thatched farmer's house from the train window on our way to Oita from Sasebo Port. We laughed about how great the plain white rice tasted after almost a year of eating *kaolian* (sorghum) and *paomee* (millet). We laughed and celebrated our safe return "home" in our own way.

We found out that my second-oldest brother, Kay, who had been in Southeast Asia with the Japanese army, had come back alive. My third older brother, Takashi, who had been attending college in Tokyo, also had survived the bombing of Tokyo, and was about to finish college. Kay and Takashi had come to Father's birthplace in Oita soon after the war, hoping to find some information about us in Manchuria. Ever since we had learned to read and write, all of us children had been taught to memorize the address of Father's birthplace in case of an emergency—a precautionary measure of the colonial pioneers. They had been able to find out nothing about us in Manchuria, but Kay and Takashi had found each other there. They were gone by the time we came back to Japan; Takashi back to Tokyo, and Kay to Ashiya in the northern prefecture of Kyushu. Everybody in the family had survived. No one had even been hurt. What more could we want? We were one of the luckiest families in Japan, to have the whole family survive the war unharmed. We were grateful.

Once we were settled in our apartment, the next thing was for each of us to find work, except my younger sisters, who had to be transferred to a high school in Oita. One day, I responded to an ad for a job that I saw in a local newspaper, and was hired. My employer was supposedly a publishing company. I was not sure what was expected of me, but my position seemed to be that of a receptionist. In a small front room, I sat behind a desk, facing the entrance, reading the morning papers that my employer had handed me. There was nothing else to do. I was alone in the room. I was to call my employer, who had disappeared into the back room, should anyone come in. I was getting bored when I noticed a tall figure walking back and forth in front of our office, suspiciously peeking in. I got up, ready to call my employer if needed, then realized that it was my brother Kay.

"Kay-*neesan* (older brother)!" In a flash, I flew outside and into his arms. We cried, laughed, teased, and thanked God all at the same time. Kay had been my best playmate when we were young, although he was six years my senior. At one time, Kay and I had organized a theatrical group among the neighborhood children, the two of us being the main part of the group. Kay was a born comedian and an artist, a perfect master of ceremonies as well as the artist who produced the backdrops; Takashi, who was taking *Kenbu* (the Japanese sword-dance) lessons for health reasons, performed the gallant warrior dances and recited the Chinese warrior poems that went with *Kenbu*; Michiko, my younger sister, was a natural singer and a talented piano player who could also perform expertly in the dramas, assisted by my youngest sister, Toshiko, our little cousins, and the neighborhood children. I choreographed simple movements to children's songs for my little troupe to perform; made up the dramas, mostly out of Japanese folktales; and directed my little actors and actresses. When we were ready to perform for the "public," we would send out invitations to our relatives and neighborhood friends, who would come, obligingly, and enjoy the refreshments that Mother would serve.

"Can you leave your office for a few minutes?" Kay asked anxiously. We had a lot to talk about, a lot of catching up to do, to fill in the blank of the last three years.

"I don't know. There isn't anyone else in the office, you know. And this is my first day. I don't really know what's going on."

"I think I know what's going on," Kay said, walking into the office ahead of me. He proceeded to open the door that led to the back room.

"Oh, no. Don't open that door!" My employer, a fiftyish skinny little man, had told me not to come into the back room, but instead to call him if I needed to talk to him. He heard our conversation and came out, closing the door tightly behind him like a guard. "What can I do for you?" he asked, somewhat annoyed. Kay introduced himself rather coldly and asked if he could take me out for lunch since it was close to lunchtime. This was all right with my employer.

"So how's Takashi doing?" I asked Kay as soon as we settled in a small noodle stand.

"All right, I guess. He is really something else. Hardheaded as ever. He is determined to finish college, which is good. The job is guaranteed then."

Takashi was majoring in meteorology. Meteorological observatories were run by the government. He could get a job with the government at graduation.

"How did he manage it financially? There's been no communication between Dairen and Tokyo for the last two or three years, you know."

"We earned it, by God. We sweated for every penny of it. Takashi and I worked as day laborers for the construction of occupation forces' bases. We were ditch diggers."

121

Tears welled in my eyes. Takashi had always been pale and very fragile. Kay smiled apologetically and patted my hand.

"Takashi is a big boy. He's got muscles now."

"Didn't anybody help you?"

"Help? Are you kidding? When I was released from the army, I went straight to Father's family home, hoping to find out something about you guys. They didn't know any more about you than I did, but I found Takashi there, lost and scared like a church mouse. He cried when he saw me, the poor kid. All he wanted was to get the hell out of there."

"I don't understand. What did they do to him?"

"Nothing. That's what they did. Nothing. Except to tell us that we were eating their rice! The hell with rice! We are not beggars. I told them so. I told them off, and we left."

"Oh, my word. No wonder they were cool to us when we got there."

"They were? If they had mistreated you or Mother, I would go and wring their necks!"

"Oh, calm down. They were decent enough. They just made it clear that this was not the best time to visit them. It's just that everybody is having a hard time surviving."

"Not those farmers. They are the ones who are hoarding all the rice, jacking the price up sky-high. Our cousins are the biggest farmers in the area, did you know that?"

"They may be. But let's face it. They hardly know any of us, and if it weren't for the war—I mean, the way it ended—we would probably have never even met them. We don't mean any more to them than they do to us. You know, I've been thinking about them. We are worse than strangers, because they must feel guilty about us, deep down. We are their family, after all. That's why they resent us. Their guilty conscience."

Our cousin Taro's constant effort to categorize us as "the repatriates" rather than as a part of his family made sense in that light.

"Well, whatever," Kay said. "But who needs them?"

Kay came back to my office around five o'clock, just as I was getting ready to leave.

"Where is your boss?" he whispered.

"In his office, I suppose." I looked at the forbidden back door. Kay walked over to the door and stood close to it, listening closely. Then, to my astonishment, he slowly turned the handle and opened the door. The flow of music, women's laughter, and the clattering sound of glasses flooded in through the open door. Kay motioned for me to stay put, and disappeared into the room, closing the door quietly behind himself. I was frightened for him, and thought of calling the police, but Kay came out while I was still hesitating.

"Let's go." Kay pointed to the door with his chin, protectively leading me out of the office, and started walking, somewhat agitated.

"Hey, wait! What happened?" I turned to him, puzzled and annoyed.

"I got you fired. That's what happened." He grinned. "Those are black market gangs behind that 'office.' You were just a cover. You don't want to get mixed up with those people. Stay away from them."

That was the end of my first "career."

The American occupation forces had been building their army, navy and air force bases in the crucial spots on all the Japanese islands. Most of the construction had already been completed, but some were still under way. Kay was one of the subcontractors for U.S. Air Force Base construction in Ashiya. He talked me into going there with him. There were job possibilities there, and he wanted someone from the family to meet his wife, Haruko, whom he had married soon after his repatriation.

"She is a year younger than you," he told me. "A local girl from Oita prefecture. Not much education, but no dummy. Her mother rented rooms, and took me and Takashi in when we had no place to go. They literally saved my life when I came down with malaria. So be nice to her, will you?" Kay was seriously concerned.

When I was introduced to Haruko, I called her "*Onay-san* (older sister)" without hesitation. Kay nodded to me with delight, and chuckled at Haruko's embarrassment.

"Oh, dear," Haruko giggled, "do you have to call me that? I don't know if I can live up to it. Kay has been telling us how smart you are."

"Of course I will call you *Onay-san*. You are Kay *nee-san*'s wife. Besides, I already like you."

And I really did. She was a tiny girl with big dimples, alert and quick moving, and obviously adored Kay.

The town of Ashiya was bustling with working people. It was reassuring. There seemed to be a kind of a positive life there. I decided to stay with Kay in Ashiya, for a while anyway, and went to the Japanese government personnel office overseeing the construction of the U.S. Air Force Base. I was interviewed by a Japanese man in charge of the personnel office. As he read my resume, his face tightened.

"This part here, the Japanese Red Cross Nurses Corps. We must do something about this." He talked to himself, but out loud.

"I beg your pardon?" I had joined the Japanese Red Cross Nurses Corps during the war and had included the fact in my resume. But so what?

"Well, let me see," the man went on, totally ignoring me. "This *Futaba Gakuin*, it's a private college, isn't it?" He put down my resume and looked me over thoughtfully.

"Yes, it is a private college for girls."

"We could stretch this another year and erase this Red Cross thing . . . Yes, that's what we will do." Without waiting for my consent, he crossed out the Red Cross Nurses Corps with a bold line.

"Why don't you rewrite your resume without the Red Cross?" he said, handing my resume back to me. I looked at him with resentment, with hurt pride, but met only his blank face. I picked up a fresh sheet of paper and rewrote my resume, omitting the Red Cross Nurses Corps as suggested, and handed it back to him silently. I understood him. This was my personal share of "war crime," which the man thought should be concealed and considered it small enough to be erased. From then on, I never mentioned the Red Cross in any of my resumes or to any of my new friends.

It rained a lot in Ashiya. I had bought a pair of *ama-geta* (Japanese wooden platform thongs made for rainy days) instead of regular rain boots. They had taller supports under the wooden sole than regular *geta*, (traditional Japanese wooden thongs) to keep one's feet above the puddles, and had small hoods shielding the front half the feet, to protect them from splash. I was attracted to them because they were a novelty to me. In Dairen, we had grown up dressed in Western clothes, except on special occasions such as new year's days or family weddings. I walked in the rain, watching the tiny red hoods over my feet turn a brighter shade of red as they got wet. They were bright red, shiny, and smooth. I decided then that red was my favorite color, exciting bright red, and wondered why my mother had never let me wear red. I remembered the black velveteen dress with white satin collar that I had worn to the school recital when I was in the first grade. It had drawn comments from the teachers and the mothers of my friends, but not from my peers. Had I had had my way then, I thought, I would have worn red all the time.

The shiny red hoods, however, were not much protection, even in this soft rain in the early spring. My toes were getting wet and cold. When I reached the entrance hall to my office, I slipped the *ama-geta* off my feet to change into my shoes and found that my toes were pink and numb from the cold rain that had seeped through.

"You need rubber boots to survive here," Arthur said, standing over me with a big grin.

"I know. I should have bought the rubber boots, but they are so ugly. These *ama-geta* are pretty, aren't they?"

Arthur laughed. He was one of the interpreters on the base. He was a trilinguist—English, German, and Japanese—having been born in Kobe, Japan, to a German father and a half-German, half-Japanese mother. He and I were the same age, and we had become close friends since I had started working here a few months previous. I had been hired as a time-keeper for the Japanese government's engineering branch, which was overseeing the contractors working on the base.

I had moved out of Kay's place when I had earned my first paycheck. I was crowding his little home. Haruko's mother was living with them, and men came to their home almost every night to drink and play cards. I had never known Kay to drink or to gamble. It made me uncomfortable to see Kay drink with other "roughnecks" and play cards with them. His language had become as rough as that of any of these men, his voice as loud if not louder.

"What do you think of Hiro?" Kay asked me one night. Hiro was one of his friends who came regularly.

"Hiro? He is all right. Polite and clean. Better than some others."

"Better than some others, eh? He'd better be. He is my right-arm man. He is a hard worker. He'll make it big some day. Do you like him?"

"What do you mean?" I was getting suspicious.

"He is good looking, isn't he?" Haruko said, coming in from the kitchen.

"He is OK. Why?"

"Kay promised you to him," Haruko giggled.

I turned to Kay. I was stunned. Speechless. Kay laughed uncomfortably. "Don't take it seriously. We were both drinking."

"But Hiro is most serious," Haruko said. "He is falling in love with Kaz-chan."

"He can't be. He doesn't even know me!" I cried out in disbelief.

"Oh, your brother has told him plenty, how pretty and smart you are and all that."

I swallowed my anger and went outside. *What is this? What has happened to Kay? promising me to somebody over a few drinks?* It suddenly seemed a lifetime since Kay had left home to enlist in the Imperial Japanese Army. The transformation that had taken place in Kay's maturation process while in the army and while he coped with its defeat was heartbreaking. My affectionate, artistic, and fun-loving brother had not survived the hard years. I had a stranger for a brother now, a coarse, blunt, and insensitive man. This stranger might even sneer at my memory of "the performing art group" we had once created together. Or he might not even remember it. That had been another world.

"Are you angry with me?" Kay's shadow appeared quietly by the fence in the bleak moonlight. I looked away. No, I was not angry with him. I was choked with loneliness. I was lonely for the brother I had once had, lonely for the home I had once had, lonely for the world I had once lived in. Before the war. Yes, it was before the war, a lifetime ago, before the war had smashed everything called happy. As if someone had inadvertently touched a kaleidoscope, the world had suddenly started to revolve rapidly, in all colors and all shapes, and we in it, out of breath. Then it had stopped, as suddenly as it had started. And now I was standing here with a broken kaleidoscope in my hand.

"I am sorry," Kay muttered in monotone, "I must have been out of my mind. But you see, he and I worked closely together, like brothers, you know, and I was talking about you guys all the time. God, I missed you . . . all of you. I remembered *Yamasaki Shinbun* (Yamasaki Newspaper) we used to put together to send to Mamoru, pasting pictures, writing articles about every little thing that was going on at home. Remember the cartoon I drew of Michiko's "mushroom" haircut? They were filled with happy and funny news, weren't they . . . and I wished, oh I wished to God that something like that would be sent to me, something to tell me that you were all right. But deep down, I knew something terrible was happening to all the Japanese in Manchuria. And I tried to fool myself, damn it. I pretended that everyone was safe and sound. Happy like we always were. And I pretended that you were marrying my friend, happily ever after. Like a game, a stupid game. I am sorry."

It was soon after this miserable incident that I had moved out of my brother's home.

"You won't have much to do today," Arthur said. "They are still at it, the strikers. Nobody's working at the construction site. It's blocked off."

"Oh, dear. I wonder how long it'll go on."

"Probably another day or so, and then they will compromise. They don't scare me, but I would stay clear of it. I don't want to get caught in the middle of it again. I learned my lesson when I was in Kobe. Asa is stuck with the job this time."

Asa was short for Asahara, who was another one of the interpreters on the base. I had heard a rumor that he was a former officer in the Imperial Japanese Navy. His athletic, swift movements and knowledge of English seemed to support the rumor, but no one openly talked about it. He came to our office sometimes but kept his distance.

"What do you mean that you learned your lesson in Kobe?"

"The strikers lost out and blamed it all on me. They claimed that I didn't take their side and interpret right, and they were going to beat me up. Those are rough guys, the construction workers, you know."

"So, what happened?"

"They said that they wanted to talk to me, and I met them in a schoolyard. Ten or fifteen of those tough guys. It was getting dark and I was scared to death. I tried to reason with them but it didn't work. They were getting more and more agitated, you know. So I shouted at them, 'OK, kill me if you want to, but remember that I am not Japanese!' They stopped short, and one by one they all went home."

"Just like that?"

"Just like that. And was I glad that I was a foreigner! They think twice before they beat up a foreigner."

"Because it would be an international issue?"

"No. They are just scared of all foreigners, including Koreans. The Americans and other foreigners have everything over the Japanese now. The Japanese got it in their heads that the war and everything was all their fault and that they owe everything to everybody, especially to Americans. And I look like an American, you see. Do you know that I can cuss just like an American GI? That was the first thing I learned when I started working for the Occupation Forces."

"Oh, Arthur."

"But it works. I was only eighteen when I got the job and I didn't want the workers to know it. So I acted like a GI and cussed like a GI."

My boss, Shima, came into the office just then with an umbrella, a raincoat, and rain boots—the whole works. He ignored Arthur but gave me a twitching smile, mouthed a "good morning," and disappeared into the office.

"He hates me," Arthur said with an easy chuckle.

"Does it matter?"

"Nope. The poor guy. He doesn't know how to be a young man."

127

"Because he is not a young man."

"He is young. I'd say maybe twenty-seven or eight. Thirty at most."

"Thirty? That's old. He makes me uncomfortable."

"I know. The poor guy's in love with you."

Often Arthur and I took a walk down the river bank. The river was half dry, and we could walk on its bed as if on a beach, though it was rocky. We would hop from one rock to another, Arthur one step ahead of me and helping me follow him. We had found our favorite sandy "hideout" which we could reach only by hopping over the rocks. It was secluded, quiet, and peaceful. We'd stretch out on the white sand, eating tangerines or apples and talking about whatever came to our minds, mostly about our childhood memories and families. I don't recall either one of us talking about any future plans. Neither one of us had any. The only "future" story that Arthur mentioned was his brother's pending marriage to a Japanese-American woman who was teaching at an American dependent school on an American army post in Kobe. Arthur showed me a picture of his brother. He was blond and had clear blue eyes, while Arthur had chestnut-brown hair and dark brown eyes to go with it.

"We used to be Hitler Youth, my brother and I."

"In Japan?" This reminded me of my Red Cross days, but I did not mention it.

"Yeah, in Kobe. There used to be a German community in Kobe. "

"What did you do? I mean, in the Hitler Youth."

"Nothing much. We got dressed up in uniforms, and learned to march."

"Playing soldiers . . . " I murmured. "You liked it, didn't you?"

"Yeah, I think I did. I felt like a big shot." Arthur laughed, but then fell silent.

I understood. I had played soldier myself in my Red Cross days, which had now become my "war criminal" secret. A tacit agreement prevailed among the population in postwar Japan that everyone must act as if the war had never occurred, as if no one was ever interested in the past war, and as if we were, and had always been, peace lovers, with only a handful Japanese military responsible for the war.

Arthur never mentioned the Hitler Youth again, and I never asked him about it. I would not make light of the patriotism we both once had believed in, or laugh about it, any more than I would make him feel guilty about it, or feel that he had to conceal it, as I was doing. There was a certain understanding between us, a bond because we were the product of the same society and had been shaped in the same mold.

Arthur was a rich baritone, and carried a tune perfectly. Among the many songs that he taught me, the one that I loved best was the one that was sung to the familiar tune of Beethoven's minuet: "There's a land that lies beyond the sea, far away, far away; there's a land that lies in happy hours, long ago, long ago . . . " I preferred to have Arthur sing it alone, rather than to sing it with him.

The strikers compromised after a few days, as Arthur had predicted, and I settled into the routine of my daily life, keeping busy with my job and writing letters to many of my friends from Dairen, who had scattered all over Japan. Letters and radio announcements were the only way to find lost friends and relatives at that time. Radio programming was constantly interrupted by these "lost and found" announcements. I had lost contact with most of my Red Cross friends, but had found one of my *Futaba Gakuin* classmates, Kimiko, right there in Ashiya. She was engaged to marry Asa, the interpreter who worked with Arthur. Kimiko and I once had shared the responsibility of class president at *Futaba*. The transition from city life in Dairen to the small town of Ashiya did not seem to bother Kimiko. Unlike me, she had always been reserved and taciturn, probably most obedient to her parents also.

"I've heard some things about you, Kaz," she said one evening, after showing me her secret book of illustrations, which was to prepare her for the upcoming marriage.

"Oh, what is that?"

"That you are dating a German playboy."

"Arthur?"

"I believe that was the name I heard."

"He is just a friend. A very good friend." I laughed. A German playboy, indeed!

"Well, you don't want a bad reputation. You'll have to get married someday too."

My friendship with Arthur had become "the talk of the town," and my "reputation" had become the concern of the people in my office also. I had sensed it on several occasions, especially from my boss, Shima. So when Shima asked to meet me somewhere after work for a little talk, I knew what his agenda was going to be. I suggested the playground of an elementary school. Shima seemed to be taken aback, but agreed. The school playground was my favorite spot and I had spent many evenings there, riding a swing alone. It was a tall, sturdy swing, which seemed taller than the houses around the school because it stood on a small hill at the corner of the schoolyard. The swing was just like the one that my brothers and I used to ride at the beach in Dairen. When we were tired of swimming, we would come out of the water for a cup of hot toddy called "ame-yu" that waited for us, and then take turns riding the swing. Riding the swing at the corner of the schoolyard in Ashiya, I saw again the ocean of Dairen; the deep blue-green ocean with its sparkling white ripples, teasing children to delighted screams and laughter, and I smelled and tasted the hot "ame-yu" spiced with ginger.

I arrived there long ahead of the appointed time, so that I could ride the swing before Shima showed up. I stood on the narrow seat, with my legs slightly apart for balance, and gripped the rough ropes with all my might, for my life literally depended on them. I would bend low when my back reached the highest point, parallel to the top of the swing's frame, then push the swing forward as hard as I could, cutting through the breeze to the other side of the parallel. The air felt clean and light up in the sky, and it carried me back to the beach in Dairen.

I caught sight of a man by the post as I swished by and knew it was Shima. I slowed down but did not stop swinging completely. I swung back and forth in front of him, conscious of his anxious eyes following me.

"Can we talk, Miss Yamasaki?" Shima shouted to my fast-moving shadow. I sat down on the swing, stretching my legs to reach the ground and stop. Shima grabbed the rope for me, but then I swayed to the side and almost kicked him.

"Excuse me!" I laughed, but noticed that Shima did not laugh or smile. He was staring down at me, steadying the rope.

"It's about Arthur, isn't it?" I asked impatiently.

"Yes," he said.

I nodded knowingly and started to swing again, but he held on to the rope.

"You know everybody is concerned about you."

"Why?" I was annoyed, and did not try to hide it.

"Arthur is a playboy. We are afraid that he might hurt you."

"How?" I was honestly puzzled. What could, or would, Arthur, or anybody, do to hurt me?

"Well, he could hurt your reputation, for one thing."

Reputation. Must we live for reputation? But I did not say anything.

"Besides, he is a bad influence on you, I am afraid."

"You don't know him," I sighed, looking up the evening sky. Poor Arthur.

"I am afraid I do. I've known him longer than you have."

"Not in the same way I do. Arthur and I understand each other."

"Are you in love with him?"

"I love him as I do my best friends." I looked up at Shima with a smile, confident that he would understand.

"He may take advantage of that. You are too trusting," he said, unsmiling.

Too trusting? I remembered Kimiko saying something to that effect. She had said that I was vulnerable and surprisingly naive, and that she hoped nobody would take an advantage of it. I remembered Arthur saying something similar also, that I had a heart of crystal. "What do you mean?" I asked, perplexed. "It's so clean and clear that I can see right through you," he had said with a tender smile.

"Everybody needs a friend," I said with a sigh, feeling desperate. Could he not understand Arthur's need, my need?

"Yes, we all do. But you must be careful in selecting your friends. Keep in mind that Arthur is a foreigner, won't you? Please don't be too trusting."

A foreigner! I winced. *Beware of foreigners! Don't "beat him up," but don't trust him either. Oh, Mr. Shima, how admirably Japanese you are. And thank you for your advice, but I think I will pass this time.* I started the swing, yanking the rope out of his hand. He did not leave, but stood there, leaning against the pole, his hands thrust into his pants pockets. I felt his eyes following me back and forth as I swished in front of him. When he finally left without another word, I suddenly felt a pang, like a child about to be abandoned. *Wait! I am Japanese too!*

I watched his tall figure walking into the hazy evening dusk, without turning once. I remained seated on the swing, and turned to listen to the song, Arthur's song, which had been echoing in my mind—there's a land that lies beyond the sea, far away, far away; there's a land that lies in happy hours, long ago, long ago—did Arthur sing this, dreaming of Germany, which "lies beyond the sea, far away?" Did Arthur's father sing this, reminiscent of the "happy hours, long ago?" Arthur's family would probably never go back to Germany, just as I would probably never see Dairen again.

CHAPTER 11

Call of the Cicada

WHEN THE CONSTRUCTION of the Ashiya Air Base was completed, I came home to Oita, where my family had settled. My brother Mamoru, in a partnership with a friend, was trying to start a private high school, which years later would turn out to be one of the best high schools in Oita. My father was still unemployed, except for helping Mamoru to finance and organize his project. I went to the local employment office, looking for work. The employment office referred me to Camp Chickamauga, one of the U.S. Occupation Force bases in Japan. It was located in Beppu, a town about five miles north of Oita.

Camp Chickamauga was built on the hills that enhanced the town, a spacious area commanding a view over the Beppu Bay, with rows of barracks, office buildings, clubs, a church, and dependent quarters on the easy slope covered by lush green trees and shrubs. I saw American soldiers—GIs—for the first time. I walked by their dependent school, with an American flag teasing the soft breeze in the sun. Children were running about, screaming and laughing. I saw American family cars and army jeeps passing by leisurely. I heard pleasant, light music flowing out from some of the buildings. This was a world of order and affluence that I had forgotten still existed.

I was to meet a Captain Denton at the engineering office. The engineering office was a large room filled with desks and drafting tables occupied by shirt-sleeved soldiers. I stood by the door quietly, not knowing which way to turn. There was no receptionist. I noticed a few oriental-looking soldiers, and wondered if they were the Japanese-Americans

133

called Nisei. Then one of the soldiers, who had been bending over a blueprint, put down his pen and ruler, stretched himself, and headed toward where I was standing. I realized then that I happened to be standing by a coffee maker. The soldier came to the coffee maker, helped himself to a cup of coffee, and winked at me. I was embarrassed and frightened, but somehow managed a vague smile.

"May I help you?" the soldier asked casually. *Is he about my age, twenty or twenty-one?* I wondered.

"Yes. I am looking for Captain Denton." I had to check my paper to recall the unfamiliar American name.

"Captain Denton? His office is over there." He indicated the direction with a slight movement of his chin, all the while looking me up and down over the steam of his coffee. I felt uncomfortable, but his hazel eyes were smiling, somewhat encouragingly. I mumbled a thanks and walked in the direction indicated, feeling the soldier's hazel eyes glued to my back.

The adjacent smaller room was even more quiet than the large front room. There were only two desks and a few filing cabinets. One desk was occupied by a young soldier typing a document. The woman, who was not in uniform, at the other desk, looked up. She looked Japanese. Wondering if she was Japanese or Nisei, whether I should address her in Japanese or English, I placed my job application on her desk without a word. She took a quick look and said in smooth American English that Captain Denton was out of his office at the moment. *Should I wait for him or leave?* I hesitated. She repeated the statement in Japanese, and I hurriedly said, "Yes, I understood you," in English, and the Nisei woman and I both laughed.

Just then, Captain Denton walked in. He was a man of about thirty or thirty-five, with a blond crew cut and a light mustache. The Nisei woman handed him my application. He glanced at it as he proceeded toward his office.

"Come in." He opened the door to his office. I went to the door and waited for him to go in. He did not move.

"Come on in," he repeated, holding the door open for me. Helplessly I turned to the Nisei woman. It was totally against Japanese culture to enter into a room ahead of someone your senior. The Nisei woman understood this. With a chuckle, she briefly explained it to the captain, who smiled and mocked a polite bow, then almost pushed me into the room.

"Where did you learn to speak English?" he asked, studying my application.

"Dairen, Manchuria."

"Were you born there?"

"Yes. The area was a Japanese colony. That is, until two years ago." The captain nodded. It was now 1947, two years after the end of World War II.

"When did you get back?"

"Last February. About six months ago."

"How was it in Manchuria?"

"Well, . . . it was pretty hard . . . " What could I say? That a million and a half Japanese residents were caught in the middle of the battlefield without any means of self-defense? That the defenseless Japanese were attacked by Russian soldiers, Chinese soldiers—both Nationalists and Communists—and native Manchurian guerrillas as well? All I could do was stare at him with a question. What do you want to know?

"Never mind," the captain said shortly and changed the subject. "Can you type?"

"Yes, but . . ." I hesitated. Thanks to my Aunt Masu who had had an export-import business in Dairen, and had shown me how, I could type. But at a one-letter-at-a-time kind of speed.

"Very slowly," I added meekly.

"Hmm. Can you file?"

"I am not sure." I was not sure what he was talking about. File what? Fingernails? A file, to me, was a pile of documents in a folder. At this point, the captain closed my application.

"So you can't type, you can't file. What do you propose to do in my office?"

I looked at him, bewildered. But he was smiling teasingly.

"I can learn," I said tentatively, feeling a warm blush spreading to my ears.

"Good. Come with me." He led me out of his office, his arm around my shoulders.

"Corporal, set up a desk for this young lady. Typewriter and all. But don't give her any work. Just let her go through the documents, show her how to file, and let her practice typing."

Thus I was hired. Everyone in the office became my teacher. One soldier was a self-appointed specialist in teaching me American idioms. He would come to sit at the corner of my desk, and say something like,

"You're always on the ball," and I would gravely look at my chair and say, "On the ball? This is my chair."

I did not stay in this office very long, however. I was "snatched" by another captain within a month. A supply office was to be added to the warehouse, and a young captain, Captain Lamb, was assigned to head the office. He walked into the engineering office one day, whistling a song, swinging a metallic rod of about a foot long, and wearing dark green sunglasses. He was heading toward our office as I watched him with disapproval—whoever heard of singing or whistling in an office?

He stopped at the doorway to our office, and after a quick survey, came straight to my desk and stopped short, looking down at me intently as if the whole idea of coming here was to find me. No longer whistling, he took off his sunglasses and stood there staring at me. I was annoyed, but noticed that his large, clear blue eyes were gentle and intelligent. I liked the way he stood: relaxed but straight. I also liked the slightly tilted way he wore his cap. He then stepped back to read the nameplate on my desk, and abruptly disappeared into Captain Denton's office.

He came out shortly, and sat down at the corner of my desk, uninvited, and said,

"Hi, Suzie Q!"

"I am not Suzie Q," I protested.

"You are now, because I am going to call you Suzie Q."

"But I don't work for you."

"Yes, you do. I just talked to Captain Denton. He said I could have you."

"He did? But you haven't asked *me*."

"All right," he grinned, "Suzie Q, would you be my secretary?"

"But you don't understand. I am in training. I am learning to file, type, answer the phone, and all other things . . . "

"That's all right. I can teach you all that. Hey, relax! Give me a smile!" I smiled. I liked him.

The supply office was a bare and small room, walled off at the corner of the warehouse. There was a fiftyish Japanese foreman, Joe, who had been in America before the war and could speak the language. I called Joe "Oji-san (uncle)" out of respect, as was customary in Japanese culture. He was about my father's age, which deserved my respect. Oji-san and a burly sergeant worked in the warehouse, but they hardly ever came in to our office. I was mostly alone with Captain Lamb. He told me to call him Charles, but I could not bring myself to be on such a friendly terms with him. To me, he was a "grown-up," while I still considered myself a college student temporarily interrupted.

Unlike the first impression he had given me, Captain Lamb was very reserved when we were alone in the office. No singing or whistling, not even teasing. He behaved like a very serious-minded college professor, and I suddenly found myself tongue-tied and painfully self-conscious. The first thing Captain Lamb and I did was to furnish the office. There were two desks, one for him and one for me, with a typewriter and all the office supplies. He chose the desk closer to the door, as if appointing himself to be my guard, and asked me if we needed anything else. I asked if we could have curtains for the window and a picture to cover the bare wall. He brought an armful of large pictures the next day, all of which turned out to be pictures of horses. I knew he loved horses because he often came to the office on horseback and kept his horse tied to a tree by the office. But a picture of a horse was not exactly my taste in wall decoration. A picture of a basket of fruits, of flowers in a vase, or of a snow-covered landscape, maybe, but not a picture of a horse. With an effort, I finally chose a close-up of a horse's face. "I like his innocent, large eyes," I commented. He agreed seriously and put it in a brown wood frame and hung it on the wall. Then he took the window's measurements and came up with some soft green curtains in the matter of a few days, and seemed to be quite pleased to see my approval.

The office became my safe haven from the harsh reality. As long as I was in the office with the captain, I could pretend that the world was back in order, that nothing drastic had ever happened. In reality, however, once outside the camp I constantly encountered the reminders of war—the lost war. Almost daily, the homeless former soldiers of the disbanded Imperial Japanese armed forces, maimed and still clothed in the soiled white cotton army hospital gowns, would hop onto the streetcars to collect donations for dubious organizations. Begging on the street was forbidden by law, and this was their way of forcing public support. Some collected quietly, some with dramatic speeches. I would get up to stand by the door, pretending to view the bay, pretending to shut it all out of my mind. But how could anyone ignore them, the maimed ex-soldiers disowned by their government? Their suppressed anger, their painful despair filled the silent street car. Then one morning, on my way to the office, I accidentally saw my father walking a block ahead of me. He was carrying bamboo products—brooms, baskets, whatnots, on his back and under his arms. A street vendor? I could not believe my eyes. As far as I could remember, my father had always been a government official, which was a position bigger than life in colonial Dairen. But there he was, his steps uncertain, his back and head bent forward under the awkward load of bamboo brooms and baskets. I wrestled with this new image of my father all day at the office. I did not mention this to my father when I got home that night, nor have I mentioned it to anyone to this day. I knew that repatriates of my father's age and professional background were having a hard time finding suitable jobs in postwar Japan. But to see my father walking with a load of bamboo products on his back was as unbearable as seeing the homeless ex-soldiers begging in streetcars.

My favorite pastime, or an escape then, was rowing a boat in the Bay of Beppu. I would rent a boat and row with all my might into the bay all alone, returning hours later, feeling exhausted but renewed. Sometimes I just sat in the boat, watching the horizon where the sky and the waves merged, waiting for the sky to suck us all up into its nothingness. I also remember manicuring my fingernails fervently, shaping them long and narrow and painting them bright red. Red was the color that lifted my morale, temporary and superficial though it might be. And the red shoes. One time, Captain Lamb went to Yokohama for a week. He brought back two pairs of shoes for me; one pair in beige, and another in red. They were a perfect fit, as if he had once held my foot in his hand and knew my size. I was almost too embarrassed to thank him. Of course, they were my favorite for a long time.

It was about this time that I started going to a Catholic church in Oita, and took up private Catechism lessons with the priest of the same church. All because I had found out that the captain was a Catholic. I wanted to breathe in his culture, I wanted to reach out to him as far as I was allowed. I knew there was a line between the members of the American occupation forces and the Japanese. The American army was strict about its men's interactions with Japanese women, especially for officers, and so was the Japanese public. Japanese women seen walking with American men instantly became social outcasts in Japanese society. We were watched from both sides. I sensed that the captain was seriously cautious in his personal relationship with me. He was gentle and sweet, but extremely prudent and respectful. Once, two of his friends came into our office, "just to say hi to Suzie Q." The captain seemed to have expected them. Both were young officers, one a captain and one a lieutenant. They casually asked me a few questions in an attempt to start a conversation with me. It didn't work. I was nervous and too tense for a casual conversation. I also sensed that I was being observed, or evaluated, by his friends, and I resented it.

Christmas came, and the members of the church that I had been attending were invited to attend the midnight mass at Camp Chickamauga Chapel. I went with them, though I was not a formal member. Captain Lamb was one of the hosts, meeting us and seating us. As I knelt down and crossed myself, I felt someone watching me, and looked up. The captain was watching me from a distance, with a faint and tender smile at the corners of his mouth. After the holidays, however, Captain Lamb seemed to have disappeared. He simply did not come to the office any longer. Another captain came to take over his place. He told me that Captain Lamb had been transferred to Shikoku, another island in Japan, and gave me his new address. I never used it. I played with the idea of "surprising" him by following him to Shikoku, but never was able to muster the nerve. I waited for him to call me.

Beppu was only five or six miles from Oita, but its atmosphere was completely different from that of Oita, probably because it had always been a tourist town with hot springs, and now was crowded with GIs. It was one of those towns that slept during the day and came alive at night. Night clubs, dance halls, restaurants, and movie theaters colorfully illuminated the downtown night after night. When I wanted to see a movie in Beppu, I always chose to go for matinees on Saturdays. One of those Saturdays, I went to see a movie called *The Red Shoes*. Moira Shearer played the heroine ballerina whose magic shoes nearly danced her to death. The movie was filled with ballet and ballet music. I had loved ballet since I was a small child. My youngest maternal aunt, Aunt Kiku, had been an aspiring ballerina in our happy days in Dairen, and my mother had bought tickets from Aunt Kiku whenever she performed. The story of *The Red Shoes* was romantic and sad. The ballerina was torn between her career and love, and I cried with her. When the movie was over, I sighed and remained seated, unwilling to leave the world of fantasy. When I finally began to get up, reluctantly, the movie started again for the evening performance, and I sat back and watched it all over again.

It was getting dark when I came out of the theater. I was hungry. I had not eaten anything since lunch. Avoiding the noisy main street, I went to a small restaurant on a backstreet for a light meal. I had to hurry home. My parents would worry about me. As I headed toward the main street, after a bowl of noodles, to catch a streetcar back to Oita, a jeep came up to me from behind, and stopped in front of me.

"Get in," a soldier with a military police armband jumped out of the jeep and ordered me. *What is it?* I looked into the jeep. A young Japanese woman, who looked like a streetwalker with her heavily painted face and flashy dress, was hugging herself in the backseat.

"What happened? Is anything wrong with you?" I hurriedly climbed into the jeep and looked into her painted face with concern. The woman drew back with obvious distrust. After giving me a long, searching glance, she turned away with a sneer. I even felt hostility from the woman.

"What is it? What's going on?" I asked, tapping the shoulder of the soldier in the front seat of the already moving jeep. The jeep stopped in front of the military police headquarters before the soldier could give me a clear answer.

The woman and I were taken to a big room on the upper floor of the headquarters. About thirty women were either sitting or standing around, doing nothing. They seemed to be waiting for something. Most of them were heavily made up and were dressed somewhat provocatively. Were they streetwalkers? I looked around with genuine curiosity. Then I noticed that a corner of the room was sectioned off by white curtains, and that the women were called in, one at a time. Some kind of questioning seemed to be conducted behind the curtain. When I saw a nurse peeking out to call in another woman, however, it finally dawned on me what might be going on behind the curtain.

"What is this? Would you tell me?" I asked the nearest woman, who reacted to my question in exactly the same way as the woman in the jeep had: with a sneer and silent hostility. She made it clear that I wasn't her friend. I walked over to the MP who was standing by the door and asked to see whoever was in charge. The MP opened the door to an office where a sergeant was sitting behind a desk. I went in and showed him my identification card, which had my name, my picture, and my job title as an interpreter at Camp Chickamauga.

"What was an interpreter doing walking around the backstreets of Beppu at night?"

"I came to Beppu to see a movie," I said indignantly.

"Alone?"

"Yes."

"No boyfriend?"

"No."

140

"Where do you live?"

"In Oita with my parents."

"Your parents probably have no idea what you are doing in Beppu."

"They know that I came to see a movie."

"You'd better come up with something better than a movie. You're going to run out of excuses sooner or later." Apparently he was enjoying himself.

"You are mistaking me. I am not what you seem to think I am."

"That remains to be seen. Anyway, we've caught a lot of girls tonight. You aren't the only amateur here. We caught a lot of amateurs tonight too. It's no big deal. You see, there's been a lot of VD going around. It's good to have yourself checked. It's for your own good." Then he added, "There's no charge," and laughed.

"I don't need to be checked."

"What do you mean?"

"I, er . . . " How could I tell him? that I had never slept with a man? My heart pounded with embarrassment and anger, and the thought of Captain Lamb suddenly came to my mind. With one telephone call, he would storm in here and rescue me. He had been extremely protective toward me. GIs around me had always treated me with respect and reservation. He had taken over my personal protection where my family was unable to reach. But I was alone now. The thought of the captain blurred my vision instantly, as it always did in those days. Ever since I had seen the captain from the streetcar window one afternoon, my tears had been hopelessly free flowing. He was riding in the back seat of an open car, with cocked cap and dark sunglasses. There were five people in the car: two American women and three American officers, probably two couples and one bachelor—Captain Lamb. Apparently he was back in town, visiting his friends. They were heading toward Oita, the same direction that I was going, headed to a quieter restaurant in Oita, most likely. Their car and my streetcar ran parallel for a while. I could almost hear their laughter. A carefree group of young American officers and their wives, in a world where he belonged and I did not. I watched the merry open car passing by, blurred and deformed by my unreliable tears.

"It would be much easier and quicker, if you'd just go ahead and get it over with," the sergeant said. I left his office in silence, and "got it over with" in silence.

As I left the MP headquarters, someone caught up with me from behind.

"You are a repatriate, aren't you?" the young woman asked. "Repatriate" had become a proper noun for those of us who had returned to Japan from Japanese colonies after World War II, to distinguish us from native Japanese.

I recognized her as a repatriate also. Somehow, we were different from the native Japanese.

"From where?" she asked.

"Dairen."

"Oh, my God! I am from Port Arthur." Port Arthur had been a naval base for the Japanese Imperial Navy, about thirty miles west of Dairen. We were practically cousins!

"I saw you at the MP station a while ago, and I knew right away that you were a repatriate. I was a freshman at Port Arthur Teacher's College. Which college are you from? When did you leave Dairen? And where are you living now? Oh, we have so much to talk about!"

"Did you say that you were in the MP station a while ago?"

"Yeah, but you didn't see me. You didn't see anybody, or anything. Boy, were you mad! Raging mad!" She laughed, a cheerful and lively laugh.

"I am sorry." I tried to wipe away the trace of the bitter tears.

"That's all right. I understand, though I quit crying a long time ago myself."

Her name was Miyako. She had her own apartment in Beppu, where a group of young repatriates congregated often. I was welcomed into the group readily. One repatriate accepted another without question. They were mostly from Manchuria, although there were one or two from Korea, which had been under Japanese occupation, and from Taiwan, another lost colony. We talked about everything: movies, books, schools, jobs, families, and current incidents. Whatever the topic, however, the conversation somehow always ended up in memories of the colonies— our hometowns. "Ah, the acacia. Remember the fragrance of acacia? It filled the whole city, the whole summer." "Yeah. We tried to make a bottle of perfume out of it once. It didn't work." "What did you do?" "We packed a bunch of acacia flowers in a bottle with water and some alcohol. They rotted." "Stupid!" We missed our hometowns, as would anyone. Only we knew that our hometowns were lost to us for good. Once, the colonies were the frontier symbols of Japan's international power, and we, the children of the colonial pioneers, had grown up with an extra dose of national pride. Now we represented the war crimes of Imperial

Japan and were made to feel ashamed, as if we had invaded China ourselves.

"We don't even have a burnt down house to rebuild," someone at Miyako's place said with a mock grumbling, and we laughed. We were young. Material losses did not really matter to us. What we needed was some kind of a focal point, something to believe in, something to fill the vacuum we suddenly found in ourselves. We turned to meaningless daily excitement or dreaming, or both. Miyako dreamed of becoming a ballerina. She had a well-balanced, athletic figure, befitting Port Arthur Teacher's College, which had been known for its athletic performances, especially floor exercise. She had a parallel bar fixed on the wall of her apartment, exercised regularly, and worked as a taxi dancer at night at one of the dance halls in downtown Beppu.

Miyako and the others who congregated at her place were about my age. If they were older, it was only by a few years. Yet they seemed more mature and worldly than I was. I suspected that I might have been somewhat sheltered and felt the need to catch up with them. I wanted to grow up. On my own. Most of all I wanted to become a woman, no more "goody two-shoes." I decided to move to Beppu, and found an apartment close to Miyako's. My father was not pleased with the idea of my moving, but did not try to stop me. I had noticed that my parents, since we had reached Japan, seemed to have abandoned their parental authority over us children, especially over me, at an awkward age. But a free rein did not give me any sense of freedom. Instead, I remember feeling lost without my parents' authority, though I might have rebelled had they tried to stop me. I am not sure. As I understand now, this was a postwar phenomenon in Japan. When Japan had surrendered to the Allies, many Japanese parents, though temporarily, seemed to have relinquished their parental authority over their children. It seems that they blamed themselves for the fate that had fallen on their children because of the consequences of the war, and thus "disqualified" themselves as parents. But didn't they realize that they were depriving us children of guidelines or role models when we most needed them? Or were they lost themselves?

Miyako and I became close friends. Sometimes I followed her to the dance hall, where I met other dancers and the manager. One day, I decided to be a taxi dancer myself. The dance hall represented the world of adults, filled with women's intimate secrets—the world that I had never known. This was an irresistible temptation to me. An older dancer called "Shanghai," a repatriate from a former Japanese concession in mainland China, taught me the dance steps, and Miyako's dressmaker made me two evening gowns. I was ready for the adventure of my life.

The dance hall was located on the top floor of a warehouselike building along the Beppu Bay. One could enjoy the night view of the bay, shimmering under the rotating beams from the lighthouse. Along the windows, there were tables and chairs for patrons from the hot spring hotels as well as local men of all ages and occupations. No American soldiers were there because the place was an "off limit" area for GIs. The band played on the stage, in front of which the dancers sat in a semicircle, waiting to be asked for a dance in exchange for the tickets the customers had purchased at the entrance. No cash was used. Sometimes patrons would send a waiter to ask certain dancers to come sit at the table with them, just for a chitchat. I was seated between Miyako and Shanghai. They were both popular, and I was often left alone. Most of the dancers seemed to have old customers who would ask for them by name, but I was a novice, awkward and uncomfortable at dancing as well as at table conversation. I was almost always the customers' last choice. Often I was asked, to my chagrin and embarrassment, if I were a college student. My long gown and painted fingernails did not fool anybody. So when a waiter came to tell me that someone was asking for me to come to his table, I could not believe it.

A heavy-set Caucasian man in a suit and tie was sitting at the table by himself. When I approached his table, the man jumped up noisily, spreading his arms with exaggerated surprise.

"So it *is* you! I couldn't believe my eyes when I first saw you sitting there. What in the world are you doing here?" I finally recognized him by his voice. His name was John, and was one of the civilian engineers working for U.S. Army in Camp Chickamauga. I had seen him, or rather heard him, once when I went to Captain Denton's office. He was shouting at Captain Denton, it seemed, but then I realized that he was simply talking to everyone in the office about the strike we had just had in the camp. Swinging his arms around, snapping his fingers in the air, I would have expected a fight had he not roared in laughter.

John was a big man, tall and husky, but unexpectedly light-footed. A good dancer. Not at all like the Japanese men, whose performance was neat and accurate, he danced simply to enjoy the dance. I found myself more relaxed dancing with him than with any Japanese man. He didn't like to tango but loved to jitterbug and to polka, which suited me fine. I had never enjoyed the tango myself, but loved the quick-moving jitterbug and the lively steps of the polka. I squealed and laughed as he turned me around freely in the jitterbug or "romped" around with me to the merry beat of the polka until I was pleasantly exhausted. He started coming to dance with me every night after that. Then sometimes we sat by the window, watching the night view of the bay. He had been in the navy in his youth and showed me the tattoo on his right forearm. The name of his ship, *Reno*, was in the center of a wreathlike design.

"Marry me, Suzie. Would you marry me?" John asked, in the middle of a dance.

"All right. How about tomorrow?" I laughed.

"I mean it. I love you." He stopped dancing.

"You know we can't," I said, frowning.

"I know. But the law will pass. Maybe in another year or two. It's going to pass."

A law had been passed allowing GIs to marry Japanese women if they obtained their commanding officer's approval, but he was a civilian, a California resident. The California state law of antimiscegenation would have to be repealed before he could marry me. I told him I would think about it. He was sixteen years my senior, twice divorced, with no dependents. I discussed this with Miyako.

"Why not?" Miyako said. "Do you have anything else going for you?"

"No." I had long ago given up the idea of going back to school.

"Do you want to be like Shanghai, dancing in a dance hall all your life?"

"No," I laughed. Dancing in a dance hall was, to me, nothing more than a whim, a capricious fantasy. I had it in mind that I could always go back to being a translator when and if I wanted to.

"Well? The guy's nuts about you. That's obvious. He'll take a good care of you. He might even help you go back to college. What are you waiting for?"

"I don't know. I'm not sure. Anyway, we'll have to wait for the law to pass."

"Are you kidding? Go live with him. Now."

"Like tomorrow?" I laughed again, but rather nervously. Miyako was serious.

"Yeah. Tomorrow. Tell him you want a nice house and a maid. He'll get them for you."

Well, why not? I thought to myself after Miyako had left. Miyako was right. There was nothing "going on" for me. Nothing. All had been lost.

We lived in a world with no order, no future. The town of Beppu was filled with nightclubs, bars, dance halls and streetwalkers. The street-walkers who catered to GIs were called *pan-pan* and I was afraid that people were already looking at me as if I might be a *pan-pan* because I spoke English and dated John. Once you were seen walking with an American, you had stepped outside your society. There was no turning back. And I did not want to turn back. I knew I was a misfit in Japan. I had known it since my first step on Japanese soil in Sasebo; since my first meeting with my cousins in my father's old home. No, I did not want to turn back and conform to a culture in which I knew I would not belong. I had no choice but to go ahead with this one direction open to me. Marry John. And get out of this whole mess and disappear into the land of freedom called America.

"I will marry you, John, as soon as we can. But in the meantime, get me a house and a maid, and we'll live together," I told him the next night when he came to dance.

And of course he did. A small but a newly built house on the hill behind the camp, and a maid to keep me company.

The news traveled fast. My brother Mamoru came looking for me.

"Nice place."

"Thanks."

"So what does he do? Is he a military man?"

"No. He is a civilian. An engineer working for the U.S. Army."

"You aren't married, I mean, legally, are you?"

"No. But we probably can in a year or so."

"Maybe. He may change his mind."

"Or I may."

"Suppose you're left with his kids. Then what?"

"He's been married before, and never had children. We probably won't, but if we do, we do. He'll be happy."

"You hope so."

"We'll be all right. I'll be all right. How's Father? and Mama?"

"They aren't pleased with this. There's been a rumor. A stupid rumor that we have sold you to a wealthy American."

"Oh! For how much?"

"That's not funny. Father is really hurt. He said . . . "

"What did he say?"

"He said for you not to come home to Oita."

"You mean he wants to disown me?"

"He's hurt. Upset. Just don't come home for a while."

"Mama will talk to him."

"Mother said that all of her sons have survived the war, but she has lost a daughter to it."

Mama! Lost me to the war? Like a war-casualty? But I am not dead, Mama. . .

I remembered her weeping softly day and night when I had announced my decision to join the Red Cross Nurses Corps in order to dedicate myself to my country, one year before Japan's unconditional surrender. Now I was hurting her again. *Oh, Mama. Maybe this was a mistake. . .*

"Tell Mama I miss her, will you?"

"I will."

Then we had nothing more to say to each other.

So Mama considers me a war-casualty and Father tells me not to come home, I thought as I fought back my welling tears.

"Sorry." Mamoru hung his head like the bow of a defeated samurai warrior, then left the room. I didn't get up. I heard him exchange a few words with the maid and then close the door. I sat there looking out, listening to the hollow call of the cicada, and noticed that it was coming from a tree over the patio. The low but persistent call of the cicada. Reverberating but hollow. There is no music in the call of the cicada. No joy, no life. It is a gloomy and irritating noise, made by the scraping of their membranes, amplified by the hollow space in the insect's abdomen. They live only long enough to mate and lay eggs.

CHAPTER 12

Temptations

THE HOUSE ON the hill behind the camp where John and I now lived was in a quiet community laid out in the woods on the hill, allowing each house a fair-sized yard of its own. The air was clean and the neighborhood quiet. It was an ideal surrounding for a pleasant, peaceful home, like the one that I had once enjoyed. But I soon realized that John had quite a different idea about home life. The alcove, *tokonoma*, where a scroll of painting or calligraphy and a flower arrangement were usually displayed, was now turned into a home bar. He also set up a record player, blasting out songs like "Your Cheating Heart" and "It's Only a Paper Moon." He brought his friends home at any time for a few drinks, and these parties usually lasted deep into the night, sometimes until the early morning. Still, I did not complain. I was determined to make it work. I had to prove to myself that I had made the right choice.

The Korean War had started that summer, the summer of 1950, and the officers and servicemen of the United Nations Armed Forces were in Japan on R & R—rest and relaxation—so John brought home soldiers and officers of all ranks and nationalities. He would meet them at the downtown bars or at the officer's club on Post and invite them home. He would roll up his shirt sleeve to show his proud tattoo, declaring, "I was in the United States Navy!" and everybody would toast to the honor of the United States Navy as they commenced another night of merrymaking.

One such Saturday evening, he brought home two young Turkish officers. When they saw our record player, one of them went back to their hotel to get a Turkish record. Their music strangely reminded me of

Japanese folk songs, offbeat and deliberate, songs sung in a husky and hoarse asexual voice. When the music took on a faster and more rhythmical tune, one of the officers got up to dance and I was amazed at the dance's similarity to the Russian folk dances that I had seen in Dairen. He would squat down and jump up the next second, snapping his fingers to the rhythm, turning and kicking, his face flushed and excited. The other officer and I clapped our hands to the music while John helped himself to his favorite whisky and coke. The Turkish officers stayed in our front room that night, happily exhausted; John stretched out on the couch in a drunken stupor.

Our house was turning out to be a playground of a gala festivity. It was far from the home I had in mind, but I kept my chin up, especially when Mother came for visits. I showed her the pictures that John had taken of me, dressed up to go out, laughing on the beach, or just sitting in the sun on the patio—proof of my "happy" life.

"Is Father still angry with me?" I finally managed to ask.

"He was never angry with you, Kazuko. He was angry with those people who would start such a malicious rumor. He was just waiting for the rumor to die down."

"Did it?"

"Those things take time. But don't worry about it. If you ever need us, if anything goes wrong, Kazuko, you can always come home. Your father wants you to know that."

I emphatically assured her that everything was fine and that I was happy with John. I wanted to believe it myself.

Miyako, who was still working in the dance hall downtown, came to see me one day. She was leaving for Tokyo. It was time that she tried her luck in the big city, she said. Then she lowered her voice and asked me if John was coming home every night.

"No, he isn't," I said. "You see, he has a room in B.O.Q., bachelor officers' quarters, and he stays there sometimes."

"Hmm . . . " She took a sip of her coffee, looking me over thoughtfully. "You never grow up, do you, Kaz?" She sighed.

"What are you saying, Miyako?"

"I am saying . . . I am telling you to watch your step."

"I don't understand . . . "

"Listen. John has another woman. Right under your nose."

She gave me the name and address of the woman. I was stunned. As if to prove Miyako right, John did not come home that night or the next. I probably would not have thought anything of it had it not been for Miyako's words. But I decided to check the address, at least. Maybe it was just a rumor. The dance hall downtown was a pool of rumors and vicious gossip. Maybe Miyako was wrong.

The woman who answered to the name was very pretty. Her narrow and sensitive face surprisingly resembled that of Sanjo Miki, one of the most popular actresses in Japan at that time. Her calm manner told me that she was more than a few years older than I, and much more worldly. Bracing myself, I introduced myself and asked to see John.

"Are you his friend or something?" The woman looked puzzled. I nodded like a child.

She turned around and yelled for John, who promptly, and innocently, came out, but stopped dead when he saw me, his eyes almost jumping out of their sockets. The woman became alarmed.

"Who is this girl?" She demanded. John introduced me to her, and her to me, rather foolishly. I automatically smiled and bowed politely.

"What do you want?" The woman was indignant.

"I want to talk to John, if you don't mind."

"Well, talk to him."

I looked at John's quickly sobered face and felt sorry for him. Like a goldfish fighting for air, he was breathing hard, looking around as if searching for a hiding place or wishing his six foot one inch, 210 pound frame would diminish to nothing.

"Will you come home, John? I need to talk to you."

"Home?" the woman cut in sharply. "Are you married?"

"No, but we are going to be. That is, I thought we were."

"Johnny, is it true?" The woman turned to John. John nodded gravely.

"You love this girl? Not me? Tell me, which one of us do you love?" The woman was fuming, ready to scratch my eyes out. John swiftly came to stand between us, facing the woman, covering me. "I love Suzie."

The woman screamed and ran into her room. Then a record flew out of her room like a flying saucer and hit the wall in the hallway, missing John closely. Then another. And another. John and I ran outside. I left him standing there barefooted.

I did not waste a minute when I reached home in a taxi. I packed my clothes and went home to Oita. Father had said I could come home, hadn't he? For all I cared, I could gift wrap John and send him to that pretty Sanjo Miki look-alike.

"He is an alcoholic and unfaithful to me," I told my parents.

"Now, don't be too hasty in judging others, Kazuko." My father was as calm as usual.

"He drinks every day, Father. Almost every day."

"A man can take a few drinks now and then."

"And pass out?"

"Well, he probably went overboard a couple of times."

"He has another woman. I met her. And she is very pretty."

"Kazuko, Japan is, these days, filled with temptations for men, especially American men. Those attractive Japanese women are all over Americans. It must be hard to resist them. Be patient. He'll come around."

John came after me the following day, with his interpreter George, a Nisei who had happened to be visiting Japan when the war had started and was now fighting to get back his American citizenship so that he could go home to his parents in Seattle. I had learned that there were many Nisei "stuck" in Japan as he was. John was trying to help him, and in return, George was John's faithful assistant. It could have been George's idea to appeal to my father. He knew the patriarchy of Japan and its chauvinistic double-standard culture.

Sitting on the *tatami* floor, his legs folded under him Japanese style, John bowed deeply to my father, admitted that he had made a grave mistake, and swore that it would never be repeated. He also told Father that he loved me "from the bottom of his heart" and would always do so.

"Why don't you go home with him?" Father asked me gently.

"Home? We have no home. The place is a barroom. And I refuse to be a bar girl. Not any more."

John asked George to translate what I had said to Father.

"Sweetheart, I will quit drinking. I swear to God. Believe me just this once."

George translated this to my father, who obviously believed and accepted John's apology. My father respected a man's words.

"There, he said he will even quit drinking for you, didn't he?" Father turned to me in all sincerity. "One must learn to forgive. Forgive him this once, and trust him."

I gave up and went home with John. *Maybe I was too hasty in judging John,* I thought. *Maybe all American men are like that. Maybe I have a lot to learn about American culture.* I was uncertain but decided to give it another chance.

John became a model husband. He treated me royally. We had people over for dinner but no alcoholic beverages were served. We went out often, as John would get restless, but not to the officer's club, where everybody, young and old, men and women, gathered together to toast to any excuse. We became close friends with Dr. Watanabe and his wife, who were nondrinkers, of course, and related to our landlord. Mrs. Watanabe was an accomplished cook, and taught me the art of cooking, including tongue stew, which was Dr. Watanabe's favorite and became John's favorite also. I learned to cook Western dishes as well as Japanese dishes. John loved sushi, sashimi, oysters on the half shells, lobsters, and frog legs, all of which I learned to prepare, and John showered me with compliments, often accompanied by loud finger snapping.

Our life was that of a model newlywed couple—that is until we met Colonel Tippins, one of many temporary bachelor officers. He did not live in B.O.Q. but lived in a large Japanese-style house on the beach, requisitioned by the U.S. Forces just as my aunt Masu's house in Russian-occupied Dairen once had been. John and I were invited there often. I loved the house because of the endless sound of waves and the salty moist air blowing through the pine trees in the spacious Japanese garden. The pine trees were uniformly bent toward the house, like a line of faithful disciples kowtowing to their unseen master. Rocks of different sizes and shapes were placed sparsely between the pines, and I often sat on a rock to pose for John's picture-taking sessions. We swam, fished, rowed a boat, played cards, and enjoyed outdoor cooking. And, of course, John started taking a few drinks just to be sociable, which seemed harmless at first. John was not drinking as much as the others, which pleased me at first but puzzled me later. It puzzled me because it did not seem to take very many drinks for John to end up falling off to sleep unconsciously in the corner chair. I would get upset, but everybody would say, oh, let him sleep it off, he'll be all right, and I'd resign. I did not know anything about alcoholic beverages and their effects. My father had always been a teetotaler and except for the small cup of ritual *sake* on new year's day there never was any alcohol in our house. I could not really tell the difference between a normal sleep and a stupor, but I was uneasy. I knew something was wrong.

"I fell off to sleep and couldn't make it home" became John's favorite excuse every time he didn't come home. Sometimes it was at Colonel Tippins' house that John had to "sleep it off," sometimes it was at the B.O.Q. and finally it was at one of the bars downtown. Two women in fancy kimonos brought John home in a taxi one night. He was drunk, and passed out as soon as he came into the living room. The women were giggling and asked for water. I thanked them for bringing John home.

"That's all right. He is a good customer." They waved it off.

"A good customer?"

"Oh yes, he comes over just about every night."

I stayed up all night, listening to John's irregular snoring. In the morning, before John awoke, I left him for the second time. This time, I did not head home to my parents. I had decided to go to my Aunt Kiku's place in Yamaguchi, about six hour's train ride north from Beppu. Aunt Kiku, the youngest of my mother's three sisters, was the closest to my age, and I liked her husband, uncle Hiroshi also. Aunt Kiku, an aspiring ballerina in her youth, had given up dancing to marry uncle Hiroshi. They were young and more likely to understand my despair, my anger, and my disappointment in John.

"I know it's my own fault, Auntie. I closed my eyes and threw myself into his arms when I didn't even know him. He is what he is. If I don't like what he is, I ought to leave him. But Father says I must be patient and forgive him."

"Do you love him?"

"I have thought about it, and I don't know."

"What do you mean you don't know?"

"In a way, I am attracted to him. He is so American, I mean, spontaneous and outgoing, fun-loving and so sweet. But then, he is like a child. I have to mother him and be constantly forgiving. Aunt Kiku, I want someone mature, someone I can respect and follow."

"Like your father?"

"Not really."

"Didn't you say he was sixteen years your senior?"

"Aunt Kiku, age doesn't mean a thing! He stopped growing when he was a teenage sailor."

I was not blaming John for any of my misery. Rather, I felt guilty about him. Guilty for using him in my attempt to escape the despair of postwar Japan. I felt guilty and hoped that John would understand and let me go.

There was a field office of the Counter Intelligence Corps of the American occupation forces in Yamaguchi and I was able to get a job as a translator there. They also gave me a room in the employee's dormitory in a huge Japanese house surrounded by a tall wall and a roofed gate with a thick brush-stroke sign that read *Noda Goten*—Noda Palace—one of the few buildings that had escaped the bombing, obviously requisitioned by the U.S. occupation forces. I wondered if the "palace" had once belonged to a feudal lord or a wealthy landowner. My room was bare and gloomy but I did not mind it. It was my castle.

I was also given a small "castle" all to myself at the office because I was the only female translator. I had access to all the geographical dictionaries, listing the names of every existing city, town, and village in Japan, which lined the walls of the translator's pool, but my desk was set in a small adjacent room. I liked this setup and the job. It was almost like working on a research project by myself. Every morning, I would find material to be translated into English in my basket marked "IN." Mostly they were newspaper articles or reports of local meetings and gatherings. The articles that needed to be translated were circled in red. I was allowed as much time as I needed. I would keep them in my "HOLD" basket until I was through with them, then I'd sign my name and the date and put them in my "OUT" basket, which would be emptied by the following morning. No one bothered me, and I did not have to depend on anyone. I liked it.

I wrote home to my parents but did not write to John. I thought it might make it easier for him to forget me if I left him alone. He found out where I was from Dr. Watanabe, however, and somehow found the phone number of the dormitory. He called and pleaded with me to come back to Beppu. I was adamant and asked him to please forgive me and forget me. The conversation always ended in an exchange of apologies from both sides, nonsensical and endless. Still, he kept calling.

One morning, I was called into the office of my superior, Lieutenant Smith.

"I understand you have a boyfriend in Beppu," He said casually, after commending me for my work. How did he know? I was taken aback, then it dawned on me that the telephone at the dormitory could easily be tapped. This was Counter Intelligence Corps, after all. Gathering information or running a personal background investigation was their area of expertise.

"Yes, I do," I said with a certain resignation.

"Why don't you take a couple of days off and go talk to him? Talking face to face is much better than arguing over the telephone, don't you think?"

I decided to take the lieutenant's advice and went back to Beppu. As I got off the train I saw John standing on the platform, his head and thick shoulders above everyone else's. He was carrying a big bouquet of flowers, his teary eyes shining. *Oh, John, don't do this to me,* I took the flowers in silence and John drove me to Dr. Watanabe's house in silence. To my surprise, the Watanabes had prepared a welcome-home dinner for me and had invited my parents.

"But I only came back to talk to John. I am going back to Yamaguchi in a few days," I protested weakly.

"We'll see, we'll see. We'll talk about it later." Mrs. Watanabe stopped me with a smile, nodding to my mother, who smiled politely but avoided meeting my eyes. *So John had been working on Watanabes to get through to my parents, who might then persuade me to come back to him.* I was quietly seething with anger but felt helplessly trapped at the same time. The dinner went smoothly and the conversation was pleasant and casual. Mrs. Watanabe and Mother were lamenting about the high price of food while Dr. Watanabe and Father exchanged small talk on local politics. John and I were rather quiet. John did not have his faithful George with him. He had learned to understand some Japanese himself but not enough to join in the conversation. Then I overheard Dr. Watanabe.

"You are right, Mr. Yamasaki, she might as well stay with him and make the best of it. What decent Japanese man would marry her now?"

I was startled, but checked myself from turning to them. I was startled because of the cruel honesty of his statement. But then, the doctor was only agreeing with my father. My father was the one who had initiated the statement. So that was why he had talked me into going back to John when I had first wanted to leave him. And he was right. I had run off to live with an American, a foreigner, thus branding myself an outcast from "decent" Japanese society. What other choices did I now have?

"Let's toast to the reunion of Kazuko and John," Dr. Watanabe cheerfully suggested.

"But I am not coming back to Beppu," I said with an effort. "Everybody in town knows about John and his way of living."

John caught the word Beppu and read my expression.

"Sweetheart, I hate Beppu too. I have already applied for a position in Kobe. I am pretty sure that I'll get it. Will you come to Kobe with me?"

"Kobe?" I thought of Arthur, the Japanese-German boy I had met before I came to Beppu. Kobe was an international city. It might, just might, resemble Dairen.

"I'll go to Kobe, John, but I am not going to live with you. Not until we are legally married," I said.

I was now determined to marry him, if only to divorce him the next day. It was now my family obligation to make things right.

CHAPTER 13

Secret Funeral

ON 25 SEPTEMBER 1952, soon after the McCarren-Walter Act passed the U.S. Senate, allowing Americans to marry Japanese, John and I were married in Kobe. Mr. Manning, the vice consul at the American Consulate, Kobe, Japan, where I had worked as a translator until the day before, married us in his office.

As I had promised myself as well as John, the first thing I did upon coming to Kobe was to secure my independence from him. I found myself a job and a modest place to live within my income, both of which turned out to be surprisingly easy. I went to the personnel office of U.S. Army Headquarters in Kobe and was immediately hired at the personnel office as a translator, and found, on the same day, a sunny room with a large window on the upper floor of a quiet home where I was the only boarder. The family was a well-to-do retired couple with an adopted little girl and a maid. They took me in right away, without any questions. Their son, who was an intern in one of the hospitals in Kobe, came home to visit his parents once in a while. Other than that, they led a rather secluded life, which was more than agreeable to me.

The area must have survived the bombing of the war. The wood-framed house was surrounded by a tall board fence that had its own ornamental narrow thatched roof over it. The front gate was a sliding door of weathered, latticed wood also covered by a thatched roof, reminiscent of Taisho era Japan, (1912–26) which I had seen only in movies. The alley that I walked down every day from the house to the main street was a layer of worn-out bricks, as if transplanted from the street of an old

European country. I was fascinated with the house and the alley, but the best feature of my new abode, I found, was the sound of the heavy iron gong, which traveled from a Buddhist temple half hidden in the woods behind the house. Every morning I woke up to the deep and deliberate resonance of the iron gong, walked down the old brick alley, and caught a streetcar in front of a barbershop on the main street. I often saw a fat and baldheaded man sitting at the register of the barbershop on Saturday afternoons on my way to town, and wondered if the man was Chinese. His ruddy face and shiny head reminded me of a manager in the Chinese restaurant in Dairen where my family often went. I felt a certain kinship toward the man, but never managed to gather enough nerve to smile at him.

In the downtown area, Kobe was a bustling business town, not unlike Dairen. But it was more like postwar Dairen, crowded and noisy. The city was sufficiently recovered from the raven of the war. After five years, people were getting back on their feet.

The personnel office to which I was assigned was located on the ground floor of an eight-storied white building in downtown Kobe, close to the shoreline. My job was eight-to-five routine office work and I soon made friends and became a part of the staff. The personnel office was divided into two departments: the Indigenous Personnel Office, which handled the affairs of all locally hired Japanese and foreigners, and the Civilian Personnel Office, which handled the affairs of all American civilians such as John. John often came to the office to pick up his paycheck or to talk to someone in that section. We said hi to each other pleasantly, like strangers.

From the information network among the girls in the office, I learned more about John than I cared to know: that he was the highest paid American civilian in the area and that he was one of the most popular figures in downtown bars and nightclubs because of the money he flaunted. The money exchange rate was 360 yen to one U.S. dollar then, which virtually made all Americans "rich" in Japan at the time. On weekends, I visited him at the B.O.Q., which was a requisitioned hotel called Fuji Hotel. We had dinner and dance dates and we came to know another couple like us, an American civilian and his Japanese girlfriend. The four of us, Bob, Fumiko, John, and I, went out together often. Wherever we went, restaurants or nightclubs, we met the most enthusiastic welcome because of John's popularity. "This is my fiancée," John would introduce me to the *mama-san* (madam) of the place, who would then hug me with exaggerated delight while flashing her quick eyes to survey me from head to toe. Fumiko, I soon learned, had been working in one of those nightclubs when she had met Bob.

"I am Korean," Fumiko told me one day, almost challengingly.

"Really? But you don't have a Korean accent." I had known many Koreans in Dairen and most of them had had a Korean accent in their Japanese.

"I was born and raised in Japan. Actually, I am more fluent in Japanese than Korean. I just wanted you to know it before you heard it from someone else." She smiled, anxiously watching my reaction. I understood her sentiment. Koreans had been treated as second-class Japanese until their country was liberated from the Japanese military at the end of World War II.

"So now I know where you got that smooth complexion," I smiled teasingly. Fumiko was an attractive young woman with large, sensitive, dark eyes and stylishly cropped hair.

"Oh, I don't know about that." Fumiko laughed happily and I knew I had gained a new friend.

Fumiko and Bob had an apartment close to the Fuji Hotel, and I started stopping by to see her on my days off.

"What's this 'four days ecstasy' that Bob mentioned the other night?" I asked one day when I dropped by on my way to see John.

"Oh, that . . . I don't know. I don't know what he meant . . . " Fumiko said, averting her eyes.

"You and John got upset when Bob mentioned it, remember? Obviously, it was a slip on Bob's part, wasn't it?" I insisted. "I have some idea what it might be. But let me tell you that it doesn't really matter to me. It won't surprise me. Not at this point. I am just curious to know what he meant."

"All right, I'll tell you. It's something that happened before you came to Kobe. I didn't know about you and John. I thought John was free."

It was a four-day excursion taken by Fumiko, Bob, John, and Fumiko's friend, who was also a hostess at the same nightclub where Fumiko was working at the time. It was right after the "meeting" that John and I had had in Beppu with Dr. and Mrs. Watanabe and my parents. Hadn't John said he'd be all right once he got away from the temptations of Beppu? Apparently, bigger and better temptations had awaited him in Kobe.

"I am sorry. You aren't mad at me, are you?"

"No, of course not."

"You are mad at John. And I don't blame you."

"Mad at John? No, I don't think I am."

I honestly did not think I was angry at him. Rather, I felt that I had known it all along. I excused myself and left her apartment. I needed time. Alone. I walked to Fuji Hotel and went straight up to John's room. The door was unlocked. When I walked in, he was still in bed, about to get up.

"Oh, hi, sweetheart." He blinked his eyes.

I looked down at him, noticing his thinning hair, his scalp "shining" through like that of the man at the barbershop. Without a word, I took off the skin tight leather gloves I was wearing and slapped his shiny head with them. Once, twice, and ready for another hit.

"Hey, hey! Stop it. What's this for?" He ducked.

"It's for your four days ecstasy." I walked out of his room.

No, I told myself, I was not angry at him. If anything, I was envious of him, I insisted. I was envious of his freedom, the complete absence of a sense of obligation, a sense of honor. He was the one man I knew who walked freely, without the fetters of our civilized society, fetters of which I would probably never be free.

"You owe no explanation, no justification to anyone, not even to yourself, for living your life as you see fit," was the favorite phrase of Nancy, a coworker with whom I often shared lunch times. John and Nancy, free of fetters. How lighthearted their lives must be!

"Are you free this weekend?" Nancy asked me one day, shortly after the incident.

"Maybe. Why?"

"I'm looking for a blind date for this cute, young guy. A newlywed draftee who misses his wife terribly. Could you come along to the picnic in Awaji Island with us this weekend?"

I went with the group without a second thought. We rode horses and swam on the beach. I heard myself laughing and giggling as I had laughed and giggled as a youngster on the beach of Dairen. *Hey, I am laughing! How long has it been?*

The "cute, young guy" worked in the military personnel office on the second floor of the same building. He was a clean, all-American boy, smelling of shaving lotion but very homesick. I dated him several times after that. He was not as light-footed as John in dancing and his conversation was limited to talk about his hometown, especially his young bride. I understood his homesickness. I was acutely homesick myself. I had been homesick ever since we had left Dairen on a frosty February morning in 1947. It had been nearly five years. Five years in exile. I had learned to live with it, never expecting the pain of it to go away. Japan was my country, but I belonged to Dairen, the lost colony.

I had been suffering from insomnia for some time then, experimenting with one drug after another. I could doze off, but before falling asleep I would hear the heavy resonance of the morning gong from the Buddhist temple, and a few unsuspected tears would quietly trickle down. Still I kept going. I worked hard at the office and went to movies at night. I found out that the old war movies and newsreels of the last wars in Pacific and in China were being played at one of the small back-street theaters. They fascinated me. For hours I would intensely watch them, the stories of the wars of the lost cause, and let my tears flow freely—along with a theater full of others sitting in silence in the dark, like attending a secret funeral.

I was wearing myself down. One Saturday afternoon, I gathered all my sleeping pills and left for Awaji Island without telling anyone.

I checked in at the Japanese inn hanging over the water, had supper, took a hot Japanese bath, read for a while, and then took all the sleeping pills I had, hoping it would be enough to keep me asleep forever. I simply did not want to wake up to face another day. *Maybe I should write a note or something,* the thought crossed my mind, then—*What for? This is no big deal, I just want to forget the whole thing, like I never existed.*

A woman's voice woke me. I didn't know how long the woman had been calling me through the *shoji* screen. "Telephone for you. At the office downstairs. Please come down to the office."

I got out of bed, surprised that I had been sleeping, and went out into the hallway. I walked straight down the hallway but the walls banged into me from both sides, from left and from right. I realized that maybe I was walking in a zigzag, then tried to walk with one hand tracing the wall, almost leaning on the wall. When I came to the top of the staircase, however, I knew that I would not be able to make it to the bottom. The stairs and everything else were swerving and strangely out of focus. I sat down, held on to the rail, and in this sitting position, managed to make it to the bottom of the stairs, one step at a time. When I finally reached the phone, I found myself unable to speak. I was just breathing into the phone.

"Hello, hello! Suzie! Are you there?" Fumiko's voice was urgently shouting from afar. People in the office realized then that something was wrong with me and took over the phone. After a short conversation—or was it a long conversation?—they told me that my friend was coming over. Then they carried me back to my room and I fell back to sleep.

Fumiko and her brother were there when I opened my eyes to the sound of waves. They took me back to Kobe, to Fumiko's apartment, and called a doctor. The doctor asked me what I had taken but I did not know. Just a bunch of over the counter sleeping pills. He gave me some kind of a shot and told me to sleep it off. John came, looking totally confused. It was an accidental overdose of sleeping pills, they decided, and I agreed and fell back to sleep. *"Lucky that we have survived," someone at Miyako's place in Beppu had said one night. We had shuddered in silence, remembering the postwar terror in the lost colonies. All of us at Miyako's place were colonial-born repatriates. Then someone quietly raised a question, "Is surviving lucky?" turning everyone's mind into a hushed darkness. Then a mournful groan came out from the darkness, "Lucky were those who have died in glory." "Yeah, had they believed in it," quickly responded a cynic. "They did! I know they did!" an angry voice hissed at the cynic.*

The following week, the Kobe American Consulate sent in a request to our office for a translator to help out in handling the visas for the war brides. The number of Japanese wives and children of U.S. servicemen who were allowed to enter the United States as nonquota immigrants under the War Brides Act had increased in the area, and the Kobe American Consulate had become shorthanded in issuing visas for them. I volunteered to go. I needed the change.

The visas that we issued them then were accompanied by chest X-rays and detailed personal histories, not only about themselves—where they had been born and lived and what they had done every minute of their lives—but also about their parents, siblings, and relatives. This gave me a chance to meet many young women, from all walks of life, and I was deeply impressed by their enthusiasm and excitement about America. To them, America was not merely an escape, as it was in my case. They were looking at America as their hope, their dream, and their future home. Many of the women had small children, obviously their pride, their reason for living, their reason for venturing into the new world. I was impressed.

CHAPTER 14

Reason to Live

"WAIT! PLEASE WAIT." I stopped Tomoko, Junko's mother, from calling out to her.

I had spotted Junko and wanted to watch her. She stood out in the crowd of neighborhood children playing baseball in the empty lot where Tomoko and I could watch from the upstairs window. Not only was she the only half-Caucasian among the Japanese children, she was also the only girl among the players and the youngest at six. Tall for her age and slim, her cinnamon hair in two ponytails hanging over her ears, she walked with the confidence of an athlete, graceful and intense. She was walking toward home plate, holding her own. The coach handed her a bat thicker and longer than her well-tanned slender arm. She stood straight at home plate, weighing the bat in her hand like a professional baseball player surveying the whole situation.

"She is a tomboy," Tomoko smiled, proud and apologetic. I nodded in silence. I knew I had fallen in love with the fiercely intense tomboy. There was nothing on her mind at that moment except the ball the pitcher was warming up with the serious circling motion of his arm. She missed the first strike. And the second. Every time she missed it, she licked her lips and pursed them tight, ready for the next, oblivious of the jeering spectators. I liked that. When she missed the third strike and her last chance, Tomoko called out to her from the window and told her to come in.

"Junko, say hi to Mrs. Johnson."

Junko looked up at me, straight into my eyes, without a word, without a smile.

"Hi," I smiled. "Are you mad at me or something?"

"No." She shook her head, her steady gaze still fixed upon me. Had Tomoko told her about me? A possible new mother? I wondered.

"Go wash your hands," Tomoko told her, "and your face."

"Face too?" Junko grimaced and Tomoko and I laughed. She actually needed a shampoo and a good bath.

"Don't go away!" She commanded me and dashed out.

Tomoko and I went back to sit at the table. Two Japanese women around thirty meeting for the first time, the fate of a six-year-old girl in their hands.

I had first heard about Junko from my maid, who lived in the maid's dormitory on Post, where gossip and information were actively exchanged. I was now living in the dependent housing at ASA (Army Security Agency) Camp Kuma in Hokkaido, Japan. John and I had been married for seven years, and we had just come back from a trip to San Francisco to obtain my American citizenship. The immigration law then was that if you had been married to a U.S. government employee working overseas for more than five years, the five year residence within the United States, which was normally required, was waived. We had stayed in San Francisco for a week, long enough for me to pass the citizenship test and to be sworn in. After spending a couple more weeks in Phoenix, Arizona, visiting John's family, we came back to Japan and I immediately renounced my Japanese citizenship. This was not required by law but was important to me. I had made a choice and I wanted to declare to myself and the world that there was no turning back. I did not want to keep dual citizenship. Now I was making another lifetime commitment—adopting a child.

"You like books," I remarked, looking around the room. The room was clean and bare except for a low bookcase, which was packed with paperbacks, new and old.

"I got in the habit of reading because of my long illness," Tomoko said. Her voice, low and husky like the voice of an eighty-year-old woman, was almost inaudible.

"Yes, I heard about your health problem."

Tomoko had suffered from tuberculosis for years and was now facing surgery to remove one of her lungs.

"If it weren't for my illness, I wouldn't give up Junko."

"Of course not. I understand." Then I ventured, "The surgery might help you."

"Or kill me."

I looked away. Her hauntingly quiet voice, resigned and yet unwavering, sank into my skin.

"I have no relatives to look after her while I go through the surgery and the follow-up treatment, which could take years. When I heard about you looking for a mixed-blood baby or small child, I decided to meet you."

"Why me? There must have been others. Junko is a pretty girl. She seems to be quite intelligent and in good health."

"Yes, many people have wanted her since her birth, but I have resisted them all. They were all Caucasian Americans, you see. They look down on us bar girls. They may mistreat Junko."

A child out of wedlock doesn't deserve respect? Love? A fair chance at life? Tomoko looked into my eyes searchingly and I nodded in silence. I understood her. I saw myself in her.

Shortly after John and I were married, without any warning, I coughed up blood one evening. It was not a little blood. It was a flow of bubbling blood gushing out of my mouth. I used up a box of tissue while John was running around, getting me a towel and a glass of water, not knowing what else to do. It stopped as suddenly as it had started, but I was taken to the emergency room on post right away and then flown to American Army Hospital in Tokyo. I was diagnosed with tuberculosis. I was not totally surprised, as if I had been holding it in secrecy. It had been eight years since I had been dismissed from the Red Cross nurse training school for suspected tuberculosis. For eight years, I and everyone else in the family had forgotten about my tuberculosis in the chaos of the war's aftermath, while it was steadily ticking within me like a time bomb. How many times had I tried to walk out on John? I could have been left with his child and my tuberculosis. I was kept at the American Army Hospital in Tokyo for nine months, taking streptomycin treatment. Then I was an outpatient for the next two years. Suddenly, the table was turned and I owed my life to John and America.

Call it luck of the draw or a trick of fate, there I was about to adopt a child born to a woman who could very well have been me. No doubt, there was an undeniable bond between the two of us, Tomoko and me. We were of the same generation, survivors of the lost generation of World War II. I had lived through the war and its destruction. So had she.

"You are Japanese," Tomoko read my thoughts. "You understand."

"Of course I do. Please don't apologize for . . . for anything. I understand."

In spite of her illness, Tomoko had continued to work in a downtown bar to support herself and Junko. This was the only way of making a living available to her. Junko's father, an American soldier, had been killed in the Korean War, she said, and I did not probe any further. It was the summer of 1959, six years after the end of the Korean War.

On the day before the Fourth of July, Junko came to live with us although the legal procedure for adoption was not yet completed. I changed her name from Junko to June Marie. She was pleased.

"I am an American," she declared proudly. I smiled and nodded. She had waited for six years since her uncelebrated birth to find a place to which she could feel a connection. *Her cinnamon hair and hazel eyes.* I was almost in tears.

I took her to the P. X. (post exchange) to buy her a few necessities such as jeans, T-shirts, and sneakers. A transformation, the creation of an "American" girl. Then I noticed. I noticed that in her old neighborhood Junko had stood out, looking Caucasian, and now in her new neighborhood on the American army post she looked surprisingly Japanese. My friends smiled at her and whispered to me, "She is beautiful. What nationality is she?"

Dressed in her new American outfit, she and I paraded around the P.X. looking for more pretty things for June Marie, my daughter. I had never spent much time in the children's dress department before, but now I peacocked around with my little girl. I stopped by the rack and gingerly picked out a party dress of pale green with an overlay of white organza. Then I saw a sudden gleam in June Marie's eyes. Look! Her hazel eyes flashed green with excitement! I took her to the dressing room and dressed her in this pale green dress with short puffed sleeves and billowing skirt overlaid with white organza.

"Do you like it?" I had to ask her. She was expressionless.

Standing in front of the full-size, three-sided mirror, staring at herself, she nodded gravely. I decided to purchase it, but noticing her hesitation to take off the dress, I told her she could wear it home. I went to talk to the saleswoman. As I turned to point out the dress to the saleswoman, I saw June Marie moving around in front of the mirror, intensely examining herself from all angles. She was holding up her arms as if on a tightrope, turning halfway to catch the back view, from left and from right, and then turning in a full circle to let the billowing skirt float in the air, turning faster and faster, from left and from right, her lips parted in wonderment. Before we left the P.X. June Marie was fully dressed in the pale green party dress, black enamel shoes, matching small purse, lacy bonnet, and white gloves, ready for Cinderella's pumpkin carriage.

The next day, we were to go to the Fourth of July picnic at the officer's club. When I went to wake her up, she was already fully dressed. She was dressed in the party dress with hat and gloves. Thus we went to the Fourth of July picnic, we in shorts and T-shirts, June Marie in her pale green organza party dress. She joined the other children in a hayride in an open cart, sitting prettily among the hay, John chasing after the cart, taking snapshots one after another.

June Marie was taking everything in a stride. There was no hesitation in her calling me Mommy and John Daddy from day one. She was doing her best to adapt herself to our lifestyle, seriously minding my every word, to the point that it made me wonder what kind of a "good talk" Tomoko had had with her. One day I was compelled to tell her that it was all right for her to say no to me if she didn't like what I, or anybody for that matter, told her. She nodded thoughtfully.

One sunny afternoon, June and I were sitting on the bench in the playground. She was coloring in her new coloring book while I was reading. Then a girl about her size came over and stood in front of her, inspecting her from head to toe, watching what she was doing.

"Hi, what's your name?" I asked her, but her mind was on June and June was totally ignoring her. Then suddenly the girl snatched the crayon out of June's hand and stepped back a few steps, staring at June challengingly. June stood up and gave me a quick glance. I got the message and nodded my OK. The girl was already running, a few yards ahead of her, with the crayon in her hand. June dashed out. They ran around a swing, around a slide, and around a tree. The girl was fast but June was determined. She finally caught up with the girl and pushed her down. Leaving the girl on the ground, June walked back with her crayon. She sat down by her book and resumed her coloring, and I went back to my book. I had been talking to the first grade teacher about sending her to the first grade in September, and the teacher had recommended that I send her to kindergarten for a year. But after this incident I was sure that June could handle the first grade. She was bright and independent. The only handicap she would have at school was the language barrier. So I started speaking English to her. I would say whatever I wanted to say to her in slow English first, then follow it in Japanese. Everything: "Do you want to eat rice?" followed by *"gohan tabe tai?"* or "let's go outside" followed by *"soto ni iki masho,"* and so on. We also stacked up picture books, ones with large simple objects made for two or three year-olds. We would sit together and play "repeat after me" games. I also encouraged her to go outside to play with other children. Often I watched her from the upstairs window with concern but she was fast becoming one of the "American" children on the army post.

One day she brought a friend home and introduced her as "My best friend, Debby." I had known Debby before June came to live with us because her mother, Eleanor, and I played bridge together. Eleanor's husband was a doctor, both were well-educated African Americans, and Debby was a bright child. Debby and June were followed everywhere by Debby's little brother Charles. Little Charles declared one day, "You know, Mrs. Johnson, we don't have to be scared of Gary anymore." "Oh yeah?" I asked. "Why is that?" "Because June can beat him up." I had to talk to June about "beating up" boys, or anybody for that matter, but I was secretly chuckling to myself. What a tomboy I had for a daughter! At the same time, however, this was a bitter sign of the life she had had to survive as an illegitimate half-white child in a world of Japanese children. A dreamy Cinderella in a pale green dress and a tough fighter who would "beat up" a neighborhood boy—all in a neat, tiny package.

A few days after she started school in September, I walked into her classroom just to see how she was doing. The teacher had invited me to come anytime. June was sitting right in front of the teacher and smiled at me proudly like she might be the leader of the class. I looked around and noticed that there were many drawings posted on the wall. I checked each one, looking for June's drawing, but could not find one with her name. The teacher noticed my puzzlement and informed me that the one signed "Marie" was June's.

"June decided to be Marie for a while," the teacher said in mock seriousness.

"Oh, why?" I turned to June.

"Because they call me June-bug and I don't like it." June announced and looked about the room. No one laughed. I bowed my acceptance. Maybe this was a serious business in a first-grade class.

One afternoon, Helen, my closest friend, called and asked me to go downtown with her to see her dressmaker. She was having a communication problem with the Japanese seamstress, she said. Helen was the wife of Lieutenant Colonel Gavin, who was the chief of the engineering section where John worked. We bowled, played bridge, and went to parties together. When Helen came to pick me up, I saw Eleanor and another one of the officer's wives' club members.

"So, everybody on the post is going to your dressmaker's," I said.

"Yeah, all these nosy people want to see my new dress."

When we drove by the officer's club, we noticed many cars lined up in the parking lot. Quite unusual for this time of the day. A weekday at that, too.

"Hey, what's this? Something is going on. Let's go in and see what's going on," Helen suggested. We walked in, but nobody was in the dining hall area or at the bar. The backroom was partitioned off as if a secret meeting was being held, so we, all four of us, decided to investigate the room.

"Surprise!"

The roomful of women stood up, laughing and dashing toward me. The room was decorated with balloons and colorful tapes, and on the center table among the gift-wrapped packages, was June, looking somewhat pale. I was stunned, and just stood there gaping. A surprise "baby shower" for my June? The room was filled with warm and earnest welcome and acceptance of June and me. I turned back, fumbling to cover my face. My easy tears! John came out of nowhere and gave me his hand-kerchief.

"Oh, John! Why didn't you tell me! You didn't tell me anything!"

"Helen would have killed me if I had."

I walked over to June and hugged her. She looked frightened.

"It's all right, sweetheart. This is just a party to surprise us." I picked her up and put her down. We were seated in the middle of the room like royalty, or more like two lost kids.

Helen, Eleanor, and some others had planned and worked on this surprise "baby shower" for June for the last couple of weeks, never giving me a hint. They had invited every member of the officer's wives' club, and none of them, not even their husbands or the employees of the officer's club had given me any hint.

"I didn't even have a chance to get dressed," I complained through my tears.

"This is an ASA (Army Security Agency) camp, Sue. Don't trust anybody," laughed Helen.

Epilogue

It was about a year after June Marie's adoption that Helen's husband Ed was transferred back to the United States. Then within a few months we heard from Helen that Ed had died of a heart attack. This was not a total surprise to anyone on the post. Ed had become an alcoholic while stationed in Japan. It was like a set alarm going off, not unexpected but still startling. John and Ed had been drinking buddies all the while that Ed had been in Hokkaido. John had always been good at finding a drinking buddy wherever we went, and it was not hard to do so in postwar Japan. Alcoholic beverages of all kinds were available on U.S. Army posts at low cost; time was on their hands now that the Korean war was over and Vietnam was far away; welcome parties for the newcomers and *sayonara* parties for the ones going home were formal affairs on a monthly basis, the attendance of which was a requirement for all officers. It was the lifestyle of the U.S. Army post in Japan at the time and I blamed John's drinking problem on it. I wanted to pull John out of Japan.

By the time I finally succeeded in getting John to leave Japan and to accept a job in Fort Leonard Wood, Missouri, however, John was already an alcoholic, beyond help. He tried to control himself and I hung on to false hope. But we were helpless, or ignorant. He had his first mild heart attack one day, then a very serious one, serious enough for him to be kept under an oxygen tent for some time, followed by a month of hospitalization and outpatient treatment. The day the doctor told him that he was fully recovered and could go back to work, he happily reported back to work. Three hours later, the commanding officer and chief engineer

173

came to see me. John had had a final heart attack at his office. It was one week before Christmas in 1962.

Instead of going back to Japan to my family, I went to Phoenix, Arizona, where John's family lived, attended a business college, and found myself a job as a legal secretary. I was determined to raise June as an American.

In February 1965, I married my present husband, Yoso, whom I had met while John and I lived at ASA Camp Kuma in Hokkaido, Japan. He was there as the head of MID (Military Intelligence Detachment) Agency. John and I used to invite a few bachelor officers on post for Thanksgiving or Christmas. Yoso was one of our guests at one time, and was now back in the United States, stationed in Seattle, Washington. He was one of the first ones to send me a letter of condolence. I remembered seeing him often at the officer's club at ASA Camp Kuma, never touching a drink and always quietly friendly, quite the opposite of what John had been. After a year and a half of correspondence and phone conversations between Seattle and Phoenix and one date in San Francisco, we were married in Phoenix, Arizona, in Judge Tang's office, with John's sister Boo and her daughter Linda as our witnesses.

In November 1982, my father passed away at the age of 92. I was then living in a small town called Ontario in the state of Oregon with Yoso, now retired from the army, and our daughter Yoko. June was married to her college sweetheart and living in Los Angeles at the time. I flew back to Japan alone for his funeral, regretting bitterly that I had not been there at his final moment. But he had left me forty pages of memoirs. As was his way with everything, he had meticulously started the memoir with his birthplace and birthdate, then had gone on to his boyhood in Japan, the youthful dreams that had sent him to Manchuria, his marriage and his children, and the tragedies of the war and its ending. When he came to the Furanten incident, however, he had stopped short, saying that he was unable to go on objectively and would come back to it later. He never did. His memoirs went on to the repatriation and the hardship our family had gone through in postwar Japan, thanking each of his children for their struggle in a tone of apology as if he were somehow responsible for the fate that had fallen upon us. But the page for the Furanten incident was left blank. After more than thirty years, he was still unable to talk about it. It seemed only natural that he had turned to Buddhism, seeking inner peace, and had remained a devout Buddhist for the last twenty years of his life.

After his funeral my sister Michiko and I stayed at my youngest sister Toshiko's place for two weeks, taking turns at Mother's bedside. It had been a long time since all the members of our family had gotten together. The private high school that my oldest brother Mamoru had started some thirty years ago had become, according to him, the best in the city of Oita and was expanding every year. My second brother Kay had died in a car accident and left his wife with four children, but they were doing all right in northern Kyushu. My third brother Takashi had become the head of one of the meteorological observatories run by the government, but had recently gone through surgery for stomach cancer. (He died shortly after our reunion.) Kunio, my friend who had hand-delivered his letter to me while I was in the Red Cross, was a high school classmate of Takashi's. According to Takashi, Kunio had survived the war and had become a journalist, and was then the secretary of the Japan Journalists' Federation in Tokyo. Takashi gave me Kunio's address and phone number but to this day I have not contacted him. We had found our ways of survival in different ways, so far apart. My sister Michiko was married to the president of an export-import company, trading with American general stores such as K-Mart, and had two daughters. My youngest sister Toshiko was married to a veterinarian and had three daughters. Since Michiko lived in Tokyo and Takashi in another city, Toshiko and my brother Mamoru's wife Hisako were the ones who had been taking care of my parents on a daily basis. The hospital where my parents had been staying was a private hospital and the doctor who owned the hospital was Mamoru's golf friend, so the doctor had made special arrangements for my parents to stay in one private room. Because Father died so quietly, without any suffering, Mother, who was right there in the next bed, did not even know what was going on until Hisako gently broke the news to her. She had been ill longer than Father and the doctor warned us of the effect that Father's death might have on her condition. Although she was still coherent, her heart had turned extremely weak and she was in and out of a light sleep day and night.

One afternoon, I was sitting by my mother's bed, watching the news on television while she slept. The news included a segment about Japanese orphans who had been left behind in the hands of native Chinese in Manchuria at the time when their families escaped. They were babies and small children then, but now they were close to forty, unable to speak Japanese and unable to remember their Japanese names. They still came to Japan, looking for their families. The program showed each of them, one by one, an announcer asking them through an interpreter for whatever they could remember to help identify themselves. Some showed a fragment of the clothing they had been wearing when they were left behind, some showed toys that they had kept for all those years, some remembered their first names, or even a part of their last names. They looked lost and frustrated, yet they all looked healthy and most of them were happily married. They had been well taken care of and were grateful to their Chinese adoptive parents. Some of them said that they had not even known that they were Japanese until just recently. Their Chinese parents had kept their true identities secret to protect them from any harm, politically or otherwise.

I was so engrossed in this, sobbing and blowing my nose, that I did not realize my mother was awake. She had her head turned to the television, gazing into the screen, streams of tears quietly running down from the corners of her eyes.

"Shall I change the channel, Mama? It's not good for you to get upset."

But Mother shook her head and we watched the program to the end. She reached out for tissues to wipe her tears and sighed.

"The poor children . . . "

"I know." I held her small hand. *I know, Mother, that the war did not end in the summer of 1945.*

As I watched her fall back to sleep, I was thinking of my father's memoir; the blank spot and his tone of apology. An apology—yes, it was the tears of apology that I had seen streaking down his face. Never before and never again, but I had seen him cry that one time in Furanten. And I could still see him impatiently brushing off the new tears with the back of his clenched fist as he cleaned the bloodstained faces of the slaughtered *gakuto* boys, buttoned their tattered shirts, lowered their bodies into the crude hole, and covered them with old newspapers and dirt at the corner of the schoolyard in Furanten.

The blank spot in his memoirs was not blank. It was heavily filled with his silent apologies to us, the sacrificed generation; with the unasked questions to his government; and with the lonely anger that he had kept to himself—the deep complexity that he and his generation of Japanese had taken to their graves.

As I bid farewell to his picture, smiling slightly at Mother's bedside, I looked at the mole on his face, the button that had beeped for me long ago, the bouncy, soft button that beeped no longer. *Rest in peace, Father, for I have long come to terms with it all and with myself. But, oh, not without remorse.*

Afterword

by Dr. Kathleen Uno

FIVE DECADES AFTER defeat in World War II brought about the dissolution of the Japanese empire, Westerners studying Japan are beginning to investigate the social and cultural history of Japanese colonialism.[1] *Manchurian Legacy*, the autobiography of a young Japanese woman born and raised in Manchuria, makes several important contributions to understandings of the pre-1945 Japanese overseas expansion. First, although Manchuria was both an early frontier and a crucial, late addition to the formal empire, very little is known about women's experiences there. While it has been the conventional wisdom that Japanese women of the colonies differed from those of the mainland, little has been recorded about women's lives in the longer occupied lands of Taiwan and Korea or in Manchuria.[2] Second, in contrast to existing Manchurian narratives, Kuramoto's memoir is the story of an individual outside the controlling circles of the army, bureaucracy, or large corporations.[3] The perspective of those beyond government or semiofficial circles also tells us much about daily life in Manchuria during the 1940s. To be sure, Kuramoto was a member of the colonial elite. Her father was a minor official, and her immediate family and relatives were wealthy or in responsible positions in the South Manchurian Railway Company. Yet no one was immune to terror, desperation, and despair in the closing months of World War II and its aftermath. Kuramoto's story reveals the forward looking, spirited character and great intelligence of a woman who lived through moments of decision, adaptation, and quiet happiness. Hers is not merely a tale of woe or a uniformly bleak narrative of dark and tragic events. She makes accessible to English readers her individual outlook and experiences as a young Manchurian Japanese woman and a range of norms and interactions in urban colonial society. Third, Kuramoto exposes the disruption and moral confusion of early postwar Japan, and the special economic, social, and spiritual losses sustained by those who were repatriated from the colonies with little more than their lives.[4]

Fourth, the experiences of Japanese who migrated to the overseas colonies can be compared to those of Japanese who settled in regions not controlled by Japanese, for example the United States, Canada, Brazil, and Peru. It contributes to the study of Japanese and Asian American diaspora. Finally, the epochal event in Kuramoto's life, the end of the war in the Pacific, was also a major milestone in Japanese history. Vivid recollections of anti-Japanese sentiment unleashed overseas by defeat; the horrors and hardships that former soldiers, officials, company managers, agricultural settlers, and their dependents endured until repatriation back to Japan; the difficulties of adjusting to life in the ruins of empire; the bombed out, impoverished environment of early postwar Japan; and the distinctive outlook of repatriates previously unavailable in English burst out of the pages and etch themselves into the reader's memory. *Manchurian Legacy* is an unforgettable individual story that illuminates the little known worlds of colonial Manchuria and mainland Japan in the initial years of the Allied Occupation.[5]

Kuramoto came of age in Manchuria at a time when Japanese expansion was at its height. Although Japan had had ancient footholds on the Korean peninsula, and Toyotomi Hideyoshi had attempted to invade the Asian mainland in the late sixteenth century, Japan did not begin to acquire its modern empire until after the Meiji Restoration of 1868. The new regime sought to build a rich country and strong army to ward off Western imperialism, and overseas expansion marked Japan as a powerful nation rather than a weak region susceptible to victimization.

The settlement and administrative control of contiguous areas began in the 1870s. The neighboring islands of Okinawa (formerly the Ryûkyû Islands, ruled by their own monarch) and Hokkaidô (once known as Ezo) were incorporated into the home islands as prefectures and the Kurile Islands were acquired peacefully through treaty negotiations with imperial Russia. But more ambitious imperial expansion followed a series of wars. Taiwan (Formosa) fell under Japanese control after the first Sino-Japanese War of 1894–95. Korea, the Liaotung Peninsula, the

Southern half of Sakhalin Island, and the South Manchurian Railway were acquired after the Russo-Japanese War of 1904–5. Then the German islands of the South Pacific (technically a League of Nations Class C mandate) and Shantung, the former German leasehold after World War I (later given back to China). An opportunistic occupation of Siberian territory during the Russian civil war of 1918–22, however, yielded no permanent territorial gains. In absence of military force, Japan sought to strengthen her position on the Asian continent at the expense of Chinese political autonomy through the Twenty-One Demands made of China in 1915 and through economic expansionism during the 1920s.[6]

Kuramoto's native place became much more important in the empire after the 1931 Manchurian Incident.[7] After a failed attempt in 1928, the Kwantung Army (the Japanese field army in Manchuria) acting without orders from Tokyo seized Manchuria, which Russia had once occupied and which the Chinese considered theirs. Through advisors who supervised the Manchurian officials' every move, Japan, especially the army, controlled the puppet state of Manchukuo formed in 1932.

Leaders expected Manchukuo's development to Japanese strategic, economic, and social needs. Manchukuo, a Japanese vision of utopia that was increasingly divorced from Manchurian economic, political, and social realities, went largely unrecognized by the rest of the world. In a bid to gain acquiescence to its mainland conquest, Japan went to war with China in the second Sino-Japanese War (1937–45), and vast expanses of China came under nominal Japanese control. In the southern advance after 1939, Japan took over large parts of Southeast Asia and the western Pacific, and in 1941 Japan attacked the United States at Pearl Harbor to retain access to resources needed for the war with China. Through an ever-expanding war, the Japanese military tried to force Chinese acceptance of its conquest of Manchuria. Born in 1927, Kuramoto came of age in a world of conflict and war, although Japanese lives in Dairen were relatively peaceful and undisturbed by the surrounding turmoil until August 1945.[8]

Existing studies of modern Japanese colonialism have focused on political and economic development and policies.[9] In contrast, Kuramoto vividly describes the northern rhythm of seasons, the crisp modernity of the urban layout and facilities of her birthplace Dairen (Dalian), and its natural beauty from extensive parks, rugged coast, and nearby mountains. The tracks of the South Manchurian Railway (SMR)[10] that extended to the hinterlands from Dairen, the commercial hub and modern showplace of the empire also thread their way through Kuramoto's narrative.

The tracks, land, offices, and settlements planned by the SMR framed Japan's empire building in the 1930s and 1940s. The SMR's activities, like those of the ever vigilant, controlling Kwangtung Army (in Japanese, *Kantô gun*), were ubiquitous. Carrying freight as well as traders, military personnel, businessmen, tourists, and especially agricultural colonists, the SMR was a lifeline for commerce, mining, agriculture, manufacturing, and control. It linked small agricultural settlements to Dairen and the economy to mainland Japan. Kuramoto's uncle and cousin worked for the SMR, and it transported her and her family to the tiny community where her father took up a new administrative post in 1944.

Before the 1930s, the lion's share of colonial activity was directed at integrating Taiwan and Korea into the Japanese empire. In terms of emigrés, much of the advance guard consisted of soldiers and administrators as well as traders, representatives of major companies, lower level officials, and small shopkeepers and artisans, including female employees and entertainment workers.[11] In addition to Japanese from the main islands, migrants to Japanese settlements on the Asian continent included Chinese as well as colonial subjects from Taiwan and Korea. Official statistics from the 1930s and 1940s are probably on the low side, but provide a rough index of changing migration patterns after the seizure of Manchuria in 1931 and the expansion of the Japanese empire to China, Southeast Asia, and the South Pacific after 1937. For example, the number of Koreans increased from 238,000 in 1912 to 488,000 in 1920, then grew to 629,000 in 1931, and 1,450,000 in 1940, while the number of Japanese in Manchuria (excluding the Kwangtung Leased Territory, that is, the Liaotung Peninsula containing Dairen) was listed as 818,000 in 1940. However, the Koreans were concentrated in the less developed provinces while the Japanese tended to live in economically advanced areas. For comparison, 1940 Foreign Ministry data indicates 207,000 Japanese residing in North America, including Hawaii; 227,000 in Latin America; 1,400 in Europe; and 200 in Africa; but figures derived from the U.S. census show 258,000 Japanese in Hawaii and the U.S. mainland in 1940.[12] In any case, migration of Japanese to Manchuria overshadowed emigration to all other destinations after 1933.[13]

The colonial periphery where Kuramoto lived became central to the dreams of Japanese on the home islands during the 1930s. Amid the depressed, unstable domestic and international environment of 1930s,

Manchuria assumed a central place in Japanese strategic and economic policies, and the songs, films, and stories circulating in the mass media reveal an equally strong influence on Japanese popular culture. Government funds flowed into investment projects as well as colonization schemes, giving hope to the hard pressed at home. In 1930, the SMR estimated Manchuria's population to be 32 million, but by 1940 it had risen to 43 million. Despite a probable undercount, Chinese migration between 1925 and Sept. 1943 was pegged at 14 million, but 9 million of the migrants did not stay, leaving a net gain of 5 million. The number of Japanese in many cities in Manchuria and the Liaotung Peninsula more than doubled in the decade between 1931 and 1941, and the rate of Japanese migration accelerated from an average of 9,000 persons per year during the 1920s to an average of 83,000 per year during the 1930s.[14]

After the Manchurian Incident, an increase in the number of Japanese came to be viewed positively for several reasons. Japanese settlement strengthened the nation's claim to the territory it occupied. The rapid development of Manchurian mining, communications, and industry drew workers from China, Korea, and later Japan. There were also plans for agricultural development, however, which strongly reflected the agrarian values of yesteryear. Poor economic conditions in the cities and countryside amid the Showa Recession (1927–36) and the worldwide Great Depression after 1929, motivated Japanese emigrants to seek better opportunities overseas during the 1930s.[15]

As stories of disastrous crop failures in the countryside and farmers selling their daughters appeared in the newspapers, publicists, local elites, and longtime supporters of emigration turned in part to Manchurian settlement for a solution. As time passed, the gap between emigration quotas and the actual number of Japanese signing up to migrate to the new Manchurian territories grew ever larger, but rather than dampen the patriotic fervor with a dash of cold facts, officials, organizations, and the media, continued to laud the brave pioneers who sailed to Manchuria, to present stories of success after frontier adversity, and to trumpet Manchuria as the leading edge of Japanese progress and modernity. The uplifting exhortations to help oneself, one's village, and the nation by building Manchurian agriculture and industry gave hope to individuals, communities, and the nation in turbulent times.[16]

In this atmosphere, it is not surprising that naive teenagers like Kazuko Kuramoto responded enthusiastically to the calls to defend the empire. The empire represented the nation's future in Asia and the world, but it also was the key to their own future. Filled with youthful ambition, passion to serve her country, and determination to make it great, yet innocent of the military debacles or solicitude for the fate of Chinese, Koreans, Manchurians, or other Asians in the empire, Kuramoto volunteered for a nursing corps in 1944. Although she later became aware of the hatreds and resentments pent up in the non-Japanese residents of Manchuria during the reversal of Japan's fortunes in war, she clung fiercely to Dairen and Manchuria as her home. Kuramoto had never visited Japan, and during nurses' training her troubled interactions with women born in the main islands made her ambivalent about her mother country.

After forced repatriation in 1947, Kuramoto records both culture shock and moral anomie resulting from defeat. Imperial values and institutions were doubly discredited, by defeat in war and by the democratic zeal of the occupation authorities. The older generation could no longer exercise moral authority, and teenagers and young adults were cast adrift. Their parents, government leaders, and teachers had prepared them for a world that had ceased to exist. Amid this early postwar social and cultural confusion, Kuramoto resolved a personal identity crisis by plotting her escape from a Japan in which the repatriates, especially the women, were social misfits. The fashions, demeanor, and speech of many colonial women were too aggressive and too Western to gain them acceptance by proper women and men of the home islands. The overseas territories were gone; there was no place for those who were once the proudest standard bearers of the nation's empire, progress, and modernity. In the early postwar years, they were instead living reminders of a failed past.

Like Kuramoto, Japanese emigrants in the United States, Canada, and Peru experienced disruption and trauma during World War II.[17] But for the Japanese classified as dangerous enemy aliens in North and South America, the dislocations occurred during rather than after the war. Judged on little or no evidence to be disloyal and potentially subversive of the war effort, the male leaders were rounded up and whisked away from the community. Then, the remaining men, women, and children, including many second generation Japanese who had never been to Japan, were removed to areas away from the west coast of the Pacific United States and incarcerated in makeshift, crowded quarters for the duration of the war.[18] Their responses to their circumstances, like those of the Japanese in Manchuria, varied. In bitterness, some embraced Japan, supporting its cause, resisting administrative policies that seemed unfair, or repatriating to Japan after the end of the war. Others were determined to show themselves two hundred percent loyal to the land of their birth, and one way to do that was to participate in the fight against Japan. Still others simply endured and hoped for a return to freedom, toleration, and peace.

Although it focuses on the life experiences of a young woman from a third-generation, wealthy, urban family, by revealing the outlook, choices, and social world of an individual outside the machinery of colonialism, *Manchurian Legacy* begins to fill a void in studies of the Japanese empire. Without the perspectives of women of all ages, Manchurian born Japanese, and the cosmopolitan elite of the empire's premier city Dairen, we cannot begin to fully comprehend Japan's prewar colonial societies. Nonetheless, additional perspectives of others residing in the 1930s and 1940s territories, the agricultural families and single youths, women and men from ordinary urban households, rank and file soldiers, and the empire's subalterns (the Manchurians, Chinese, Taiwanese, Koreans, and other Asians in Korea, Taiwan, Manchuria, and Japan) are needed for a more complete social history of Japanese colonialism. In turn, analysis of social and cultural aspects of Japanese imperialism contributes to ongoing discussions in the larger interdisciplinary fields of Japanese, Asian, and Asian American studies as well as in colonial and postcolonial studies, cultural and literary studies, women's and gender studies, and the social sciences.[19]

NOTES

1. Works pioneering aspects of the social history of Japanese colonialism include Mark Peattie, "Treaty Port Settlements in China, 1895–1937," in Peter Duus, Ramon H. Myers, Mark Peattie, eds., *The Japanese Informal Empire in China, 1895–1947* (Princeton, N.J.: Princeton University Press, 1989), 166–209; The Executive Committee International Public Hearing, *War Victimization and Japan: International Public Hearing Report* (Osaka, Japan: Toho Shuppan, 1993); The Korean Council for Women Drafted for Military Sexual Slavery by Japan, *True Stories of the Korean Comfort Women*, ed. Keith Howard, (London: Cassell, 1996); Michael Weiner, *Race and Migration in Imperial Japan* (New York: Routledge, 1995); Peter Duus, *The Abacus and the Sword: The Japanese Penetration of Korea, 1895–1910* (Berkeley: University of California Press, 1995), 323–24; Carter J. Eckert, "Total War, Industrialization, and Social Change in Late Colonial Korea," in Peter Duus, Ramon H. Myers, Mark Peattie, eds., *The Japanese Wartime Empire, 1931–1945* (Princeton, N.J.: Princeton

University Press, 1996), 40–39; Wan-Yao Chou, "The *Kôminka* Movement in Taiwan and Korea: Comparisons and Interpretations," *Wartime Empire*, 40–69; Ken'ichi Gotô, "Cooperation, Submission, and Resistance of Indigenous Elites of Southeast Asia in the Wartime Empire," in *Wartime Empire*, 275–91; George Hicks, "The Comfort Women," *Wartime Empire*, 305–23; Special Issue: "The Comfort Women: Colonialism, War, and Sex," *positions: east asia cultures critique* 5, no. 2 (1997); Joshua Fogel, "Integrating into Chinese Society: A Comparison of the Japanese Communities of Shanghai and Harbin," in Sharon Minichiello, ed., *Japan's Competing Modernities: Issues in Culture and Democracy 1900–1930* (Honolulu: University of Hawaii Press, 1998), 46–69; Barbara J. Brooks, "Peopling the Japanese Empire: The Koreans in Manchuria and the Rhetoric of Inclusion," *Japan's Competing Modernities*, 25–44; Barbara J. Brooks, "Reading the Japanese Colonial Archive: Gender and Bourgeois Civility in Korea and Japan Before 1932," in Barbara Molony, Kathleen Uno, eds., *Gendering Modern Japanese History* (Cambridge, Mass.: Center for East Asian Studies Publications /Harvard University Press, forthcoming); W. Donald Smith, "Sorting Coal and Pickling Cabbage: Korean Women in the Japanese Mining Industry," *Gendering*.

The cultural history of empire is emerging in writings such as E. Patricia Tsurumi, *Japanese Colonial Education in Taiwan* (Cambridge: Harvard University Press, 1977); John W. Dower, *War Without Mercy: Race and Power in the Pacific War* (New York: Pantheon, 1986); Joshua Fogel, *Politics and Sinology: The Case of Naitô Konan (1866–1934)* (Cambridge: Council on East Asian Studies/Harvard University Press, 1984); Sophia Lee, "The Foreign Ministry's Cultural Agenda for China: The Boxer Indemnity," *Wartime Empire*, 272–306; Stefan Tanaka, *Japan's Orient: Rendering Pasts into History* (Berkeley: University of California Press, 1993); James A. Fujii, "Writing Out Asia: Modernity, Canon, and Natsume Soseki's Kokoro," *positions: east asia cultures critique* 1, no. 1 (1991), reprinted in Tani Barlow, ed. *Formations of Colonial Modernity* (Durham, N.C.: Duke University Press, 1997), 171–98; Alan Christy, "The Making of Imperial Subjects in Okinawa," *positions: east asia cultures critique* 1, no. 3 (1993), reprinted in *Formations*, 141–70; Tomiyama Ichirô, "Colonialism and the Sciences of the Tropical Zone," *positions: east asia cultures critique* 3, no. 2 (1995), reprinted in *Formations*, 199–222; Miriam Silverberg, "Remembering Pearl Harbor, Forgetting Charlie Chaplin, and the Disappearing Woman: A Picture Story," *positions: east asia cultures critique* 1, no. 1 (1993), reprinted in *Formations*, 249–94; Louise Young, *Japan's Total Empire: Manchuria and the Culture of Wartime Imperialism* (Berkeley: University of California Press, 1998); Tessa Morris-Suzuki, "Becoming Japanese: Imperial Expansion and Identity Crises in the Early Twentieth Century," *Japan's Competing Modernities*, 157–81; Kevin M. Doak, "Culture, Ethnicity, and the State in Early Twentieth-Century Japan," *Japan's Competing Modernities*, 181–205; Michael E. Robinson, "Broadcasting in Korea, 1924–37: Colonial Modernity and Cultural Hegemony," *Japan's Competing Modernities*, 358–78; Mark Driscoll, "Seeds and

(Nest) Eggs of Empire: Sexology Manuals/Manual Sexology," in Molony and Uno, *Gendering*.

2. Striking features of Japanese emigration to Asia are the well balanced sex ratios, but the most frequently mentioned female occupations were sex and service work in inns, cafes, brothels, and bars. Female entrepreneurs like Kuramoto's rich aunt also crop up in the literature. Tomoko Yamazaki, *Sandakan No. 8* (Armonk, N.Y.: M. E. Sharpe, 1998); Peattie, "Treaty Port Settlements;" Igor R. Saveliev, "Japanese across the Sea: Features of Japanese Emigration to the Far East, 1875 and 1916," *Amerasia Journal* 23, no. 3 (1997–98): 103–22. On the expansion of a culture of prostitution in colonial Korea, see Yong-ok Song, "Japanese Colonial Rule and State-Managed Prostitution: Korea's Licensed Prostitutes," *positions: east asia cultures critique* 5, no. 1 (1997): 171–217. Kaneko Fumiko, trans. Jean Inglis, *The Prison Memoirs of a Japanese Woman* (Armonk, N.Y.: M. E. Sharpe, 1991) and Hiroko Nakamoto, *My Japan, 1930–51* (New York: McGraw-Hill, 1970) describe life as dependent children in Korea.

3. See for example Takeo Itô, trans. Joshua Fogel, *Life along the South Manchurian Railway: The Memoirs of Itô Takeo* (Armonk, N.Y.: M. E. Sharpe, 1988); *Abacus*, 342–56. See also semiautobiographical fiction such as Toshiyuki Kajiyama, trans. Yoshiko Dykstra, *The Clan Records: Five Stories of Korea* (Honolulu: University of Hawaii Press, 1995).

4. Some works of fiction reflecting the anomie of the early occupation years are Jiro Osaragi, Brewster Horwitz, trans., *Homecoming* (New York: Knopf, 1955); Jiro Osaragi, Ivan Morris, trans., *The Journey* (New York: Knopf, 1967); Fumiko Hayashi, "Downtown," in Ivan Morris, ed. and trans., *Modern Japanese Short Stories: An Anthology* (Rutland, Vt.: Tuttle Books, 1962), 349–64; Fumiko Hayashi, Janice Brown, trans., *I Saw a Pale Horse* (Ithaca, N.Y.: Cornell University, East Asia Program, 1997); Fumiko Hayashi, "Tokyo," in Donald Keene, ed., *Modern Japanese Literature* (New York: Grove Press, 1956), 415–28; Osamu Dazai, "Villon's Wife," in Keene, *Modern Japanese Literature*, 387–97.

5. The central goals of the Allied Occupation (1945–52) were the demilitarization and democratization of Japan so that the United States and the rest of the world would never have to fight Japan again.

6. Overviews of Japanese imperialism include Mark Peattie, "Introduction," *Informal Empire*, 1–52; Louis Gann, "Western and Japanese Colonialism: A Preliminary Comparison," *Informal Empire*, 497–525; Mark Peattie, "The Japanese Colonial Empire, 1895–1945," in Peter Duus, ed., *The Cambridge History of Japan*, vol. 6 (New York: Cambridge University Press, 1988), 217–70; Peter Duus, "Introduction," *Informal Empire*, ix–xxix.

7. See Takehiko Yoshihashi, *Conspiracy at Mukden: The Rise of the Japanese Military* (New Haven, Conn.: Yale University Press, 1963) and Sadako Ogata, *Defiance in Manchuria: The Making of Japanese Foreign Policy, 1941–42* (Berkeley: University of California Press, 1964).

8. Regarding resistance to Japanese control, see for example Brooks, "Peopling the Empire," 30–33, 37–38; Ion Hamish, *The Cross in the Dark Valley: The*

Canadian Protestant Missionary Movement in the Japanese Empire, 1931–1945 (Waterloo, Canada: Wilfred Laruier University Press, 1999), 70, 77.

9. Key works on the Japanese empire include: Duus, Myers, Peattie, *Informal Empire;* W. G. Beasley, *Japanese Imperialism, 1894–1945* (New York: Oxford University Press, 1987); Mark Peattie, "Japanese Colonial Empire," *Cambridge History, vol. 6,* 217–70; *Abacus;* and *Wartime Empire.*

10. John Young, *The Research Activities of the South Manchurian Railway Company 1907–1945: A History and Bibliography* (New York: East Asian Institute, Columbia University, 1966); Ramon Myers, "Japanese Imperialism in Manchuria: The South Manchurian Railway Company, 1906–1933," in Duus, Myers, and Peattie, *Informal Empire,* 101–32; and Itô, *Memoirs.*

11. See Irene Taueber, *The Population of Japan* (Princeton: Princeton University Press, 1958), 191–204; Peattie, "Treaty Port Settlements," *Abacus,* esp. 289–353; Brooks, "Reading the Colonial Archive."

12. *Population of Japan,* 193, 198–99, 346; Peattie, "Treaty Port Settlements," 170–71. The total population in Kwangtung was only 1.4 million in 1940, with 192,000 Japanese among the population of Dairen, *Population of Japan,* 192; *Total Empire,* 253. Regarding numbers of Koreans in Manchuria, see also Brooks, "Peopling the Empire," 29, and for the United States, Bill Ong Hing, *Making and Remaking Asian America Through Immigration Policy, 1850–1990* (Stanford, Calif.: Stanford University Press, 1993), 54.

13. The migration of Japanese to colonial settlements in China, Korea, Manchuria, and Taiwan can be compared to migrations to non-Japanese areas in North and South America and Asia. Influenced by current interest in global migration, studies of the Japanese diaspora and race or minorities in Japan are multiplying. See Igor R. Saveliev, "Japanese Across the Sea: Features of Japanese Emigration to the Far East, 1875 and 1916," *Amerasia Journal* 23, no. 3 (1997–98): 103–22. On emigration to and settlement of destinations beyond Asia, see for example, *Abacus,* 290; Yuji Ichioka, *The Issei: The World of the First Generation Japanese Immigrants, 1885–1924* (New York: The Free Press, 1988); Yamato Ichihashi, *The Japanese in the United States* (Stanford, Calif.: Stanford University Press, 1932); Mitziko Sawada, *Tokyo Life, New York Dreams: Urban Japanese Visions of America, 1890–1924* (Berkeley: University of California Press, 1996); Kiyoshi Karl Kawakami, *Asia at the Door a Study of the Japanese Question in Continental United States, Hawaii and Canada* (New York; Chicago: Fleming H. Revell Company, 1914); Japan Consulate. *Facts about Japanese in Canada and Other Miscellaneous Information* (Ottowa, Ontario: n.p., 1922); Ken Adachi, *The Enemy That Never Was* (Toronto: McClellan and Stewart, 1976); Toyoko Takata, *Nikkei Legacy: The Story of Japanese Canadians from Settlement to Today* (Toronto, Canada: NC Press, 1983); C. Harvey Gardiner, *The Japanese and Peru, 1873–1973* (Albuquerque: University of New Mexico Press, 1975); Joao Frederico Normano and Antonello Gerbi, *The Japanese in South America: An Introductory Survey with Special Reference to Peru* (New York: The John Day Company, 1943); Teiiti Suzuki, *The Japanese Immigrant in Brazil* (Tokyo:

University of Tokyo Press, 1964). Works on other diasporas include Robin Cohen, *Global Diasporas: An Introduction* (Seattle: University of Washington Press, 1997); Darshan Singh Tatla, *The Sikh Diaspora: The Search for Statehood* (Seattle: University of Washington Press, 1999); Jennifer Cushman and Guwu Wang, eds., *Changing Identities of the Southeast Asian Chinese since World War II* (Hong Kong: Hong Kong University Press, 1988); Guwu Wang, *China and the Chinese Overseas* (Singapore: Times Academic Press, 1991).

14. *Population of Japan; Total Empire*, 253, 257.

15. Employment opportunities lured not only Japanese, but Japanese Americans as well to Manchuria. The second generation Japanese in the United States were shut out of white collar and professional occupations due to the Great Depression and racial discrimination. See John J. Stephan, "Hijacked by Utopia," *Amerasia Journal* 23, no. 3 (1997–98): 1–44; Yuji Ichioka, "The Meaning of Loyalty: The Case of Kazumaro Buddy Uno," *Amerasia Journal* 23, no. 3 (1997–98): 45–72; Eriko Yamamoto, "Miya Sannomiya Kikuchi: A Pioneer Nisei Woman's Life and Identity," *Amerasia Journal* 23, no. 3 (1997–98): 73–103. Regarding nisei (second generation) Japanese Americans who were trapped in Japan during World War II, see Mary Tomita, *Dear Miye: Letters from Home* (Stanford, Calif.: Stanford University Press, 1996); Sen Nishiyama, "Unexpected Encounters," *Amerasia Journal* 23, no. 3 (1997–98): 125–42; Mary Tomita, "Coming of Age in Japan," *Amerasia Journal* 23, no. 3 (1997–98): 164–80; Nobuyo Yamamoto, "A Nisei Woman in Rural Japan," *Amerasia Journal* 23, no. 3 (1997–98): 182–96.

16. There were several stages of Manchurian settlement during the 1930s. In the first, prospective settlers were recruited from all over Japan. In the second stage, colonists were recruited from a single village or rural district in household units. In the final stage, male youths between the ages of 16 and 19 went to Manchuria for a three year period, after which they had the option of remaining permanently. See Sandra Wilson, "The 'New Paradise': Japanese Emigration to Manchuria in the 1930s and 1940s," *The International History Review* 17, no. 2 (1995): 221–86; *Total Empire*, 241–414, esp. 394–95; both authors also cite Thomas R. Havens, *Farm and Nation in Modern Japan* (Princeton, N.J.: Princeton University Press, 1974).

17. Regarding World War II as a time of trial and disruption for Japanese Americans, see for example, Mine Okubo, *Citizen 13660* (New York: Columbia University Press, 1946), reprinted (Seattle: University of Washington Press, 1986); Bill Hosokawa, *Nisei: The Quiet Americans* (New York: Morrow and Co., 1969); John Okada, *No-No Boy* (Seattle: University of Washington Press, 1976); Paul Spickard, "The Nisei Assume Power: The Japanese American Citizens League, 1941–1942," *Pacific Historical Review* 52 (1983): 147–74; Peter Sano, *One Thousand Days in Siberia: The Odyssey of a Japanese American POW* (Lincoln, Neb.: University of Nebraska Press, 1997). Minoru Kiyota, trans. Linda Klepinger Keenan, *Beyond Loyalty: The Story of a Kibei* (Honolulu: University of Hawaii Press, 1997). Kibei (literally, returned to America) are

U.S. born Japanese who were sent back to Japan to live, while nisei (second generation) refers more generally to the children of Japanese who emigrated to overseas.

18. For overviews of the internment of Japanese American internment and its aftermath, see Michi Weglyn, *Years of Infamy: The Untold Story of America's Camps* (New York: Morrow, 1976); Roger Daniels, *Concentration Camps U.S.A.: Japanese Americans and World War II* (New York: Holt, Rinehart, and Winston, 1971); Jeremy Irons, *Justice at War* (New York: Oxford University Press, 1983); Peter Irons, ed., *Justice Delayed: The Record of the Japanese American Internment Cases* (Middletown, Conn.: Wesleyan University Press, 1989). For the experiences of Japanese in Canada and Latin American countries, see Roger Daniels, *Concentration Camps, North America: Japanese in the United States and Canada during World War II*, 1981, 1989; reprinted (Malabar, Florida: Krieger Publications., 1993[1981, 1989]); Forrest Emmanuel La Violette, *The Canadian Japanese and World War II: A Sociological and Psychological Account* reprinted (Toronto, Ont.: University of Toronto Press, 1987 [1948]); Barry Broadfoot, *Years of Sorrow, Years of Shame: the Story of the Japanese Canadians in World War II* (Toronto, B.C.; Garden City, N.Y.: Doubleday, 1977); Ann Gomer Sunahara, *The Politics of Racism: the Uprooting of Japanese Canadians during the Second World War* (Toronto, Ont.: Lorimer, 1981); Roy Miki, *Justice in Our Time: the Japanese Canadian Redress Settlement* (Vancouver, B.C.: Talonbooks; Winnipeg: National Association of Japanese Canadians, 1991); Robert Katsumasa Okazaki, *The Nisei Mass Evacuation Group and P.O.W. Camp 101: The Japanese-Canadian Community's Struggle for Justice and Human Rights During World War II* (Scarborough, Ont.: Markham Litho Ltd., 1996); C. Harvery Gardiner, *Pawns in a Triangle of Hate: The Peruvian Japanese and the United States* (Seattle: University of Washington Press, 1981); *Crystal City 50th Anniversary Reunion Album: Monterey, California, October 8–10, 1993* (n.p.: n.p., 1993) discuss the World War II internment of Japanese in Canada and Peru.

19. See for example *Formations; Total Empire; Japan's Competing Modernities*; Haruko Taya Cook and Theodore Cook, *Japan at War: An Oral History* (New York: The New Press, 1992); Saundra Pollock Sturdevant and Brenda Stoltzfus, eds., *Let the Good Times Roll: Prostitution and the U.S. Military in Asia* (New York: The New Press, 1992); Frank Dikotter, *The Discourse of Race in Modern China* (Stanford, Calif.: Stanford University Press, 1992); Partha Chaterjee, *Fragments of the Nation* (Princeton, N.J.: Princeton University Press, 1996); Michael Weiner, ed., *Japan's Minorities* (New York: Routledge, 1997); Tessa Morris-Suzuki, *Re-Inventing Japan: Time, Space, Nation* (Armonk, N.Y.: M. E. Sharpe, 1998). Beyond Asia, see Maria Mies, *Patriarchy and Accumulation on a World Scale* (Atlantic Highlands: Zed Books, 1986); Mary Poovey, *Uneven Developments: The Ideological Work of Gender in Mid-Victorian England* (Chicago: University of Chicago, 1988); Ann Laura Stoler, *Race and the Education of Desire: Foucault's History of Sexuality and the Colonial Order of Things* (Durham, N.C.: Duke University Press, 1995); Frances Gouda, *Dutch Culture Overseas:*

Colonial Practice in the Netherlands Indies 1900–1942 (Amsterdam: Amsterdam University Press, 1995); Anne McClintock, *Imperial Leather: Race, Gender, and Sexuality in the Colonial Contest* (New York: Routledge, 1995); Lisa Lowe, *Immigrant Acts: On Asian American Cultural Politics* (Durham, N.C.: Duke University Press, 1996); Dorinne Kondo, *About Face: Performing Race in Fashion and Theatre* (New York: Routledge, 1997).